Cooking for Good Health

Creative Recipes Without Added Fat, Sugar, or Salt

Gloria Rose

AVERY PUBLISHING GROUP INC.

Garden City Park, New York

Cover designer: Ann Vestal and Rudy Shur
Photo cover credit: Derik Murray, The Image Bank
Printer: Paragon Press, Honesdale, PA

This book is dedicated to my husband, Hal.
His determination, strength, patience, and, most of all, his love,
provided the constant support I needed
to complete my dream.

Cataloging-in-Publication Data

Rose, Gloria.
　　Cooking for good health: creative recipes without added fat,
sugar, or salt / Gloria Rose.
　　p. cm.
　　Includes index.
　　ISBN 0-89529-577-6

　　1. Diet therapy—Recipes. 2. Low-fat diet—Recipes. 3.
Low-cholesterol diet—Recipes. 4. Salt-free diet—Recipes.
5. Sugar-free diet—Recipes.　　I. Title.

RM222.R68 1993　　641.5'63　　　　　　　　　QB193-617

Printed in the United States of America

10　9　8　7　6　5　4　3

Contents

Letter to My Readers,   v
Acknowledgments,   vi
Introduction,   1

Interviews

Arthritis Interview,   6
Cancer Interview,   11
Cholesterol Interview,   17
Diabetes Interview,   22
Heart Disease Interview,   29
Hypertension Interview,   34
Weight Control Interview,   43
Nutrition Interview,   47
Exercise Interview,   55

Basic Nutritional Information

Daily Meal Plans,   60
How to Choose Foods Low in Cholesterol and
   Saturated Fat,   64
Controlling Your Sodium Intake,   73
The Sweet Facts,   76
Calcium Equivalents,   77
Nutrition Labels,   78
Fiber—Which Is Best for You?,   80
Weight Loss Diet & Weight Loss Maintenance Plan,   81
The Pregnant Woman,   124

Recipes

"Our" Homemade Basics,   133
Appetizers,   145
Soups,   157
Seafood Entrees,   181
Meat Entrees,   196
Poultry Entrees,   210
Vegetarian Entrees,   238
Salads,   254
Vegetables,   271
Pasta, Rice & Grains,   300
Breads,   312
Dressings, Spreads & Sauces,   321
Desserts & Snacks,   335

Everyday Measurements,   365
Approved Products,   366
Index,   372

Letter to My Readers

Dear Reader:

I write this letter with two thoughts in mind. First, this book is not primarily a cookbook—it has been designed for those who have health problems. Until now they have been unable to find a way to prepare delicious meals yet keep within their medical needs. And second, this book will aid those fortunate individuals who do not have health problems, but wish to continue to seek a proper nutritional way of life.

Therefore, you will not find the typical explanations usually discussed, such as how to mix or blend, how to store and freeze certain foods, how to carve and cut, etc. I assume the individual reader has knowledge of kitchen techniques so that we can get onto more important information.

Heathfully yours,

Gloria Rose

Gloria Rose

Acknowledgments

My sincerest thanks and warmest appreciation to all of those who labored so diligently to help create a book that makes me immensely proud. To Drs. Stephen J. Fischl, Michael Gutkin, Mary T. Herald, David E. Klein, Richard Podell, James C. Salwitz, David A. Worth and Sharma Sharda for giving me their precious time, knowledge and consideration in making the medical section so outstanding; to my staff nutritionists, Judi Scher Spector, R.D. and Joyce Cieslak, R.D., for their endless hours in breaking down the nutritional information for each and every recipe; to George Wehrmaker, whom I could not do without, for his patience, imagination and creativity; and to Natalie Lopes for taking my scribbles and making them come alive on the computer.

And to Barbara Dunn for her tireless effort and sincere dedication in assisting me in reaching my deadline.

And finally, to my daughter Hermyne and my son Barry Paul for the best recipe of all — love, encouragement and enthusiasm.

Gloria Rose

Introduction

Now for the most important question on your mind—how can we prepare delicious foods without the use of *fats, sugars* or *salt?* I am going to try to make it as simple and as easy as I can. Keep in mind all the other cookbooks printed in the last few years have used some small quantities of these "forbidden additives" in order to enhance the flavor, but now we are going to eliminate them altogether.

Please keep in mind that almost all the food products mentioned throughout the book are usually available nationwide. Check the Approved Product List in back of the book for further product information.

Well, there you are, begin to cook without fats or oils, sugar or salt using all the following information. Within a short time you will find yourself creating new exciting dishes that take very little time to prepare. Your body will thank you.

FATS OR OILS

Let's begin with the fats or oils. In other cookbooks when a shortening or oil is listed in the first three ingredients, 90 percent of the time that shortening will be used only for sautéing. By eliminating that oil or fat we have already made a drastic change! We are going to sauté with stock. Not just any stock but a delicious homemade stock that you can make yourself. Notice how many French recipes recommend "sautéing the onions until they are translucent, not brown." Well, a small amount of our stock will accomplish just that and enhance the flavor at the same time.

There are certain recipes and times where a little oil must be used.

1

When oil is needed, I use canola oil, which has been proven to be heart-healthy.

The use of a No Stick cooking spray, a little stock or water, or a little wine (NEVER COOKING WINE) will make your food creations a culinary delight!

SUGARS

The craving for sweets in our daily intake has been with us since the Stone Age. In recent times, if mommy didn't reward us for being good with a chocolate chip cookie or a handful of jelly beans, how different the quality of our lives would be. Doctors tell us that sugar, honey or any other refined sweetener can help lead to tooth decay and the possible formation of the buildup of plaques in the circulatory system which can ultimately lead to heart problems. So let's eliminate refined sugar from our daily consumption!

I believe our sweet tooth must be satisfied in order for us to remain on a permanent health program. Desserts, for example, are just as important to our daily meal as our entree. Finishing a meal with a fresh fruit cocktail is not my idea of pleasure. Our desserts consist of cheesecakes, cookies, parfaits and frozen desserts prepared without the use of artificial sweeteners or additives—in its place we substitute all varieties of frozen fruit concentrates. The most commonly used is apple juice concentrate. It can make your lemonade sweet without added sugar as well as help create wonderful desserts. More and more varieties of frozen fruit juice concentrates are appearing in supermarkets. Check the labels to be sure no sugars are added—that includes fructose, sucrose and corn syrup.

Date sugar, purchased in a health food store, can also give you sweetness in certain recipes. Because of the consistency, it will not melt in a batter or mixture, so use it when a smooth texture is not necessary.

Two excellent products that can be used in place of sugar are barley malt syrup and brown rice syrup. Both contain no cane or beet sugar but have the sweetness from processed barley and rice. Believe it or not, you'll wonder how you ever did without them. Look under Approved Products, pages 366-370, for those I think are the best.

Apple butter, other fruit butters and no sugar added preserves, jams and jellies can also do wonders for cakes, pies and pudding.

SALT

Of all the categories, salt is probably the easiest to find substitutes for. Some of the seasonings I am about to discuss may be new to you so use them sparingly.

Miso — pick up a small plastic container in the health food store. I use the light miso which resembles peanut butter; after experimenting you will find the varieties are endless in both color, texture and taste. For those of you that have a strong liking for salt, miso will do the trick. It has an unlimited versatility — use it in soups, casseroles, stews, etc. Because of its creamy consistency a tablespoon of miso in a pot of soup will go a long way. In fact, 1 to 2 tablespoons of miso is approximately the equivalent of 1/2 teaspoon of salt.

Soy sauce — this is a synthetic product consisting of soy meal treated with acid, caramel coloring, corn syrup, salt and water. Light soy sauce and dark soy sauce are basically the same in calories, the difference is just the color. The dark soy sauce has more caramel coloring added and has been fermented for a longer period of time. Check the labels in your part of the country and only buy low-sodium soy sauce and please always dilute the soy sauce at least by twice the amount of water; that is, if you are using a tablespoon of low-sodium soy sauce add 2 tablespoons of water. When using it in a pot of soup, it is not necessary to further dilute the soy sauce.

Don't let labels fool you — even if the soy sauce says "low sodium" or "sodium reduced," read the list for other ingredients. Many companies use sugar or caramel flavoring. Also be sure "salt" is the last ingredient listed!

Tamari or Shoyu — this product is a naturally made soy sauce opposed to the synthetic sauce found in restaurants and markets. For those readers that have a wheat allergy there is now a wheatless tamari sauce found in health food stores giving you the pleasure of a new seasoning. Use this product only in cooking before serving since it has a very strong flavor and should not be used at the table. Dilute the same as soy sauce.

Herbs and spices — these enhance the flavor of your foods. Never keep your spices longer than six months since they either lose their flavor or change and become bitter. To find a specific spice quickly, arrange them in alphabetical order on your shelf. It really helps.

Always use fresh herbs if possible since dried herbs in jars can never give the same flavor as fresh herbs from the garden. However, there are times when we are unable to pick a fresh herb and must rely on our spice shelf; use half the amount of the dried herb. For example, 1 teaspoon dried basil can be substituted for 2 teaspoons fresh basil. So start using the familiar herbs and expand from there to the more exotic. Here's a cliffhanger—did you ever hear of fenugreek? Buy a tiny amount ground, put 1/4 to 1/2 teaspoon in a stew for a new flavor sensation.

Vinegars—A good vinegar can make a plain dish come alive. Chicken, fish and even vegetables burst with a new zestful flavor when a gourmet-type vinegar is added. Don't spend a fortune and buy ready-to-use herb vinegars—do it yourself—it's fun and less than half the money. For example, take six or eight peeled garlic cloves, place them in a bottle of red wine vinegar. Wait a few days, open, take a whiff, and judge for yourself. Do the same with fresh tarragon or any other fresh herb and your dressings will take on a whole new flavor.

Have you ever tried rice vinegar? If not you are truly missing something. It is sweet and mellow and needs no additives. Slice some beefsteak tomatoes and alternate them in a dish with a sweet onion, add the vinegar, sprinkle with fresh parsley and as they say—a dish fit for a king. You will find rice vinegar in the Oriental food section of your supermarket. Give it a try.

Flavored oils—There are many flavored oils on the market such as toasted sesame oil, chili oil, walnut oil, etc. All of these are acceptable—under one condition. Only use 1/4 teaspoon per person per recipe so that it is considered to be a flavoring not an ingredient. This includes olive oil and canola oil as well.

When the thought of this book began to germinate in my mind, I knew I had to develop a chapter that concerned the doctor/patient relationship.

I'm sure at one time or another we all have been to a doctor's office when two things occurred. First we wanted the doctor to explain to us in very simple "non-medical" language what was wrong with us. And second when we left the office we realized there were so many more questions we would have liked to have asked. But we thought the doctor was either too busy to give us a lengthy explanation or possibly we felt we were unable to understand his clinical response.

I therefore developed and directed these interviews as if you the reader are now sitting with your doctor and asking "many of the questions you wanted to know but were afraid to ask."

Gloria Rose

David Allen Worth, M. D.
Attending Consultant of Rheumatology
Overlook Hospital, Summit, NJ
Fellow of the American Rheumatology Association

INTERVIEW WITH DR. DAVID ALLEN WORTH

ARTHRITIS

Q: What is arthritis?

A: Arthritis is an inflammation or an irritation in a joint area. It could be in the back, the neck, knee, wrist, or any number of areas. Some people might have a pain in the joint and that's called arthritis or arthritic pain.

Q: What are the causes of arthritis?

A: There are many. It could be due to a virus, a rheumatoid disease or it could be due to lupus, or gout. There are multiple causes.

Q: What are the predisposing factors towards arthritis?

A: With gout it could be dietary. Eating too many high purine foods, especially meats, can result in high uric acid in the blood which can affect the joints. Organ meats, especially sweetbreads, have very high purine content. Most arthritis is wear and tear. So somebody could have wear and tear, osteoarthritis, that would increase in prevalence with age. Also arthritis is related to usage. If somebody is a jack-hammer operator, he is going to get arthritis in the shoulder; a ball pitcher will have arthritis in the shoulder or elbow; a typist might have arthritis in the fingers or the wrists; a concert pianist might get arthritis in the wrists from banging on the keys.

Q: How common is arthritis?

A: It has been estimated that between 6-1/2 and 10 percent of the adult population have arthritis or rheumatism.

Q: Does arthritis occur in children?

A: Yes.

Q: Can arthritis be inherited?

A: Rheumatoid arthritis might be inherited, especially the tendency toward it.

Q: What are the symptoms of arthritis?

A: Pain, stiffness, swelling, heat, redness, lack of use. The stiffness might be in the morning before use or in the evening after use.

Q: How can we make a positive diagnosis of arthritis?

A: On physical examination, x-rays and blood tests.

Q: What would prevent arthritis from developing?

A: The main thing that helps arthritis, prevents it or lessens it, is mild exercise that keeps the joints from being stiff. Walking, swimming, range of motion exercises, occasionally bicycle riding. You don't want to strain or stress a joint. You don't want to over abuse it; to use a joint past fatigue, past pain. You know, Mickey Mantle had a bad knee that was painful and running on it would just make it worse.

Q: Where arthritis already exists, what corrective adjustments and treatments should be made?

A: Medication, anti-inflammatory medication, for pain relief; physical therapy for muscle strengthening and learning how to protect the joint from further injury; mechanical devices, braces, to protect the joint during use. Exercise for muscle strengthening, exercising for range of motion.

Q: What point does diet play?

A: The main thing with diet is: eat a healthy diet, avoid alcohol, keep the weight down to an ideal body weight, eat adequate amounts of calcium and avoid eating too much meat protein. In terms of calcium; osteoporosis can lead to fractures and pain, so anything that's going to increase activity in the muscle mass will increase bone mass. Healthy exercise will also help maintain the bone mass and spinal integrity.

Q: Any other particular suggestions regarding health or lifestyle?

A: Obviously not to smoke, maintain ideal body weight.

Q. Does stress play a role?

A: Stress can lead to the wear and tear but is not really a cause.

Q: Is overweight a major factor?

A: Well it will tend to aggravate the joints in the knees, which can be a problem for some patients. You have to apply about three and a half times the body weight to the knees when you walk up the stairs and that's a tremendous burden on the joints.

Q: Is arthritis curable?

A: Some conditions are. Some conditions are controllable. There has got to be a partnership between the physician and the patient, they have to work together. The individual patient has to pay attention to the condition, the underlying cause and the lifestyle.

Q: Are you pleased with the results with the patients on the "Gourmet Long Life Cooking School Program?" And do you have any examples of patients of yours who've gone to the school and utilized the program?

A: Yes, very pleased. I've had some patients with arthritis, who I sent to Gloria Rose's cooking school and they have all done well.

Q: Why, just recently, have we suddenly become aware of osteoporosis?

A: I think it's been around some time, but we now have some new therapies and diagnostic methods. But it's not more prevalent.

Q: What is gout?

A: Gout is an inflammatory disease that is caused by soft tissue deposits of uric acid which cause the joints to swell. In the majority of cases it can be controlled.

Q: And gout is associated with arthritis?

A: Yes, it causes an arthritic condition.

Q: Is gout treatable?

A: Yes.

Q: Does diet play a part?

A: Yes by avoiding sweetbreads, alcohol and keeping the weight down. There are also some medications that help.

James C. Salwitz, M. D.
Medical Oncologist, New Brunswick, NJ
Instructor Robert Wood Johnson Medical School
Fellowship National Cancer Institute, Bethesda, Maryland
Fellow American Board of Medical Oncology

INTERVIEW WITH DR. JAMES C. SALWITZ

CANCER

Q: What is cancer?

A: Cancer is the disease caused by the loss of growth control. When we are babies we grow quickly but as we become older that growth slows. This slowing of growth is a controlled event. Cancer is the disease that occurs when one cell in our body loses that control and starts to double and grow rapidly without regard to function or the injury it causes.

Q: What is the cause of cancer?

A: Cancer, which is a disease caused by damage to the genes (chromosomes), has a wide range of causes. Some individuals have genetic and inherited tendencies toward cancer, but the vast majority of people have something occur during their life which causes their cancer. Such events are radiation exposure (even the chronic low grade radiation exposure which none of us can avoid), chemical exposure, various substances in our diets caused by cooking and by our normal food intake, smoking and other environmental exposures. Any of these events cause cancer by damaging the chromosomes.

Q: What are the pre-disposing factors towards cancer?

A: Any event which increases the exposure of the individual to various cancer causing agents, either dietary substances or smoking, will pre-dispose the individual towards cancer. In addition, many individuals have an increased tendency towards cancer because of the genes they inherit from their parents. Those sorts of tendencies towards cancer may in fact go back thousands of years or may run closely in a family.

Q: How common is cancer?

A: Cancer will effect more than one in three individuals during their lifetime. It affects almost 800,000 people a year in the United States and causes half that many deaths. Certain cancers are increased in certain parts of the world and in certain populations even within a single country.

Q: Can cancer occur in children?

A: While a fairly rare event, especially compared to accidents, cancers in fact do occur in children. While there are some rare forms of cancer that are directly inherited and unavoidable, however, more commonly a tendency towards cancer is inherited and an individual increases that risk with the exposures to various substances or events during his lifetime.

Q: What are the symptoms of cancer?

A: Symptoms of cancer can be summed up in the words "permanent change." An individual should be concerned about the possibility of cancer if a permanent and increasing change has occurred in their bodies. Whether this is a pain, a growth, a loss of appetite, shortness of breath, permanent change in mood, a change in the coloration of their skin or any other change, the characteristic that should most concern a person is the unexplained and seemingly permanent change which has occurred in his or her body.

Q: How can a positive diagnosis be made?

A: A diagnosis of cancer is made by a set of tests which must conclude with a biopsy of that portion of the body which is suspected to be cancerous.

Q: How can you tell if a cancer is under control?

A: This requires medical supervision with frequent physical examinations as prescribed by the patient's physician, and testing as indicated.

Q: Would cancer clear without treatment?

A: While there have been rare reports of spontaneous disappearance (regression) of cancer, this is an event which probably occurs in less than 1 in 500,000 cases and cannot be depended upon. It can be assumed that if cancer is not treated it will progress.

Q: Does cancer shorten the life span?

A: Most cancers if left untreated will shorten a patient's expected life span. With treatment, approximately half of cancers can be cured and the vast majority can be at least controlled. Some very low grade tumors (such as certain skin cancers) do not affect survival for some time.

Q: Do you have any other suggestions regarding lifestyle, diet or exercise to control cancer?

A: A wise individual will evaluate his or her lifestyle including diet, the work place, the amount of rest and the amount of exercise and try to design a style of living which allows him or her to feel the best and decrease the risk of all disease. We have nothing unless we have our health. Sadly, many people do not make these changes until it is too late and good health cannot be regained.

Q: At what age do women develop breast cancer?

A: The incidence of breast cancer in the United States increases dramatically with age. While 5 per 100,000 women will have breast cancer at age 25, this number has risen to 200 per 100,000 by age 75. Eventually 25% of women who have cancer will have breast cancer, and 7% of all women who die after age 35 will die of breast cancer.

Q: How often should mammograms be taken?

A: The American Cancer Society recommends that women without unusual risk factors for breast cancer have a mammogram at age 40, a second at age 45 and a yearly one after age 50. For women with increased risks of breast cancer (for example, a sister or mother who has had breast cancer), most specialists would recommend mammograms be started earlier as well as careful medical follow-up. There is a push within the American Cancer Society to recommend that all women have their first mammograms by age 30.

Q: Are certain races or ethnic groups more susceptible to cancer?

A: Types of cancer vary in regard to geography, country and nationality, race and ethnic group. However, each ethnic group, race and physical location appears to have certain cancers with which it is associated. No ethnic group is safe from cancer but simply different groups have different cancer patterns.

Q: What can prevent cancer from developing?

A: While a tremendous amount of research is ongoing into various vaccines or chemicals which can decrease an individual's risk of cancer, the key to prevention is in avoiding those events which can cause injury to the genes and thusly cancer. Such things to be avoided are smoking, a wide range of industrial chemicals, heavy and sudden sun exposure, diets which are excessively high or low in certain substances, certain infections (such as hepatitis) and other cancer causing factors. If a patient has been diagnosed as having cancer, the approach to eliminating this illness needs to take two fronts; these are personal and medical. It is the physician's job to work with the patient to prescribe treatment control and eliminate this cancer. This may consist of surgery, medications, immunotherapy or other medical treatments. The patient's job should be to eliminate from his or her life whatever factors have caused that cancer and, therefore, might increase his or her future risk of cancer. Such changes in lifestyle could include stopping smoking, avoiding industrial chemical exposure, sun protection or changing the patient's present diet. The role of diet in cancer is to some great extent unknown but is rapidly unfolding. Certain obvious risks occur with certain diets. For example, diets rich in alcohol greatly increase the risk of multiple tumors. Diets high in flash fried foods greatly increase the risk of gastric tumors and other upper gastro-intestinal disease. Diets high in fats are suspected, though not proven, to increase the risk of breast cancer and other tumors. Diets low in fiber are again suspected, but not proven, to increase the risk of colon cancer and possibly of breast tumors. Eliminating those factors which clearly cause cancer from one's diet when a diagnosis of cancer has been made or when an individual is concerned about causing cancer is critical.

Q: What factors do fats, refined sugar and salt play in cancer?

A: Fats are suspected to increase the risk of certain tumors (as outlined above). Sugar and salt, while they have other medical risks, have not been clearly linked at this time to cancer.

Q: Is being overweight a factor in cancer?

A: There appears to be a weak correlation with certain diets, which are high in fats, and the risk of cancer and possibly in obesity and the occurrence of cancer. However, obesity by itself should be viewed as a minor risk factor.

Q: Does high fiber help reduce the possibility of cancer?

A: There has been a link shown between societies which have relatively low fiber diets (such as the United States) and an increased risk of colon cancer and possibly other tumors. However, no study has yet been performed to study whether actually increasing fiber content of the diet can decrease the possibility of cancer.

Q: Discuss potential benefits of fiber regarding cancer. What part does fiber play in the diet?

A: At this time it is not clear whether an individual within a given society can decrease the risk of cancer by modifying his fiber intake. However, many researchers hope that by simply increasing the amount of fiber in the diet that the rate of colon and possibly other cancers can be decreased.

Q: Are you pleased with the concept taught at the Gloria Rose Gourmet Long Life Cooking School Program; that is, cooking with no added fats, sugar, salt or oil and the utilization of a high fiber diet?

A: Certainly the concept of taking control of one's life and attempting to live it in the positive manner with the least risks of various diseases can only be applauded and praised.

Richard Podell, M. D., M. P. H.
New Providence, NJ
Clinical Associate Director
The Department of Family Medicine
Robert Wood Johnson Medical School
New Brunswick, NJ
Attending Physician, Internal Medicine
Overlook Hospital, Summit, NJ

INTERVIEW WITH DR. RICHARD PODELL

CHOLESTEROL

Q: What is cholesterol?

A: Cholesterol is a chemical substance, which is found in high amounts in diseased arteries. A large amount of scientific research makes us believe that too much cholesterol tends to promote disease in the arteries.

Q: What would be the cause of high cholesterol?

A: There are two main sources: The body makes it normally, and it's also taken in through diet. There are some people who have very good cholesterol regulatory systems. Their cholesterol levels stay low almost no matter what they eat. However, for many people, the amount produced from diet, together with the amount that's produced naturally, can overload the body's system to handle it.

Q: What are the predisposing factors toward cholesterol buildup?

A: Having a high blood level of certain forms of protein bound cholesterol is a major risk. There are other factors that contribute, some of which are probably genetic.

Q: How common is the cholesterol problem?

A: In the United States probably a majority of the adult population has a cholesterol level higher than desirable. A much smaller proportion have cholesterol levels that might be called semi-emergencies.

Q: Does this occur in children?

A: Yes.

Q: Can this tendency be inherited?

A: Yes.

Q: What are the symptoms of cholesterol buildup?

A: Usually there are no symptoms, until you develop a clinical disease: in which case you develop angina, heart attack or stroke.

18

In extremely severe cases one can see cholesterol filled plaques called xanthomas under the skin.

Q: Where high cholesterol already exists, what corrective adjustments and treatments should be made?

A: You can start out with a dietary approach. Lower your intake of saturated fats and cholesterol, which will tend to reduce the blood cholesterol level. Increase your intake of the water soluble kind of fiber found in oat bran or beans. If that doesn't work and cholesterol levels remain quite high, medicines can be considered.

Q: What part does diet play in cholesterol buildup?

A: It can contribute to it. If your metabolic enzymes do not automatically adjust for your dietary intake of cholesterol, then saturated fat will tend to overwhelm the body's regulatory command. This will cause a high blood cholesterol level.

Q: What factor do fats, refined sugar and salt play?

A: Animal fats tend to promote blood cholesterol, while vegetable fats like corn oil tend to lower it. There is some evidence that if you are on a high saturated fat diet, that excess sugar will tend to modestly raise the cholesterol further. Salt has a minor effect on cholesterol.

Q: Would high cholesterol clear without treatment?

A: No, it would tend to get worse with age if you don't change something.

Q: Do you have any other suggestions regarding lifestyle?

A: Obviously cholesterol is only one part of a dietary or heart disease prevention approach. The other parts would include: not smoking, keeping your weight under control and adjusting your mental attitude to avoid increased hostility, tension and stress. There may well be other pertinent interventions, but these are the ones that have been best studied.

Q: Is this condition curable?

A: Most people can control it through diet. The few who cannot be controlled through diet can usually control it through drugs.

Q: Are you pleased with the results of the patients that you've put on the "Gourmet Long Life Cooking School" program? Are there any examples or thoughts related to the cholesterol?

A: For people who want to keep cholesterol down and still eat well, Gloria Rose shows them how they can do it.

Q: Why do you think most doctors are not aware of proper nutrition?

A: I think most doctors are aware of cholesterol. Indeed, the Federal Government is making a major public relations campaign on this, everyone will be more aware. Cholesterol awareness is where we were with tobacco and high blood pressure ten or fifteen years ago. There is a fair interest that is growing rapidly.

Q: What do you consider "high cholesterol" in numbers?

A: "High" is a term that depends on several factors for its meaning. Thus, I will accept 250 mg of serum cholesterol as acceptable in a 70 year old, but not in a 40 year old. Usually, we like to see most adults at or below 200 mg HL. This assumes, of course that we have also analyzed the cholesterol into its "good" (HDL) vs. "bad" (LDL) components.

Q: Please define HDL and LDL.

A: HDL or High Density Lipoprotein is a blood protein which combines with cholesterol. Higher levels predict less heart disease. LDL or Low Density Lipoprotein, when high, predicts a higher risk of heart disease. You'd like to have a low LDL and a high HDL for the best cholesterol profile.

Q: Do you believe young children should have their cholesterol checked?

A: If there is a family history of high cholesterol or early heart disease, begin checking the children during childhood. If not, then I would wait until adolescence.

Mary T. Herald, M. D., F. A. C. P.
Associate Director of Internal Medicine, Overlook Hospital
Associate Professor of Clinical Medicine, Columbia
University College of Physicians and Surgeons

INTERVIEW WITH DR. MARY T. HERALD

DIABETES

Q: What is diabetes?

A: Diabetes is a disorder that is characterized by an elevated blood sugar. All foods that we take in are converted at one time or another into sugar because sugar is the unit of fuel that the cells of our body need. Sugar cannot get into most cells without insulin providing entry. An absolute deficiency of insulin or an insensitivity to insulin action leads to an elevated blood sugar.

Q: What are the causes of diabetes?

A: In an insulin dependent diabetic, the cause of diabetes is the destruction of the part of the pancreas that produces insulin. These patients must provide insulin by injection. The cause of the more common kind of diabetes, which we call "non-insulin dependent", is an excessive amount of weight and an intake of an excessive amount of calories which leads, in susceptible individuals, to an inefficient use of the insulin they have available.

Q: How common is diabetes?

A: It affects about 5 percent of the population of the United States.

Q: Does diabetes occur in children?

A: Yes. The form that occurs in children is the one where they have lost the capacity to make insulin.

Q: Can diabetes be inherited?

A: The predisposition to diabetes is inherited but not every diabetic has diabetic children. But there's obviously a much higher incidence of diabetes in children of diabetics. Other factors modify the expression of that inheritance.

Q: What are the predisposing factors toward diabetes?

A: Heredity, as mentioned, and chronic consumption of excessive calories with consequent obesity or overweight. I think we're seeing more and more diabetics in the United States because overweight is such a problem.

Q: What are the symptoms of diabetes?

A: In the insulin dependent type, diabetes is usually characterized by weight loss, tremendous thirst and increased urination, occasionally lethargy and even coma. These patients need insulin replacement.

With the more common, non-insulin dependent kind of diabetes, there may be very few symptoms: it may just be fatigue, some increased thirst and urination, not nothing too marked. We have a lot of people with blood sugars of 250 or greater, who say they feel fine. They don't know until we get their blood sugars down to normal that they really have been sluggish, more fatigued than they realize.

Q: How can a positive diagnosis be made?

A: The simplest way to do it is by a urine test screening for sugar, which is done for all children and most adults when they see a doctor for a checkup. It's also very simple to get an assessment of what the blood sugar is by doing a finger stick blood test. Now, if a patient is a suspected diabetic and the random blood sugar is inconclusive, the patient takes in a specific amount of sugar in a meal or in a liquid to measure how their body responds to that carbohydrate load. A normal individual will put out enough insulin to handle the large amount of sugar, and there will barely be a difference in the blood sugar level. In the diabetic, if there is not enough insulin or the insulin is inefficient in release or action, the sugar cannot be disposed of appropriately. Elevated sugars can last for hours.

Q: Does the presence of sugar in the urine always mean a patient has diabetes?

A: Usually, any sugar in the urine indicates a blood level of more than 150 mg. HL. Normal blood sugar is from 60 to 120 mg. HL. During pregnancy, however, you can have sugar in the urine without diabetes due to changes in kidney filtration. All urine sugars, however, should be investigated with a blood level test at least once.

Q: Does the absence of sugar in the urine eliminate the possibility of diabetes?

A: No. There can be wide swings in the blood sugar not reflected in the urine. As a screening procedure it's good, but it's not totally accurate.

Q: What would prevent diabetes from developing?

A: In the insulin dependent type we don't really know. It seems to be a self-destruction or auto-immune disease where the body inactivates that part of its own pancreas responsible for insulin production and release. What triggers this is unclear, although viral infections have been implicated.

Q: Where diabetes already exists, what corrective adjustments and treatments should be made?

A: For patients requiring insulin, obviously you institute insulin therapy to normalize blood sugar, and try to arrange an opportunity to exercise and a diet that will not make them overweight. Maintaining a healthy level of exercise and normal body weight is the key to the body's efficient use of insulin. The non-insulin dependent patient has a limited insulin responsiveness that can be maximized by proper diet and mild to moderate conditioning. Such a regime may prevent the expression of the elevated blood sugar. The main goal is to restrict the caloric intake. We can demonstrate an improvement in the blood sugar by restricting the caloric intake before any significant weight loss has occurred. The response seems to be directly related to the excessive number of calories and the tremendous demand that places on a limited system. Occasionally, medication is used to assist in the body's response to sugar.

Q: Do you have any other suggestions regarding lifestyle or exercise?

A: The word exercise scares a lot of people into avoidance. The exercise does not have to be vigorous. It can be something as simple as walking 2 to 3 miles a day at a moderate pace. It's keeping active. You don't have to jog, you don't have to swim 25 laps. It's really a general conditioning that is needed. Obviously, smoking in these patients should be avoided because that potentiates problems with cardiovascular disease. The use of alcohol is limited too because alcohol is a form of sugar.

25

Q: What factor do fats, salt and refined sugar play in diabetes?

A: Fats are extremely high in calories, so in and of themselves they are a problem for people who have to watch the number of calories they consume. They are the highest calorie-containing substances that we eat. Diabetics also have a higher incidence of atherosclerotic cardiovascular disease. They are more predisposed, presumably, because the level of sugar in the blood also has an influence on the way that fat is handled. A fat restricted diet can help limit calories and cholesterol, too.

Salt intake is really not so much a problem unless the patient has concurrent hypertension.

Refined sugars are empty calories. They're utilized extremely quickly by the body and are not handled particularly well by the diabetic. These create wide swings in the blood sugar level because of rapid absorption demanding a larger insulin response. In contrast, if you eat a sandwich, as the nutrients are absorbed and converted into sugar the blood level goes up on a smoother curve and is handled more easily by injected insulin or by the sluggish insulin response of the overweight diabetic.

Q: How can you tell if the diabetes is under control?

A: We can monitor the blood sugar. This is done very easily by the patient applying a drop of blood from the prick of a finger to a chemical strip. This method allows you to determine your blood sugar in the matter of a minute. Patients can do it four times a day if they need to. We usually do blood sugars before meals and at bedtime, and then one can adjust insulin therapy accordingly. Non-insulin dependent diabetics can be checked less frequently.

Q: Does diabetes shorten the life span?

A: Uncontrolled diabetes does. It predisposes individuals to athersclerotic heart disease and cardiovascular disease so the incidence of heart attacks, strokes and complications in the cardiovascular system are much more common. We are able to demonstrate that if you control the patient's blood sugar, and if you control hypertension, you can slow that process. Essentially, by controlling the blood sugar with proper diet and exercise, you can prolong someone's life.

The other complications of diabetes seen more often in the insulin dependent type, kidney and retinal disease, seem to demonstrate improvement if you control the blood sugar. Good control is beneficial but doesn't avoid complications completely.

Q: Are you pleased with the patients that you put on the "Gourmet Long Life Cooking School Program?"

A: It helped to make their adjustment to their new food plan easier, a little bit more exciting. One of the reasons I got involved with this at all was to facilitate my patients' compliance with a difficult task—changing lifestyle eating habits. Nutritionists and dietitians can turn patients off by talking to them too clinically, focusing on food in other than creative ways. Gloria's wonderful program has made it a creative challenge to cook in an interesting and tasty way. There is nothing more dull than looking at a diabetic diet. . . it tells you that you can have a half slice of this and so many ounces of that, and it's very "ho hum." Most of us live in a less controlled situation than that, and we're not into weighing our foods and calculating the amounts. Gloria's program teaches you to substitute things, and all preparations are with no fat and minimal sugar. You have to know about the exchanges in a diabetic diet as a basic outline, but the rest is your own adaptation of favorite recipes, etc. The patient feels more in control, and consequently, compliance has to be better. Gloria's guidance and reinforcement is marvelous. She advises about eating out in restaurants, teaching how to make the choices as to what to substitute or what to order on the menu. I am very pleased with the "Gourmet Long Life Cooking School."

Q: Are there any particular examples of people you sent to her cooking school who had helpful results?

A: Yes, I had a man of about 45 who had bypass surgery at 38 and in recent years had regained his weight and was running blood sugars of 250 to 300, a very high-pressured accountant. He does everything compulsively at work and could not stand a structured diet, so he just forgot about it. Eventually his high blood sugar reached serious levels, and he began to have symptoms of fatigue and some chest pain. This finally got his attention. He had been very turned off by diet therapy before I sent him to "The Gloria Rose Gourmet Long Life Cooking School," and he got into cooking and understanding that there is a lot you could do with the diet creatively. It's a different way of cooking. I've been pleased with the results with him. His blood sugar is now under control. He has begun the weight reduction. As I said before, if you change the caloric intake, in a matter of days you can see a difference in the blood sugar but the weight takes a little bit longer to follow through.

I have a lot of younger diabetics faced with the prospect of spending the rest of their lives on a very special diet. It's important for them to know that there's a lot you can do with the diet without "cheating." Gloria teaches an awareness about the presence of fats in everything. I think this is perhaps the most valuable part of the course. I don't like to use scare tactics, but I think the American diet is awful for all of us. It would be of great benefit if we could start changing how people think about food.

Q: Is diabetes curable?

A: No. In the non-insulin dependent diabetic you can put it into a non-clinical phase. In other words, if you really restrict the calories and get the patient's blood sugar under control, they can be asymptomatic. They always have to be careful. So I tell my patients it's not curable, but with proper treatment and adherence to sound dietary practice such as taught by the "Gourmet Long Life Cooking School Program," it is controllable.

Stephen J. Fischl, M. D.
New Providence, NJ
Attending Cardiologist
Overlook Hospital, Summit, NJ

INTERVIEW WITH DR. STEPHEN J. FISCHL

HEART DISEASE

Q: What is heart disease?

A: Heart disease is a broad term which encompasses a whole series of disorders. There are many different types of heart disease. The most common heart disease in the U. S. is coronary artery disease, which is due to blockages in the arteries of the heart. These restrict the blood circulation to the heart muscle and results in conditions such as angina or heart attack.

Q: What are the causes of coronary heart disease?

A: There is no single cause of this disease but rather multiple risk factors, which vary from person to person. We don't actually know if these are causes, but we know they increase the risk of developing the disease. For coronary artery disease there are probably a dozen or more risk factors. The three most important risk factors, which have been identified, are high blood pressure, cigarette smoking and an elevated blood cholesterol level.

Q: Statistically how common is coronary heart disease?

A: Heart disease in adult Americans is by far the most common cause of disability and death. It accounts for more than half the deaths in adult Americans and Western Europeans.

Q: Does it occur in children:

A: The type of heart disease we are talking about, coronary artery disease, does not per se. It is thought, however, that some of the predisposing factors may begin in childhood, but the disease may not manifest for several decades later.

Q: Can coronary heart disease be inherited?

A: There is a genetic predisposition to coronary heart disease.

Q: What are the symptoms of coronary heart disease?

A: About 1/4 to 1/3 of people with serious coronary heart disease have no symptoms. In fact the majority of people in the early stages of heart disease have no symptoms. In the later stages of the disease the most common symptom is chest pain. Usually this chest pain occurs with exertion and occasionally chest pain occurs at rest. Another symptom may be shortness of breath.

Q: How can a positive diagnosis be made?

A: It is difficult to diagnose coronary artery disease in its early stages. As it becomes more severe it is more easily diagnosed. In its early stages it frequently requires sophisticated medical testing such as a stress electro-cardiogram, commonly called the stress test and various types of nuclear scans. The most specific way of diagnosing coronary heart disease is by an in-hospital test called coronary angiography.

Q: What would prevent coronary heart disease from developing?

A: That's a major source of debate at this point. Again since there is no one single cause of coronary artery heart disease, there is no one single method by which we can prevent it. There are still many factors at play which we don't understand that are basic causes of heart disease. But we know we can decrease the risk of developing heart disease by such measures as stopping smoking and controlling high blood pressure. Within the past few years it has also been established that one can substantially reduce the risk of heart disease in people with elevated blood cholesterol by lowering the blood cholesterol level.

Q: Where coronary heart disease already exists what corrective treatments would you recommend?

A: This really requires guidance by a cardiologist. Treatments range from medication to various types of surgery for more advanced stages. Early stages of heart disease are treated usually with diet and control of blood pressure.

Q: What part does diet play in coronary heart disease?

A: Again this is a question that has been debated intensely for the past twenty to thirty years in this country. We have found that people with elevated blood cholesterol have an increased risk of heart disease. If we can lower their blood cholesterol either through a heart-healthy diet or occasionally with medication, that risk of heart disease can be substantially reduced. The exact numbers are difficult to determine. But the National Institute of Health has estimated that for every one percent which the blood cholesterol can be lowered by either diet or drugs, the risk of dying from coronary heart disease can be lowered by two percent.

Q: What factors do fats, refined sugar and salt play in coronary heart disease?

A: The most clear evidence concerns fat and cholesterol. Diets which are high in saturated fat and cholesterol predispose to higher blood cholesterol levels and are thought to represent one of the major risk factors for coronary heart disease.

Q: Refined sugar then isn't really a big factor?

A: Refined sugar per se is not thought to be a definite risk factor for heart disease at this time.

Q: How about salt?

A: Salt may be important for people who have hypertension. It is also important for people in the advanced stages of heart disease who develop a condition called congestive heart failure. In that condition the body retains abnormal amounts of salt and a drastic reduction of salt intake becomes necessary. Also for the broad population salt may be important in preventing high blood pressure problems.

Q: Does coronary heart disease shorten the life span?

A: As I said earlier, coronary heart disease is the major cause of death in adult Americans and adult Western Europeans, and more than half the population will die of heart disease.

Q: Do you have any other suggestions regarding lifestyle, diet or exercise to control heart disease?

A: Again, just to summarize, there are three major risk factors recognized for coronary heart disease. If we can stop cigarette smoking, control high blood pressure and lower blood cholesterol down to levels which The National Institute of Health recommends, then probably the rate of death from heart disease can be cut in half within the next 20 years.

Q: Is being overweight a factor?

A: Yes, for two reasons. One is, people who are overweight frequently have elevated blood cholesterol. Secondly, it is a risk factor for coronary heart disease. Not as powerful as some of the others I have mentioned but still a risk factor. People who have heart disease are more likely to have symptoms and problems if they are overweight. Most people with heart disease should lose weight.

Q: Is heart disease curable?

A: We don't talk in terms of cure. We talk in terms of controlling and preventing progression. We don't expect it ever to go away. Most people with heart disease who receive good medical care and lead healthy lifestyles can expect to live normal lives in both quality and quantity.

Q: If a program was designed to teach people how to cook without adding salt, sugar, fats or oils, and yet have the food taste delicious, would you feel this to be of help?

A: It would be most beneficial in the long term control of cholesterol. One of the biggest problems we see is people being unable to find types of foods and cooking methods to allow them to have a beneficial decent diet that they can enjoy day in and day out.

Michael Gutkin, M. D.
Chief, Hypertension Section
St. Barnabas Medical Center
Livingston, NJ 07039
Clinical Associate Professor of Medicine
UMDNJ—N. J. Medical School, Newark, NJ

INTERVIEW WITH DR. MICHAEL GUTKIN

HYPERTENSION

Q: What is hypertension?

A: Hypertension is that blood pressure which leads to premature cardiovascular disease. There are absolute numbers that determine this but 140/90 is taken as the usual cutoff point.

Q: What leads to hypertension?

A: There are two genetic models of hypertension in the laboratory rat. One depends on an abnormal sensitivity to dietary sodium; the other involves excessive activity of the sympathetic nervous system, which is only partly dependent on sodium in the diet. We find these elements of both forms of hypertension in people, in varying proportions. There are ten constellations of symptoms recognized as distinct forms of hypertension by practicing physicians, well recognized constellations of hypertension, such as kidney disease or glandular tumors. Nine of the ten affect 10 percent of the patients. The other 90 percent of the people are loosely called "essential hypertension". But a human being that is below a certain threshold of sodium, about 200 mg per day, won't develop hypertension, no matter what his or her genetic makeup is.

Over the past couple of decades, scientists have been chipping away at the "essential hypertension" category and describing forms of hypertension that seem to be distinct. For example, a minority of that 90 percent will not have hypertension any longer if they don't drink alcohol and there may be something about their metabolism that enables alcohol to cause hypertension in them. Others may have hypertension because of nocturnal obstruction of breathing call sleep apnea.

Q: What are the predisposing factors to hypertension?

A: Family history is generally found in somebody who has hypertension, but it is not necessary to have a family history to develop hypertension. Furthermore, there's generally interaction between family history and environment; for example, hypertension is more likely to develop in patients who are obese, or who have kidney disease, if they have a positive family history. If you smoke, and that leads to a narrowing of the arteries, it is more likely to give you hypertension if you have a family history than if you don't. Similarly, if you have kidney disease on one side, you're more likely to get hypertension. There are drugs that can cause hypertension. Nose drops, cortisone and oral contraceptives can be a common cause of hypertension. Certain replacement estrogens can cause hypertension. Everybody knows that stress causes hypertension. You can cause anybody, even a person who does not have hypertension to raise blood pressure, if you stress them severely enough. People who have anxiety attacks develop hypertension at times, but they may just have a transitory raise in their blood pressure, not one disease, hypertension. If one parent has a very mild degree of hypertension, the offspring could still have more severe hypertension, depending on developmental and environmental factors.

Q: How common is hypertension?

A: Up to 40 percent of the adult population has it, depending upon race and age. In people over 60 it's probably closer to 50 percent of the population. That only means that they have elevated blood pressure numbers, which make them more susceptible to heart attack and stroke. But, those elevated blood pressures don't necessarily lead to premature cardiovascular disease. You can call an elevated blood pressure "hypertension" on a numerical basis; it may not be a disease, but only a susceptibility to disease. Similarly there are people for whom a blood pressure which everybody may think is safe, represents hypertension—for example, 130/85.

Q: Do children get hypertension?

A: Yes. If a child less than 12 develops hypertension, the chance that there's an identifiable cause, such as a kidney problem, approaches 50 percent. As children get more and more distant from puberty the chance that it is "essential" hypertension increases. In addition, there is a curious form of hypertension in adolescents called "borderline hypertension" which simply means that your blood pressure sometimes goes above 140/90 but not always (160/95 by World Health Organization criteria). Such blood pressures in young people (less than 25 years) usually do not lead to the disease essential hypertension; only 25 percent develop it. These blood pressure rises may represent transitory developmental or psychological abnormalities. In some of these young folks you can evoke a characteristic psychological profile of suppressed hostility and an "anger in" personality. There's some question whether those people really have hypertension at all. Essential hypertension usually develops around age 40.

Q: Can hypertension be inherited?

A: I think we'd have to say the tendency is inherited. If you have one parent with hypertension you have a one in three chance of getting it, if you have two parents you have a two out of three chance of getting it. But much of that is avoidable by an adherence to certain health patterns, like avoidance of sodium, maintenance of ideal body weight, and possibly a high intake of potassium.

Q: What are the symptoms of hypertension?

A: For the most part, there aren't any—that's the dangerous part about it. If people wait to hear from their bodies about their hypertension they may have waited until the disease is advanced. Some of the symptoms are: a feeling of uneasiness, feeling your own heart beat, a fullness of the face and heat, headache, a little shortness of breath or becoming easily exhausted with exertion. Some people just vaguely don't feel right. There is some evidence that high blood pressure does impair cognitive functions. Things like motor hand coordination are likely to be impaired in a hypertensive person and that gets better when they're treated. People don't complain about this, but it may contribute to a feeling that something is wrong.

Q: How can a positive diagnosis be made?

A: By observing the blood pressure symptoms, physical examination and laboratory tests.

Q: What would prevent hypertension from developing?

A: It can be prevented. We know in those cultures, where sodium intake is extremely small, hypertension doesn't develop. There are genetically identical populations living in the Polynesian islands, Puka Puka, and Roratoiga. A branch of these folk which lives in one island doesn't use salt. They cook their food in sea water on the other island. The salt eaters develop hypertension more often than the others, even though they are genetically identical people. When members of primitive societies move to Western culture and adopt Western ways, their blood pressures go up. Sometimes it's difficult to ascertain whether this is because of the salt intake or the social environment. Vegetarian diets seem to be associated with blood pressures that are lower by about 7 mm of mercury. This appears to be a function of the vegetarian diet rather than other cultural attributes of vegetarians. For example, Mormons generally eat meat, Seventh Day Adventists generally don't. Their cultural characteristics and social organization are similar in many respects yet the Mormons have higher blood pressure than the Seventh Day Adventists. The flip side of this observation is that when you go from a high animal fat diet to a low total fat diet, your blood pressure will tend to fall. However, we must caution that maintenance of lean body mass is not an absolute preventative. Thin people can get very sick from high blood pressure.

Q: So that means more vegetables?

A: There is some blood pressure lowering feature of the vegetarian diet which is hard to identify. It could be more potassium, calcium and magnesium in the diet, based on circumstantial evidence. One study, known as the NHANES study, (National Health and Nutrition Examination Survey), found data which were interpreted to show that people with higher calcium intake are less likely to develop hypertension. This was previously suggested by Dr. Francis Langford, in Mississippi, who showed that those school girls who drink more milk are less likely to develop hypertension. It may be that the high potassium and high calcium intake provided by milk offsets the effects of dietary sodium. Finally, living "clean" — not smoking, not drinking — can help prevent hypertension.

Q: What factors do fats, refined sugar and salt play in hypertension?

A: Salt is probably more important in older people than younger. A substantial minority of younger people actually have a rise in their blood pressure when they go on very low sodium diets. Sodium restriction, without a rise in the potassium intake, probably isn't a useful way to prevent hypertension in younger people unless you're down to exquisitely low intakes of salt. Fats and sugars which cause obesity and insulin resistance set the stage for hypertension. Overeating any kind of calories can cause hypertension. There is evidence in animals that low saturated/high unsaturated fat intake prevents hypertension. But this has not been satisfactorily proven in humans. Hypertension can be induced through the medium of obesity (or giving your pancreas too much to do). When you are obese, your pancreas may secrete more insulin than you need, certain parts of your body don't listen to that insulin but your kidney does, and retains salt. Body sodium content does seem to be very important in developing hypertension. Reducing body sodium content seems to be important to ameliorating hypertension. The reasons for this are unknown. There are a myriad of possibilities. Salt works in many places to alter the cardiovascular system.

Q: Where do triglycerides come into this?

A: I don't think anybody has shown that triglycerides can cause hypertension. They are commonly elevated in people who have hypertension. There's more than a chance association of obesity with hypertension and high blood cholesterol with hypertension.

Q: How can you tell if hypertension is under control?

A: That's a very hard question. Certainly you would want blood pressure lower than when they started. But it's very difficult to determine what a proper blood pressure for a given patient is or whether drug treatment is necessary to bring it down. In the old days we would say: bring it down to less than 140/90, or if a patient was very sick from the hypertension, then bring down the diastolic (resting heartbeat) to less than 80. But now it's possible to measure what effect the blood pressure is having on someone's body and repeat these measurements after treatment, and see if they're improving. For example, if somebody had a blood pressure of 138/86 and had thickening on the left side of their heart on an echocardiogram you could lower the blood pressure even more and use the point at which the heart wall thins out as the proper blood pressure to maintain. So the answer is: the doctors may not really know if blood pressure is under control. They know when blood pressure has been lowered. Lowering still may not protect the patient from cardiovascular disease, unless it is lowered further.

Q: Do you think hypertension would clear up without treatment?

A: There are varying instances showing how as many as 25 percent of mild hypertensives are said to clear after a period of treatment, or without any treatment. But it's possible that they have been misclassified from the beginning. And perhaps, their blood pressure has not been observed long enough off the medication, it may take as long as four years for the hypertension to reappear. It would be very dangerous for all patients who once needed drugs to think they can do without them forever.

Q: Does hypertension shorten the life span?

A: Sure it does. It doesn't matter what age you are, it can shorten your lifespan but it doesn't shorten it in everybody.

Q: Do you have any other suggestions regarding lifestyle or exercise or other variables?

A: Follow a diet moderately low in sodium, lower is better. Maintain ideal body weight. Don't drink alcohol, don't smoke, don't eat saturated fat and keep trim. Because, in fact, the objective of any hypertensive treatment is to prevent premature cardiovascular disease, hypertension is not the only thing that causes it. You have to view the patient as jeopardized by a constellation of factors. It isn't known for sure if exercise prevents high blood pressure. Vigorous exercise is very potent in treating high blood pressure in some patients. It's probably a good idea to engage in mild exercise if only to maintain ideal body weight.

Q: Is overweight a factor here?

A: Certainly. Some patients respond dramatically to weight reduction. And the amount of weight reduction can be relatively small to obtain a very large fall in blood pressure. But generally in those cases, further reduction in weight is not accompanied by a further fall in blood pressure. If you start out with mild high blood pressure, weight reduction may be all that you need to lower blood pressure satisfactorily. Seventy percent of people who lose weight, lower their pressure.

Q: Is hypertension curable?

A: Yes, if there is an underlying cause that can be removed. For example, if there is a tumor of the adrenal gland, that's curable. And in the sense that you can put people through measures that don't involve drugs, like a change in diet or vigorous carefully formulated exercise, and bring blood pressure down permanently without drugs, it is curable.

Q: What is a normal blood pressure level?

A: We regard 130/80 or greater as a grey zone and 140/90 to 160/95 is "borderline" by World Health Organization criteria. At 130/80 or 140/90 it's possible that somebody really has the disease, that they're just at the lower end of the spectrum of blood pressures that predispose to disease. There really isn't any normal range. People really have to be looked at for how well they're bearing their blood pressure.

Q: What is low blood pressure and is it as serious as high?

A: In the absence of symptoms there is no such thing as low blood pressure. But when people feel weak or faint, due to low blood pressure, it's because their usual blood pressure has fallen, and that can be bad for you. Some people with certain types of floppy heart valves and people with Parkinson's disease with an improperly functioning sympathetic nervous system can have low blood pressure. But, in an otherwise healthy person, lifelong low readings are actually a harbinger of longevity. In some cases, when elderly people develop heart disease, their previously normal or high blood pressure may fall with age and they develop low blood pressure. And of course that bears a very bad prognosis. Their blood pressure's falling because they're sick.

Q: Can one have temporary high blood pressure?

A: Yes. There are people who, when stressed periodically, develop high blood pressure and the hypertension goes away when the stress is removed.

Q: Why are most doctors so unaware of proper nutrition?

A: Many doctors are keenly aware of it; some aren't. In some cases, it was not emphasized in their medical school curriculum. In some cases the doctor's training revolves around hospital medicine, where the effects of any chronic treatment are not emphasized; the effects are on immediate gratification, in prompt diagnosis or response to therapy. So they have no affinity for something that isn't telescoped in time or doesn't have an immediate result.

Q: Why don't they develop a system?

A: They are finding that the more dramatic diseases are fading away, and can turn their attention to preventing chronic disease. In order to serve the current needs of the public, they are getting interested in nutrition. They are facing a population that is much healthier, which needs nutritional advice to prolong their health, and they are getting better at it.

Q: Are you pleased with the results of those patients that you've placed on "The Gloria Rose Gourmet Long Life Cooking School Program?"

A: Yes, very much so.

Q: Do you have any examples?

A: I've only just started sending patients to the school. But I do have examples of people who, when on a low-fat, low-salt, low-refined carbohydrate, high-fiber diet, have lost their hypertension completely and dropped their cholesterol. Do you know that if you keep your cholesterol less than 150 for five years, you can actually start to reverse established hardening of the arteries? We're looking at the prospect of a population that could remain healthy until 80, or later, and live without having a coronary or stroke.

Sharda Sharma, M. D.
Weight Control Center, Millburn, NJ
Family Practice
Affiliated with St. Barnabas Medical Center, Livingston, NJ
Irvington General Hospital
Hospital Center at Orange

INTERVIEW WITH DR. SHARDA SHARMA

WEIGHT CONTROL

Q: Is obesity hereditary?

A: Yes, in most cases children born to overweight parents will be more likely to become obese. Also, the rate at which a person burns calories while resting (Basal Metabolic Rate) can be passed down from parents to children.

Q: What are the different types of obesity?

A: Two different types of obesity are central obesity, also known as android obesity, and gynoid obesity. Central obesity is a form of obesity which results from an enlargement of the fat cells in a person's abdominal and upper body regions. In other words, a person's body will be shaped like an apple. This type of obesity is most prevalent in males but some females may exhibit signs of it.

On the other hand, gynoid obesity is most often found in females. In this form of obesity the distribution of fat is around the gluteal and femoral regions. In simpler terms, a person's body will be shaped like a pear.

Q: What is secondary obesity?

A: Secondary obesity results from a low thyroid hormone, which causes the body to require fewer calories. This is known as hypothyroidism. Rarer causes of secondary obesity are Cushing's disease and hypothalamic disorder.

Q: Which sex has a greater tendency to be overweight?

A: Females are more prone to being obese than males. Males are able to lose weight faster than females. This is because females burn fewer calories while resting than males (i. e., a female's Basal Metabolic Rate is lower than a male's).

Q: At what point in the life cycle do people begin putting on the most weight?

A: Weight gain begins to show up most at middle age. This is because people are less active and eat diets high in fat and calories. Also, there is a lessened caloric need in all people as they grow older and many investigators believe that people need 100 fewer calories per day for each 10 years that they advance in age beyond middle life. Thus with the same caloric intake, every 10 days a person may be receiving 1,000 more calories than they need. This can cause a gain of 1 pound a month.

Q: Do hormones play any role in weight gain?

A: Yes. During pregnancy, lactation, and before menstrual periods, females will exhibit increases in weight because of hormonal changes. For example, before a period, there is a rise in the progesterone and estrogen hormones. These hormones have a tendency to cause retention of water and salt.

Q: Do emotions affect weight gain?

A: Yes. People who are emotionally upset or under tension usually have a tendency to overeat. As a young child, we are usually rewarded with good things to eat. Consequently, we relate eating good tasting foods with the comfort and security of childhood. When emotional issues arise, sometimes we turn to food to help us feel better. Unfortunately, this overeating causes weight gain and ultimately we don't feel good about ourselves.

Q: In your opinion, is it important to watch fat grams and calories?

A: It is more important to watch that your fat gram intake is low rather than your caloric intake. For example, 13 apples have approximately 1300 calories and 2.6 grams of fat. On the other hand, one cup of nuts also has approximately 1300 calories and 100 grams of fat. A person who eats the nuts instead of the apples will have a harder time losing weight.

Q: Why do people lose weight on a liquid low calorie/high protein diet and then gain the weight back?

A: A diet low in calories and high in protein provides short term success for weight loss. When people return to their normal diets, they start taking in more fat grams and consequently begin gaining back the lost weight.

For good long term results, one should change one's lifestyle. This is accomplished by taking in low amounts of fat, high amounts of fiber, and exercising daily for one's entire life.

Q: Some people claim they eat very little yet they cannot lose weight. Could this be true?

A: Yes. People have a tendency to eat the wrong foods, ones which are high in fat grams. Therefore, this prevents them from reaching their desired weight. In control studies, it has been found that it is extremely rare for a patient to adhere to a prescribed diet and fail to lose weight.

Q: Why do certain individuals who eat huge quantities of food tend to remain thin?

A: These people may appear to eat tremendous quantities but in actuality they eat foods of low fat and low caloric volume and usually do not snack. In addition, they are probably more active physically and burn up more calories in this manner.

Q: How important is exercise in producing weight loss?

A: Exercise is vital to living a healthy life. It burns the excess calories stored in the form of fat in a person's body thus resulting in weight loss and toning muscles at the same time. Exercise also improves the blood circulation and instills a sense of well being.

Q: Is there a relationship between being overweight and coronary heart disease?

A: There is definite evidence that coronary heart disease is greater among people who are obese and who eat a high fat diet.

Q: Do you feel following the Gloria Rose Gourmet Long Life Program will help people lose weight and also keep their weight off?

A: Definitely, in this program people are taught to change their lifestyles by learning to cook foods low in fat grams and cholesterol. Since individual preferences are taken into consideration, a person can stay on this program for the rest of their lives. Besides, the foods are truly delicious! Everyone in the family will enjoy and benefit from this program of no-fat, no-sugar and no-salt recipes.

Lorri B. Katz, M. A., R. D.
Clinical Nutritionist
with The Gloria Rose Gourmet Long Life Cooking School

INTERVIEW WITH LORRI B. KATZ

NUTRITION

Q: What is wrong with the typical American Diet?

A: There is a lot wrong with the typical American Diet. It is too high in fat, especially saturated fat; too high in cholesterol; too high in simple sugar; too high in salt; too high in protein and not high enough in fiber and certain vitamins and minerals.

Q: What are the dangers of the typical American Diet?

A: The American Diet or so-called "Western Diet" promotes the development of coronary artery disease, which is the number one cause of death in the United States. In addition, it can lead to obesity, high blood pressure, the development of diabetes, cancer and gallstones.

Q: What can I eat to decrease my chances of getting heart disease?

A: Too often diets describe a list of "no-no's" without telling you what you CAN eat to help the situation. In the case of heart disease, you should limit your intake of total fat, especially saturated fat, cholesterol and total calories to maintain your ideal body weight. In addition, you should consume MORE fiber, particularly water soluble fibers, like oat bran and beans, and more plant protein found in whole grains and vegetables.

Q: Why do we continue to eat foods that are not good for us?

A: There is no simple answer, but the fast pace of our society and the desire for "instant gratification" contribute to the consumption of convenience ("fast-food") foods which generally are high in fat, cholesterol, salt and calories and low in fiber and nutrients.

Q: Where should I begin in changing my diet to a healthy one?

A: You can begin by examining your present diet. The best way to do this by keeping a food diary of EVERYTHING you consume including liquids. (You might seek the professional advice of a registered dietitian.) The first thing to examine is your portion sizes. Next, examine your intake of fat and HIDDEN fats used in cooking and in convenience foods.

48

Q: How much fat is too much?

A: A therapeutically low fat diet is 25-40 grams of total fat per day. You should not go above 60 grams of fat per day. A rule of thumb is not to consume foods containing more than 3 to 4 grams of fat per serving.

There are different schools of thought on the topic, but the national guidelines have stated that fat should be limited to no more than 30 percent of total calories per day. Our program limits fat to below this level, or to 10 to 15 percent of total calories per day. For example, if you were consuming 1500 Calories per day, 10 percent would be 150 Calories from fat. Divide by 9 to determine grams of fat. You would consume approximately 17 grams of total fat per day according to our guidelines.

Q: How can I decrease my fat intake without losing the taste of my food?

A: You can follow the cooking methods of The Gloria Rose Gourmet Long Life Cooking School which will show you how to use "chicken stock" in place of your fats and oils. In addition, there are many food substitutes which taste great to use in place of fat-laden foods. You can learn to transform your favorite recipes into "heart-healthy" ones!

Q: What about red meat?

A: Red meat contains saturated fat, cholesterol and is more caloric ounce for ounce that some other protein sources such as poultry, fish and plant protein. Included with red meat is veal. According to the United States Department of Agriculture (USDA) statistics, three ounces of cooked veal have approximately ten grams of total fat, of which five grams are saturated, and contain 84 milligrams of cholesterol. This compares to three ounces of cooked lean roast beef round which have approximately five grams of total fat, of which two grams are saturated and 77 milligrams of cholesterol. Many people do not view veal as a red meat since its color is usually pale. Refer to the chapter containing the chart comparing the composition of meat, poultry and fish.

Q: What are the benefits of consuming "fatty fish?"

A: Recently, studies have indicated the benefits derived from eating "fatty fish" or fish containing omega-3 fatty acids known as

Eicosapentaenoic Acid (E. P. A.). The consumption of these particular fish appears to have a lipid (fat and cholesterol) lowering effect. Refer to the chart listing the E. P. A. oil content in fish.

Q: How about shellfish?

A: Opinions about the consumption of shellfish are varied and change frequently. The Gloria Rose Gourmet Long Life Cooking School program allows lobster and scallops. These shellfish are lower in cholesterol than others such as shrimp and contain few calories per serving. They are also very low in saturated fats. One warning—they are high in sodium!

Q: How much sodium should I consume per day?

A: First of all, we should clarify the difference between salt and sodium. Salt is made of sodium chloride. One teaspoon of salt contains 2300 milligrams of sodium. The National Academy of Sciences recommend adults consume a range of 1100 to 3300 milligrams of sodium per day which translates into an average of 2000 milligrams per day or two grams per day. One word of warning—a food does not have to taste salty to be high in sodium. The classic example is diet soda. Many diet sodas contain a preservative, sodium benzoate, which does not have a salty taste and yet a 12-ounce can of diet soda can contain up to 50 milligrams of sodium. Multiplied by the number of cans consumed per day the amount of sodium can become significant.

Q: In which foods is sodium found and how do I know how much sodium is in a food?

A: Sodium is found in almost all foods. There is never a need to add sodium to foods. The human body requires as few as 200 to 500 milligrams of sodium per day, while many people are consuming quantities 10 to 20 times that number. Refer to the chart listing high sodium foods. A good rule of thumb to follow is to avoid processed foods, fast foods and convenience foods. Canned foods traditionally have been high in sodium, but many are available in low-sodium varieties. Manufacturers often list milligrams of sodium per serving on the food label. Consumers are urging manufacturers to list the amount of sodium on all labels. At present, the listing of sodium levels is mandatory only when the label makes a claim such as "low sodium" or "salt reduced."

Q: I've heard that fiber is good for me. What is fiber and in which foods can I find it? Also, how much fiber should I consume per day?

A: Fiber is the non-digestible portion of foods. It, by itself, has no caloric nor nutritive value; however, it is an important part of the diet. Fiber is most abundant in fruit, vegetables and grains. Fiber keeps us healthy in many ways—the secret is knowing which fiber to consume. Refer to the chart listing which foods contain the type of fiber that is best for you! For example, if you want to lower your blood cholesterol levels, you should consume oat bran and beans. If you are constipated you should increase your consumption of wheat bran such as whole-wheat bread and whole-wheat grains like bulgur and brown rice. The typical American consumes only 10 to 20 grams of fiber per day. In order to obtain optimum health, one should consume between 25 and 40 grams of fiber per day. (Be sure to check with your physician before adding bulk to your diet.) Also be sure to add fiber to your diet gradually and to increase your water intake.

Q: I sometimes get gassy from fiber. What can I do to avoid this?

A: Unfortunately, some people experience flatulence or gas from an increase in dietary fiber. One way to decrease the gas from beans is to soak them in water for 24 hours prior to cooking them. Additionally, drinking a few extra glasses of water may help. Remember, add fiber to your diet gradually and increase the amount daily as your body adapts to a higher fiber content. Most people will experience a decline in gassiness after about three weeks.

Q: What about alcohol?

A: We regard alcohol as a "no-no" because of its negative effects on the body. Diabetics and hypertensives need to be especially cautious when it comes to alcohol as alcohol may cause swings in blood sugar levels and may raise blood pressure. Alcohol is also caloric at 7 Calories per gram (compared to protein and carbohydrate which each has 4, and fat which has 9 Calories per gram).

Q: Do I have to eat lettuce, tomato and "rabbit food" to have a healthy diet?

A: No, not at all. You can learn to take your favorite recipes and adapt them to a no added fat, sugar and sugar diet by following the methods of The Gloria Rose Gourmet Long Life Cooking School. A typical example is Italian food. You can make your lasagna, stuffed shells, pasta fagioli and minestrone soup without any fat, salt or sugar! Just turn to the recipes pages to learn how.

Q: What is a good breakfast for a diabetic?

A: A good breakfast for a diabetic is the same breakfast for someone with heart disease, hypertension or someone who wants to maintain good health. The breakfast should include: protein, complex carbohydrates, non-fat dairy foods and fruits. The small amount of fat required by the body is found naturally in grains and in protein-rich foods.

Sample Breakfast: 2/3 cup cooked oat bran cereal,
                             with cinnamon
                     1 cup skim milk
                     1 small orange
                     1 slice whole-wheat toast
                     2 teaspoons non-sugar preserves
                     Herbal tea with lemon

Q: My weight has been yo-yoing my entire life. Help!

A: One of the reasons many people cannot lose weight is because they have lost and regained too much weight too many times. As you lose and regain your BODY COMPOSITION CHANGES in your disfavor. You actually become FATTER every time you lose and regain. With each weight loss you lose some water, some muscle and some fat. But, when you regain the weight, you gain principally FAT, thereby increasing your body fat percentage. And fat is very slow metabolically and is difficult to take off. To boost your metabolism you need to increase your physical activity and consume a high-fiber, low-fat diet.

Q: So, then how can I lose weight?

A: The best way to lose weight is to increase your physical activity with aerobic or calorie burning exercises. This will increase your metabolism and help you get rid of fat. Examples of aerobic exercises are: walking, running, jogging, swimming, cycling and dancing. Increasing your consumption of complex carbohydrates like grains and whole-wheat products which are high in fiber and decreasing your fat intake are more sensible and longer lasting ways to lose weight than simply starving yourself.

Q: What exactly is cholesterol and in which foods is it found?

A: Cholesterol is an odorless, white fat-like substance found in all foods of animal origin. We need cholesterol to build cell walls, hormones and for various other functions. The liver makes all of the cholesterol our body needs; hence, there is no need to consume as much cholesterol as we do. Dietary sources of cholesterol include: red meat, veal, pork, lamb, organ meats, poultry skin, luncheon meats, full-fat dairy products, egg yolks, and shellfish.

Q: What is the difference between polyunsaturated, monounsaturated and saturated fats? Which is best for me?

A: The saturation of a fat refers to its chemical structure and the presence of double bonds of carbon. Because polyunsaturated fats are beneficial in lowering cholesterol some authorities believe one should increase the consumption of these oils to help lower cholesterol. Our program does not recommend the addition of extra oil, we believe that the most effective way to lower blood cholesterol is adding as little fat as possible to the diet. All authorities agree that saturated fats are not healthy and help raise blood cholesterol. Refer to the chapter containing a list of the dietary sources of the three types of fat.

Q: How much fat and cholesterol does the average American consume and what is the recommended amount per day?

A: Too much! The average American consumes 37 percent of calories from fat compared to the eastern diet in Japan where the typical diet contains only 10 to 15 percent fat. The average American consumes about 450 mg of cholesterol per day, which is down from about 700 mg a few years ago. The Gloria Rose Gourmet Long Life Cooking School program recommends the consumption of 10 to 15 percent of calories from fat and a limit of 100 to 150 mg of cholesterol per day.

Q: Are processed foods just as nutritious as fresh foods?

A: Processed foods usually are not as nutritious as fresh foods. Although canned, frozen and dehydrated foods offer nutritional value, ingredients such as salt and refined sugar can decrease the nutritional value. Plain frozen fruits and vegetables, however, are good choices. Also, many processed foods contain saturated fat in the form of butter or lard as flavor enhancers. Lastly, beware of palm kernel, palm and coconut oils which are in many processed foods because of their long shelf life. They are saturated fats and raise blood cholesterol.

Q: Should I consume sugar for energy?

A: Consuming sugar for energy is a common practice, however, it has no validity. Somehow, consumers are convinced that sugar is an "energy food." Consuming refined sugar can actually make one feel more fatigued, as the sugar can cause a surge in blood sugar and insulin, which leads to a decline in blood sugar. The best source of "energy" is from a balanced diet containing complex carbohydrates and protein.

Q: Is salt needed in canned foods as a preservative?

A: Salt is not needed in canned foods as a preservative. This is one of the most popular food myths. Salt can act as a preservative, but its presence in canned foods is to add flavor and create a taste that is acceptable to consumers. Refer to the chart listing how processing foods adds sodium.

Q: Is it natural to gain weight as you get older?

A: There is nothing natural about gaining weight with age except to say that it is a common occurrence. The average American gains one to two pounds per year after age 20! Weight gain with age is attributed to a more sedentary lifestyle, over-consumption of calories and frequent snacking.

Q: I've heard about fructose as a sugar substitute. May I use it?

A: Sugar by any other name is still sugar! Fructose is another of sugar's aliases. It is the name for the natural sugar found in fruit. However, the body perceives fructose as sugar and it functions in the body similarly to sugar. Our program does not allow fructose. Refer to the chart listing the other aliases for sugar.

54

David E. Klein, D. P. M.
New York City, NY
Exercise as it Pertains to Health Problems

INTERVIEW WITH DR. DAVID E. KLEIN

EXERCISE

Q: How does exercise fit into a good health program?

A: Exercise is essential for a good health program. A healthy body rests on three legs: proper nutrition, proper exercise and proper rest. Exercise is part of the balance of the triangle of proper health.

Q: What are the benefits of exercise?

A: The benefits of exercise are sometimes very apparent. For instance, if you exercise you will burn up calories and lose weight and increase your stamina, but there are many other dimensions of exercise. Foremost of these is the general sense of well-being from having done something positive; an inner strength and confirmation develops from having performed some exercise. Also, with aerobic exercise there is a chemical release of endorphins which have a euphoric effect on the personality. These chemical reactions from exercise give a sense of feeling better in general and the body begins to bloom with good feelings.

Q: What exercises do you recommend?

A: I've tempered my opinion about exuberant exercise these days, and am very much in favor of brisk walking. You want to be careful about that over-exuberant amateur who goes into exercise without being prepared for it. Being prepared and starting slowly are very important points. Brisk walking is excellent; bicycling is very healthy, and swimming is the best overall exercise because of the total body involvement. I often recommend what we call "mall walking." You can drive yourself to a mall in any kind of weather, rain or shine, and take a good walk in an enclosed environment. You can always do that year round. At home, of course, you could use a rowing machine. A good stretching program is also recommended. It is best to stretch just prior to or after exercise.

Q: How does exercise affect diabetes?

A: Diabetes was first recognized in the early Chinese dynasties. The only treatment they had at that point was exercise and it has been one of the oldest treatment plans for diabetes. As such it must be done every day. Exercise enhances insulin utilization.

Q: How does exercise affect heart and circulatory problems?

A: Both heart disease and peripheral vascular disease are affected by exercise because it fosters collateral circulation. To explain this, imagine that if there is a clogged river and if you push the flow of water down that river it will overflow it and run around the blockage; in the same way the body has the ability of channeling or reaching areas around a blockage in a main artery if the exertional push continued to develop it. It has been demonstrated both in the heart and the extremities that you can do this.

Q: How does exercise affect hypertension?

A: Exercise has been shown to improve the peripheral blood flow and reduce the tension and allow for a reduction in blood pressure.

Q: How does exercise affect arthritis?

A: What happens in arthritis is that if an elbow or a knee hurts, you tend to guard movement in that joint and as a result the muscles both above and below the joint will go into spasm. So these muscles do not get exercise. If people stay active and keep their muscles toned they will be able to accomplish a lot more than if they give in to the arthritis. If a person with arthritis does not keep moving the joints just get worse and the muscles weaker from non-use. Exercise in water is very good for those with arthritis. Even if you just walk in the swimming pool it is excellent.

Q: Why is The Gloria Rose Gourmet Long Life Cooking School program beneficial to your patients?

A: So many diet programs have been very unappetizing and very regimented. However, in the Gloria Rose program people are taught how to adjust and create a food plan that is suitable for their tastes and lifestyle and yet still fits within the requirements of their particular health needs. This program is so exciting because it teaches people how to eat in a healthy way according to their tastes, without use of added sugar, fat and salt that is so detrimental. She has succeeded in making healthy eating delicious and do-able, according to each individual preference.

BASIC NUTRITIONAL INFORMATION

Compare the numbers . . . . .

The Gloria Rose
Gourmet Long Life Daily Meal Plan

BREAKFAST:
1/2 grapefruit
1/3 cup oat bran cereal
1/2 apple, chopped, with cinnamon
1 cup skim milk
Herbal tea with lemon

MID-MORNING SNACK:
1 pear
1 cup seltzer water

LUNCH:
2 slices whole-wheat bread
2 ounces cooked turkey breast
1 lettuce leaf
1/2 tomato
1 teaspoon prepared mustard
1 cup herbal iced tea

MID-AFTERNOON SNACK:
3 cups air-popped popcorn

DINNER:
1 cup Lima Bean Soup, page 168
3 ounces cooked salmon
1 cup cooked broccoli
1/2 cup cooked brown rice
1 cup fresh strawberries
1 cup herbal iced tea with lemon wedge

EVENING SNACK:
1/2 cup Banana-Strawberry Sundae, page 341

TOTAL	
Calories	1255
Grams of fat	14 g
% of calories from fat	10%
Amt. of cholesterol	69 mg

.... from a typical day's fare.

Typical American Diet
Daily Meal Plan

BREAKFAST:

2 scrambled eggs in butter
2 slices bacon
2 slices white toast
2 pats of butter
2 teaspoons jelly
Coffee with 2 teaspoons sugar and 1 tablespoon half and half

MID-MORNING SNACK:

1 doughnut
Coffee with 2 teaspoons sugar and 1 tablespoon half and half

LUNCH:

Cheeseburger (FAST FOOD)
French fries
Chocolate shake

MID-AFTERNOON SNACK:

1 ounce chocolate bar

DINNER:

7 ounce T-bone steak
1 medium-size baked potato
2 tablespoons sour cream
Green salad with 2 tablespoons blue cheese dressing
1/2 cup green beans in butter sauce
1 cup ice cream

EVENING SNACK:

1 brownie
1 cup whole milk

TOTAL

Calories	3547
Grams of fat	204 g
% of calories from fat	51.7%
Amt. of cholesterol	912 mg

What do you eat
on a daily basis? . . . . . .

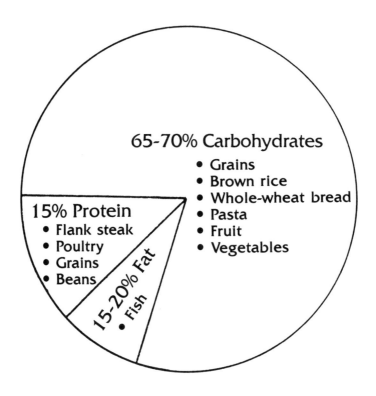

65-70% Carbohydrates
- Grains
- Brown rice
- Whole-wheat bread
- Pasta
- Fruit
- Vegetables

15% Protein
- Flank steak
- Poultry
- Grains
- Beans

15-20% Fat
- Fish

The Gloria Rose
Gourmet Long Life Cooking School

. . . . Compare the percentages

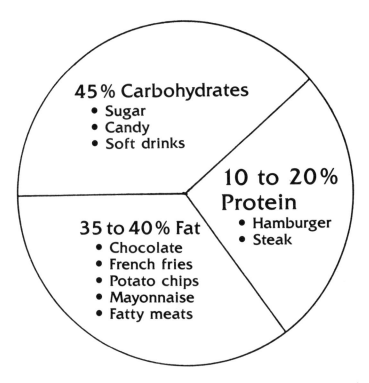

45% Carbohydrates
- Sugar
- Candy
- Soft drinks

10 to 20% Protein
- Hamburger
- Steak

35 to 40% Fat
- Chocolate
- French fries
- Potato chips
- Mayonnaise
- Fatty meats

The Typical American Diet

How to Choose Foods
Low in Cholesterol and Saturated Fat

MEAT, POULTRY, FISH, BEANS, EGG WHITES:
Chicken, turkey, Cornish hen, (without skin)
Fish and shellfish, including lobster, scallops, canned salmon, sardines and tuna packed in water
Lean meats, including beef flank steak, extra-lean chopped beef
Egg whites or egg substitute
Dried beans and peas, including lentils, lima beans, kidney beans, pinto beans, navy beans, chick peas, split peas
Tofu

DAIRY PRODUCTS:
Non-fat milk; evaporated skim milk; low-fat buttermilk; non-fat or low-fat yogurt; low-fat cottage cheese; farmer cheese; hoop cheese; "Our" Cream Cheese, page 135; "Our" Sour Cream, page 137

BREAD, CEREAL, GRAINS:
All whole-wheat or whole-grain products made without saturated fat; French or Italian bread, pita bread and rye bread; unprocessed wheat bran, oat bran; crackers and cereal without added fat; matzos, bagel, pasta, rice, tortillas, popcorn and unsalted pretzels; cakes, cookies, muffins using recipes in book.

VEGETABLES:
All varieties

FRUIT:
All varieties
Jams, jellies and preserves made without sugar

FATS AND OILS:
No Stick cooking spray
Olive oil and canola oil (only in limited amounts when needed)

BEVERAGES:
Mineral water; flavored seltzers; herbal teas; water processed, decaffeinated coffee

64

CONDIMENTS:

Herbs, spices, apple juice concentrate and other fruit juice concentrates, tamari sauce, soy sauce (diluted), miso, low-sodium mustard and sauces and toppings using recipes in book.

AVOID

MEAT, POULTRY, FISH, BEANS, EGGS, NUTS:

Duck, goose and skin from all poultry

Shellfish other than allowed

Red meat, fatty meat, veal, pork, lamb, ham, frankfurters, luncheon meats, organ meats, bacon and sausage

Egg yolks

Soybeans, most seeds, peanut butter

All nuts

DAIRY PRODUCTS:

Whole milk, 1 or 2% milk, whole-milk cheeses, cream cheese, ice cream, non-dairy creamers, whipped toppings, half and half, sour cream

BREADS, CEREAL, GRAINS:

Bread or grain made with fats; wheat germ; crackers and cereal with added fat; egg-based products; egg noodles; pastries, butter rolls, croissants, commercial biscuits and muffins, doughnuts and cakes.

VEGETABLES:

Avocados, olives. All vegetables fried in fat, served in cream, butter or cheese sauces, or canned with salt.

FRUIT:

Fruits with added sugar.

FATS AND OILS:

Butter, margarine, oils, lard, coconut oil, palm oil, palm kernel oil

BEVERAGES:

Caffeinated beverages, alcoholic beverages, carbonated sugar or diet soft drinks

CONDIMENTS:

Artificial sweeteners, salt, all sugars, steak sauces and any condiment containing sugar, salt or added fat

Choose Low-Fat Protein Sources Using Your Animal Protein Comparison Chart

ALLOWED

Animal Protein Source (3-1/2 oz.)	% Calories from fat	Total Fat grams	Total Cholesterol milligrams
Haddock	1%	0.09	60
Red snapper	2.5%	0.23	39
Cod	3.5%	0.30	50
Sea bass	5%	0.50	54
Tuna, water packed	6%	0.90	63
Sole	10%	0.80	42
Halibut	11%	1.20	50
Flounder	11%	0.80	50
Scallops	11%	1.40	52
Clams	18%	1.60	49
Lobster	19%	1.90	84
Trout, brook	19%	2.10	55
Turkey, white meat	20%	3.80	76
Oysters	22%	2.20	50
Swordfish	26%	4.00	68
Chicken, white meat	27%	4.90	87
Salmon	28%	3.70	34
Beef, round steak	29%	6.00	90
Chicken, dark meat	34%	6.50	87
Beef, flank steak	34%	7.30	90

Avoid High-Fat Animal Protein

NOT ALLOWED

Animal Protein Source (3-1/2 oz.)	% Calories from fat	Total Fat grams	Total Cholesterol milligrams
Lamb, lean	34%	7.0	99
Turkey, dark	36%	8.2	101
Steak, T-bone	41%	10.2	90
Roast, rump	44%	9.2	90
Beef, chuck	45%	9.4	90
Veal	46%	11.2	101
Pork, loin	50%	14.1	88
Beef, lean ground	55%	15.0	90
Crab	29%	3.0	100
Shrimp	8%	.8	160

References:
1. Pennington. J. A. T. and Church, H. N. *Food Values of Portion Commonly Used,* 14th Ed.
2. Nutritive Value of American Foods in Common Units, USDA TB#456, 1975
3. Krause, Barbara. *The Dictionary of Sodium, Fats, and Cholesterol.* Grosset & Dunlap, New York 1974.

OILS AND FATS

Type of Oil or Fat	Percent Saturated Fat	Percent Polyunsaturated Fat
SATURATED:		
Coconut oil	86%	2%
Palm oil	81%	2%
Butter	61%	4%
Beef fat	48%	4%
Lard	40%	12%
Vegetable shortening, avg.	32%	20%
Chicken fat	29%	26%
MONOUNSATURATED:		
Peanut oil	19%	30%
Olive oil	14%	9%
Canola oil	7%	35%
POLYUNSATURATED:		
Vegetable oil, avg.	13%	40%
Corn oil	13%	58%
Sunflower oil	10%	64%
Safflower oil	9%	74%

PAINLESS WAYS TO REDUCE FAT

Don't forget—stay below
3 grams of fat per serving!

IN PLACE OF	SUBSTITUTE	Grams of fat saved per serving
8 oz. whole milk (1 cup)	8 oz. skim milk	8
4 oz. sour cream (1/2 cup)	4 oz. low-fat yogurt	22
8 oz. regular yogurt (1 cup)	8 oz. low-fat yogurt	3
4 oz. part skim ricotta cheese (1/2 cup)	4 oz. low-fat cottage cheese	9
3 oz. chicken, with skin	3 oz. chicken, without skin	5
1 oz. potato chips	1 cup popcorn	10
6 oz. veal cutlet	6 oz. chicken-breast cutlet	13
1 oz. corn chips	1 tortilla	9
3 oz. pork chop with marbling	3 oz. lean flank steak	17
1/4 cup chocolate chips	1/4 cup carob chips	12

FAST FOOD IS FAT FOOD!

Fast Food Item	Total Calories	% Calories from fat
Burger King:		
Whopper	650	51%
Double Beef Whopper (with cheese)	970	57%
McDonald's:		
Big Mac	550	53%
Quarter Pounder (with cheese)	518	51%
Wendy's:		
Triple Cheeseburger	1040	59%
French fries	240	45%
McDonald's:		
Chicken McNuggets	314	54%
Kentucky Fried Chicken:		
Fried chicken—3 piece dinner		
original	830	47%
crispy	1070	52%
Arthur Treacher:		
Fried fish	354	50%
Apple pie	240	45%
Dairy Queen:		
Chili dog	330	55%
Dilly Bar	240	56%
Jack in the Box:		
Onion rings	351	59%

Don't get caught in the trap
at the salad bar . . .

SAVE FAT AND CALORIES

Instead of	Choose	Grams of fat saved
3 tablespoons blue cheese	3 tablespoons no oil dressing	24
1/2 cup potato salad	1/2 cup chick peas	12
4 large ripe olives	10 small mushrooms	8
1/4 avocado	1/2 cup 3-bean salad	6
1/2 cup egg salad	1/2 cup cottage cheese	7
3 tablespoons bacon bits	1/4 cup bean sprouts	4

Those cocktail party snacks

Just	Adds . . . Calories
4 crackers	84
1 ounce Cheddar cheese	114
20 peanuts	210
20 potato chips	226
4 oz. of eggnog	335
1 (3-1/2 oz.) Manhattan	164
2 tablespoons cream cheese	99
1 tablespoon caviar	32
2 sardines	75
1 chocolate eclair	316

Fish Containing Omega-3 Fatty Acids

Fish 3-1/2 oz., raw	Total Fat (grams)	Omega Fatty Acids (grams)	Cholesterol (milligrams)
Bass, striped	2.3	0.8	80
Bluefish	6.5	1.2	59
Herring, Atlantic	9.0	1.7	60
Mackerel, Atlantic	13.9	2.6	80
Mullet	4.4	1.1	34
Sablefish	15.3	1.5	49
Salmon, sockeye	8.6	1.3	—
Shark	1.9	0.5	44
Swordfish	2.1	0.2	39
Tuna, bluefin	6.6	1.6	38

Controlling Your Sodium Intake

SODIUM LEVELS

- 1 teaspoon salt has 2000 milligrams sodium
- 1 tablespoon shoyu or tamari sauce has 800 milligrams of sodium
- 1 tablespoon low-sodium soy sauce has approximately 500 milligrams sodium
- 1 bouillon cube has 1000 milligrams sodium
- 1 tablespoon dark miso has 925 milligrams sodium
- 1 tablespoon light miso has 530 milligrams sodium

NATIONAL ACADEMY OF SCIENCES
DAILY RECOMMENDATION —
1,100 TO 3,300 mg
(AVERAGE AMERICAN IS EATING 7,000 mg/DAY)

OUR PROGRAM LIMITS SODIUM INTAKE TO 2,000 mg PER DAY

A lot happens from an apple to apple pie!

WHERE'S THE SODIUM?

How food processing adds sodium . . .
(mg of sodium in parenthesis)

1 apple (2)	1 cup applesauce (4)	1/8 frozen apple pie (620)
1/2 chicken breast (69)	4 oz. frozen chicken pot pie (556)	1 breast fast food chicken (564)
4" corn-on-the-cob (trace)	3/5 cup canned corn (285)	1 oz. cornflakes (351)
1/2 cucumber, raw (3)	cucumber with 1 tbsp. Italian Salad Dressing (116)	1 large dill pickle (1428)
1 medium potato (3)	10 potato chips (200)	1 cup instant potato (485)
3 oz. pork (52)	4 slices bacon (456)	3-1/2 oz. cured ham, canned (1020)
1 small raw tomato (3)	1 cup tomato sauce (943)	1 cup tomato soup (1326)

High Sodium Foods to Avoid

Anchovies
Bacon
Bouillon
Bread crumbs — seasoned
Broth
Canned products
Catsup
Caviar
Cheese
Chili sauce
Corned beef
Corn chips
Crackers — salted
"Fast foods"
Frankfurters
Ham — especially cured
Luncheon meats
Monosodium glutamate (MSG)
Mustard

Olives
Peanuts
Pickled foods
Pickles
Pizza
Popcorn — salted
Potato chips
Pretzels
Relish
Salad dressings
Salt
Sauces — steak, barbecue
Sauerkraut
Sausage
Seasonings with salt
Tomato juice — salted
"TV" dinners
Worcestershire Sauce

Foods Low in Sodium and High in Potassium

(fresh or frozen without salt; if canned, salt-free)

FRUITS
Apples, raw, whole
Apricots
Banana
Cantaloupe
Dates
Grapefruit
Nectarines
Prunes
Raisins
Watermelon

VEGETABLES
Asparagus
Beans
Cabbage
Cauliflower
Corn-on-the-cob
Lima beans
Peas
Peppers, green
Potatoes
Radish
Squash

THE SWEET FACTS . . .

Beware! Sugar by any other name is still sugar . . .

Sugar may be listed under many different aliases on food labels. Read your food labels carefully!

Some sugar disguises: honey, molasses, corn syrup, high fructose syrup, raw sugar, brown sugar, confectioner's sugar, sorbitol, mannitol, xylitol, any ingredients ending with the letters "ose" — sucrose, fructose, lactose, maltose.

BREAKFAST CEREALS . . .
How sweet they are!

CEREAL	PERCENT SUGAR
Sugar Orange Crisp	68.0%
Sugar Smacks	61.3%
Fruity Pebbles	55.1%
Apple Jacks	55.0%
Lucky Charms	50.4%
Pink Panther	49.2%
Fruit Loops	47.4%
Trix	46.6%
Cocoa Krispies	45.9%
Count Chocula	44.2%
Captain Crunch	43.3%
Cocoa Puffs	43.0%

AND BEVERAGES TOO!

BEVERAGE	TEASPOONS OF SUGAR
Ginger ale, 12 oz.	10
Lemon-lime drinks, 12 oz.	7-1/2
Cola drinks, 12 oz.	7
Root beer, 10 oz.	4-1/2
Powdered fruit drink, 8 oz.	6
Chocolate milk, 8 oz.	6

CALCIUM EQUIVALENTS

The following foods in the listed amount contain about the same amount of calcium as in one cup of milk (300 mg).

Buttermilk, low-fat . . . . .1 cup
Cottage cheese, low-fat . . . . .2 cups
Yogurt, low-fat . . . . .1-1/4 cups
Tofu. . . . . .8 ounces
Canned salmon, with bones . . . . .4 ounces
Kidney beans . . . . .3-1/2 cups
Cooked greens, turnip or mustard . . . . .1-1/2 cups

KNOW YOUR MILKS!

Where's the fat? . . .
In 8 ounces of . . .

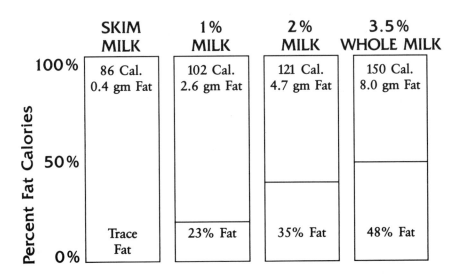

	SKIM MILK	1% MILK	2% MILK	3.5% WHOLE MILK
100%	86 Cal. 0.4 gm Fat	102 Cal. 2.6 gm Fat	121 Cal. 4.7 gm Fat	150 Cal. 8.0 gm Fat
50%				
0%	Trace Fat	23% Fat	35% Fat	48% Fat

Percent Fat Calories

NUTRITION LABELS

!Buyer Beware!

BEEF   According to USDA

- Extra lean is when a product has less than 5% fat.
- Lean or low-fat is when a product has less than 10% fat.
- "Lite", "Leaner" or "Lower fat" mean that the food has 25% less fat than a similar product.

CHOLESTEROL

- A product label may read "cholesterol free" yet still contain high amounts of saturated fats, which actually raise blood cholesterol levels more than cholesterol.

  Examples are:
  powdered coffee whitener, cracker, canned shortening

HOW TO FIGURE FAT CALORIES IN FOOD

General calories are not as important as FAT CALORIES — consider two products that both contain 100 calories — yet one could contain 60% fat calories and the other only 20% fat calories. Don't be misled by calorie count alone — remember this formula and you'll be in good shape!

GRANOLA BAR

Nutritional Information:

Per serving
Serving size . . . . 13 oz.
Servings per container 1
Calories 130
Protein 2
Carbohydrates 19
Fat 5

Use the following formula to
determine calories from fat:

$$\text{Calories from fat} = \frac{\text{grams of fat x 9}}{\text{total calories}} \text{ x } 100$$

Sample from granola bar label opposite

$$\text{Calories from fat} = \frac{5 \text{ x } 9}{130} \text{ x } 100$$

Calories from fat = 35.38 or 35%

Hints for a Slim Waistline and a Healthy Heart

☐ Drink fruit flavored seltzer water instead of fruit juice drinks and save hundreds of calories (8 oz. of seltzer water has zero calories; 8 oz. of cranberry juice cocktail has 147 Calories).

☐ Instead of eating apple pie (about 400 Calories per slice), bake an apple and flavor it with cinnamon and raisins (about 100 Calories).

☐ When serving hors d'oeuvres use sliced zucchini instead of crackers.

☐ Save the water from cooked vegetables (with lots of vitamins and minerals) and use to make soup.

☐ To get the most vitamins and minerals from your vegetables, leave the skins on. If you must peel the skin, do not slice too deeply as most of the nutrients lie just under the skin.

FIBER—WHICH IS BEST FOR YOU?

Remember . . . try to get 35 grams of fiber per day!

Column 1	Column 2
Insoluble	Soluble
Bran	Oat bran
Whole-wheat flour	Dried beans such as lentils,
Breakfast cereals	kidney beans, chick peas,
Whole grains	split peas
Kasha	Apples
Brown rice	Strawberries
	Citrus fruits
	Squash
	Cauliflower

COLUMN 1: May prevent constipation, and protect against diverticulosis, hemorrhoids and colon cancer.

COLUMN 2: Decreases fat absorption and helps to lower blood cholesterol levels. Delays glucose absorption helping diabetics.

FRUIT GROUP:

Each serving has about 2 grams of fiber

Apple	1 small
Banana	1 small
Berries	1/2 cup
Orange	1 small
Peach	1 medium

VEGETABLE GROUP:

Each serving has about 2 grams of fiber

Broccoli	1/2 stalk
Brussels sprouts	4
Carrots	1/3 cup
Green beans	1/2 cup
Potato	1 small
Tomato, raw	1 medium
Beans, canned, cooked	2 tablespoons

BREADS AND GRAIN GROUP:

Each serving has about 2 grams of fiber

Whole-wheat bread	1 slice
Grape-Nuts	2 tablespoons
Bran cereal	1 tablespoon
Oatmeal, dry	3 tablespoons
Popcorn, air-popped	2 cups
Brown rice	1/2 cup
Unprocessed bran	1 teaspoon
Shredded Wheat cereal	1/2 biscuit
Dried beans	1/4 cup

WEIGHT LOSS DIET
& WEIGHT LOSS MAINTENANCE PLAN

Every day in every newspaper across the country hundreds of ads appear regarding "Weight Loss Centers." They all guarantee wonderful results in trimming you down—it's easy—it's fast—no hunger—and, of course, they always show a picture of a 300 pound person and next to it his or her new look at 125 pounds—all done in three months!!

First of all, what they don't tell you is that if she took the "lose fat pills" for $12.95 a bottle, she has lost some weight but now may have serious health problems she never had before—hypertension (high blood pressure), migraine headaches, stomach problems, etc. Second, if she was on a liquid protein program, she lost weight as well as her bankbook! The average person on a liquid protein diet spends between $1,000 to $2,500.

But, thirdly and probably the most important problem is MAINTENANCE. They all take weight off but none of the six major weight loss programs can help you KEEP IT OFF! My office literally gets hundreds of calls telling us how within six weeks after losing the weight it comes back plus more! What is the answer!

Well, the answer is really very simple. In my opinion, they all have lost sight of one major problem. As I tell my students, you cannot expect people to maintain a program they cannot relate to. In other words, can someone who is a vegetarian or Italian or Kosher or Polish or whatever—all be put on the same maintenance program. Of course not, it's ridiculous. A maintenance program can only be successful if it custom fits each individual's needs. Any ethnic group should be able to enjoy their native dishes, eliminating fats, oils, sugar and salt without sacrificing taste.

Food is meant to be enjoyed. We are now treating the word "gourmet" as if it were a dirty word—whether it be for weight loss or for health reasons. How absurd! For food to be healthy must it be steamed veggies or broiled chicken or fish for the rest of one's life. ABSOLUTELY NOT!

Don't misunderstand, when I say "gourmet", I don't mean you should learn to cook like a chef out of the Cordon Bleu in Paris. To me gourmet means preparing one of *your* favorite delicious meals and knowing it is healthy without all the heavy butters, oils and cream! And that is what you will learn in this book.

My formula is simple—I am going to teach you how to pull out the "bad guys" from your recipe and how to replace them with the "good guys." In the beginning, it will take you a little longer to learn to substitute but I promise you within a month or two, it will become second nature. So let's begin.

SUBSTITUTES

Here is one of the quickest ways to eliminate fats from a recipe—whenever you see shortening or oil listed in the beginning of the ingredients that usually indicates something is to be sautéed. It will then say sauté until "soft" or "translucent" or "tender." Well, you don't need shortening to do that! Chop your onions or garlic fine (not diced), use a No Stick cooking spray, add 2 tablespoons chicken stock and your onions or garlic or whatever will come out perfect. In many cases that's all the recipe will require so you have eliminated 120 Calories right away. The No Stick cooking spray is only 6 calories per 2-1/2 second spray and if you spray a little longer you will not be adding hundreds of calories!

You will see that I use various oils in some recipes, but take notice they are used as a flavoring not an ingredient. For example, sesame oil, hot chili oil, et cetera—never more than 1/4 teaspoon is used for a complete recipe. In my nutrition classes, anything more than 1/4 teaspoon is considered an ingredient. When we break down our recipes for nutritional purposes, a 1/4 teaspoon for four people will come out to a trace (tr).

Next, always keep (depending upon the size of the family) a container of apple juice concentrate, in the refrigerator. DO NOT DILUTE. If you add the three containers of water, you will have apple juice and will have to use it in larger quantities—now adding more calories. We are going to use 1 tablespoon in the concentrated form for our use.

For a delicious drink, I make a large pitcher of herb tea and add 2 or 3 ounces of apple juice concentrate. The new herb teas on the market are wonderful—my family loves raspberry or orange. Add lots of ice cubes, a few slices of orange and that beats any diet cola!

In my Marinara Sauce, you will notice I add a tablespoon or so of apple juice concentrate to cut the acidity. Try it and experiment wherever you want a sweetener.

For baking I use brown rice syrup or barley malt syrup. Since most supermarkets do not stock these products on their shelves, this is one of the few items you may have to buy in a health food store.

Substituting applesauce or mashed bananas will help you eliminate most if not all of the oil or shortening from your cake, bread or cookie recipes.

Also use egg substitutes when eggs are needed–end result is the same and no cholesterol!!

For the past two years, I signed off on my television show saying "Remember nutritious can be delicious" — and that my dear readers is want I want to convey to you.

Now let's get on to the diet and maintenance plans. Following are diet plans for weight loss and maintenance for the adult male and adult female. Also included are sections devoted to the overweight child and the pregnant woman. My staff and I have done our best to present well rounded and delicious menus — the rest is up to you!

WEIGHT LOSS DIET FOR MEN

It is important to consume a variety of the right foods daily in order to achieve and maintain a desirable body weight. Your body will also work better if you have a balanced meal plan daily. The meal plans provided on the following pages for both weight loss and weight maintenance are nutritionally balanced. They were specifically designed to include the right amount of vitamins, minerals, carbohydrates, protein and fat daily. The meal plan is a guide that shows you the foods you may eat at each meal and snack time. Please keep in mind that these meal plans are flexible and any food item on a particular day can be switched and traded for another food item on the same day to accommodate your individual needs and lifestyle.

For those of you that are unable to "bag your lunch," I have designed your weight and maintenance program with that in mind. It is much easier to enjoy a "soup and sandwich" lunch than to nibble on carrot sticks or eat yogurt while out on the road. However, on weekends use the recipes in the book.

You may have to change some of your food choices and eating habits to eat in a more nutritious and healthier way. Just remember to make changes gradually. It may take longer to accomplish your goal but the changes you make will be permanent ones.

Here are a few hints to help you stick with your meal plan:

Bag Your Lunch—Take a thermos of homemade soup, or take a container of salad and homemade dressing.

Watch your meat portion sizes—it's easy to eat too much.

Drink plenty of water throughout the day!

Of course, consult your physician before beginning any weight loss diet. Also, if you have particular nutritional needs, you should consult a registered dietitian for assistance in modifying the meal plans.

Good luck on your journey to a healthier lifestyle!!

WEIGHT LOSS DIET FOR MEN
1400 CALORIES
DAY 1

BREAKFAST	CALORIES	TOTAL CALORIES
1 cup skim milk	90	
1-1/2 cups puffed wheat cereal	80	
3/4 cup strawberries	60	
1 Breakfast Muffin, page 314	120	
1 cup herb tea and lemon wedge	0	
		350

LUNCH		
1/2 cup low-fat cottage cheese on a bed of romaine lettuce with raw vegetables	250	
1 baked potato	80	
1 slice whole-wheat bread	80	
1 teaspoon fruit preserves	14	
1 cup decaffeinated coffee	0	
		424

SNACK		
1/8 honeydew melon	60	
		60

DINNER		
3 tablespoons Cucumber-Herb Dressing, page 327	34	
1 cup tossed salad	25	
1 cup Cabbage Soup, page 179	42	
1 serving Beef Stroganoff, page 200	256	
1/2 cup no-yolk noodles	80	
1 slice rye bread	80	
1 cup herb tea	0	
		517

SNACK		
2 cups popped popcorn, no butter	53	
		53

TOTAL CALORIES		1404

WEIGHT LOSS DIET FOR MEN
1400 CALORIES
DAY 2

BREAKFAST	CALORIES	TOTAL CALORIES
1 cup skim milk	90	
1/2 cup Wheatena cereal	80	
2 tablespoons raisins	60	
1 cup herb tea and lemon wedge	0	
		230

LUNCH		
1 cup skim milk	90	
1 cup Bean Soup, page 159	120	
1 cup pasta with Marinara Sauce, page 332	185	
1 slice Italian bread	80	
		475

SNACK		
1 apple	60	
		60

DINNER		
1 cup Clear Mushroom Soup, page 176	40	
1 serving Carrot Salad, page 255	205	
1 serving Chicken Hawaiian, page 218	146	
1/3 cup cooked brown rice	80	
1 serving sautéed escarole	24	
1 slice whole-wheat bread	80	
1 cup herb tea	0	
		575

SNACK		
18 Nabisco Snack Well's Cheese Crackers	60	
		60

TOTAL CALORIES		1400

WEIGHT LOSS DIET FOR MEN
1400 CALORIES
DAY 3

BREAKFAST	CALORIES	TOTAL CALORIES
1 cup skim milk	90	
1 serving Mexican Fiesta Omelet, page 252	91	
1 peach	60	
1 slice rye toast	80	
1 teaspoon fruit preserves	14	
1 cup herb tea and lemon wedge	0	
		335

LUNCH		
1 cup skim milk	90	
3 oz. tuna with lettuce and tomato	250	
3 tablespoons reduced-calorie dressing	67	
1 slice bread	80	
		487

SNACK		
1/2 cup fresh pineapple	60	
		60

DINNER		
1 cup tossed salad	25	
3 tablespoons Basic Vinaigrette, page 322	9	
1 cup Creamy Tofu Tomato Soup, page 161	119	
1 serving Confetti Macaroni Bake, page 239	158	
1/2 cup cooked spinach	25	
1 slice Italian bread	80	
1 cup herb tea	0	
		416

SNACK		
3 small Health Valley Fat Free Cookies	75	
		75

TOTAL CALORIES		1373

WEIGHT LOSS DIET FOR MEN
1400 CALORIES
DAY 4

BREAKFAST	CALORIES	TOTAL CALORIES
1 cup skim milk	90	
3/4 cup oat bran flakes	80	
1/2 cup blueberries	60	
1 cup herb tea and lemon wedge	0	
		230

LUNCH		
1 cup skim milk	90	
3/4 cup vegetable soup	80	
Chicken sandwich (3 oz. meat, lettuce, tomato and mustard)	385	
		555

SNACK		
1/2 cup cantaloupe	60	
		60

DINNER		
1 cup Soup a la Athens, page 177	29	
1 cup cooked broccoli	25	
3 tablespoons Creamy Artichoke Dressing, page 324	36	
1 serving Salmon Surprise, page 191	210	
1 serving Mushrooms in Wine, page 286	72	
1 slice multi-grain bread	80	
1 cup herb tea	0	
		452

SNACK		
1 Banana Nut Pop, page 340	89	
		89

TOTAL CALORIES		1386

WEIGHT LOSS DIET FOR MEN
1400 CALORIES
DAY 5

BREAKFAST	CALORIES	TOTAL CALORIES
1 cup skim milk	90	
2/3 cup cooked oat bran cereal	80	
1/2 grapefruit	60	
1 slice whole-wheat toast	80	
2 teaspoons fruit preserves	28	
1 cup herb tea and lemon wedge	0	
		338

LUNCH		
1 cup skim milk	90	
1 cup bean soup	160	
1 cup tossed salad	25	
2 tablespoons reduced-calorie dressing	45	
1 medium-size baked potato	80	
1/2-inch slice honeydew melon	60	
		460

SNACK		
1 peach	60	
		60

DINNER		
1 serving Egg Drop Soup, page 164	33	
1 serving Stir-Fry Chicken, page 230	189	
1/3 cup cooked brown rice	80	
1 slice whole-wheat bread	80	
1 cup herb tea	0	
		382

SNACK		
2 servings Banana-Strawberry Sundae, page 341	166	
		166

TOTAL CALORIES		1406

WEIGHT LOSS DIET FOR MEN
1400 CALORIES
DAY 6

BREAKFAST	CALORIES	TOTAL CALORIES
1 cup skim milk	90	
1/2 cup Shredded Wheat cereal	80	
1/2 banana	60	
1 cup herb tea and lemon wedge	0	
		230

LUNCH		
1 cup skim milk	90	
Chef salad (3 oz. meat, 2 cups vegetables)	275	
1/4 cup reduced-calorie dressing	90	
1 slice bread	80	
		535

SNACK		
1 orange	60	
		60

DINNER		
1 cup tossed salad	25	
3 tablespoons Creamy Garlic Italian Dressing, page 326	24	
1 serving Minestrone Soup, page 172	108	
1 serving Vegetable-Topped Baked Fish, page 195	153	
1/2 cup cooked linguine	80	
1 serving Garlic Basil Green Beans, page 282	19	
1 slice Italian bread	80	
1 cup herb tea	0	
		489

SNACK		
18 Nabisco Snack Well's Cinnamon Graham Crackers	80	
		80

TOTAL CALORIES		
		1394

WEIGHT LOSS DIET FOR MEN
1400 CALORIES
DAY 7

BREAKFAST	CALORIES	TOTAL CALORIES
1 cup skim milk	90	
2 pancakes	80	
1/2 cup raspberries	60	
1 slice whole-wheat toast	80	
1 teaspoon fruit preserves	14	
1 cup herb tea and lemon wedge	0	
		324

LUNCH		
1 cup skim milk	90	
1 turkey sandwich (3 oz. turkey, 2 slices bread, lettuce, tomato and mustard)	385	
		475

SNACK		
1 pear	60	
		60

DINNER		
1 cup tossed salad	25	
2 tablespoons Greek Garlic Dressing, page 330	18	
1 serving Brazilian Holiday Chicken, page 214	233	
1/3 cup cooked brown rice	80	
1 serving Green Peas with Curried Mushrooms, page 285	40	
1 slice rye bread	80	
1 cup herb tea	0	
		476

SNACK		
1 serving Pineapple Cloud Parfait, page 355	126	
		126

TOTAL CALORIES		1461

WEIGHT MAINTENANCE DIET FOR MEN
1800 CALORIES
DAY 1

BREAKFAST	CALORIES	TOTAL CALORIES
1 cup skim milk	90	
2 waffles	160	
3/4 cup strawberries	60	
1 slice whole-wheat toast	80	
2 teaspoons fruit preserves	28	
1 cup herb tea and lemon wedge	0	
		418

LUNCH		
1 cup skim milk	90	
1 cup vegetable soup	80	
1 chicken sandwich (3 oz. meat, 2 slices bread, lettuce and tomato)	385	
		555

SNACK		
1 large tangerine	60	
		60

DINNER		
1 cup raw vegetables	25	
3 tablespoons French Dressing, page 329	21	
1 serving Lima Bean Soup, page 168	138	
1 serving Macaroni Salmon Loaf, page 188	245	
1 serving Baked Zucchini, Eggplant & Tomatoes, page 274	82	
1 slice whole-wheat bread	80	
1 cup herb tea	0	
1 apple	60	
		651

SNACK		
1 serving Pears with Fruited Yogurt Sauce, page 354	131	
		131

TOTAL CALORIES		1815

WEIGHT MAINTENACE DIET FOR MEN
1800 CALORIES
DAY 2

BREAKFAST	CALORIES	TOTAL CALORIES
1 cup skim milk	90	
2/3 cup cooked oat bran cereal	80	
2 tablespoons raisins	60	
1 slice whole-wheat bread	80	
2 teaspoons fruit preserves	28	
1 cup herb tea and lemon wedge	0	
		338

LUNCH		
1 cup skim milk	90	
1-1/2 servings Minestrone Soup, page 172	162	
Turkey sandwich (3 oz. meat, 2 slices bread, lettuce, tomato and mustard)	385	
		637

SNACK		
1 orange	60	
		60

DINNER		
1 serving Creamy Tofu Tomato Soup, page 161	119	
1 cup tossed salad	25	
3 tablespoons Creamy Garlic Italian Dressing, page 326	24	
1 serving Spinach Mushroom Lasagna, page 244	298	
2 slices Italian bread	160	
1 serving Garlic Basil Green Beans, page 282	19	
1 cup herb tea	0	
		645

SNACK		
1 serving Pineapple Orange Pie, page 357	120	
		120

TOTAL CALORIES		1800

WEIGHT MAINTENANCE DIET FOR MEN
1800 CALORIES
DAY 3

BREAKFAST	CALORIES	TOTAL CALORIES
1 cup skim milk	90	
1/2 cup Shredded Wheat cereal	80	
1 peach	60	
2 slices multi-grain bread	160	
2 teaspoons fruit preserves	28	
1 cup herb tea and lemon wedge	0	
		418

LUNCH		
1 cup skim milk	90	
3 oz. tuna with raw vegetables	250	
1/4 cup reduced-calorie dressing	90	
1 slice whole-wheat bread	80	
		510

SNACK		
1/2 cup cubed cantaloupe	60	
		60

DINNER		
1 serving Mulligatawny Soup, page 173	156	
1 cup tossed salad	25	
1/4 cup Basic Vinaigrette, page 322	12	
1 serving Szechuan Beef with Noodles, page 208	406	
1 slice whole-wheat bread	80	
1 serving Green Bean Stir-Fry, page 292	37	
1 cup herb tea	0	
		716

SNACK		
8 Nabisco Snack Well's Wheat Crackers	80	
		80

TOTAL CALORIES		1784

WEIGHT MAINTENANCE DIET FOR MEN
1800 CALORIES
DAY 4

BREAKFAST	CALORIES	TOTAL CALORIES
1 cup skim milk	90	
1-1/2 cups puffed wheat	80	
1/2 cup blueberries	60	
2 slices rye toast	160	
1 tablespoon fruit preserves	42	
		432

LUNCH		
1 cup skim milk	90	
1-1/2 cups cooked pasta with Marinara Sauce, page 332	275	
1 cup tossed salad	25	
2 tablespoons reduced-calorie dressing	45	
1 slice bread	80	
		515

SNACK		
1/2 cup fresh pineapple and 2 tablespoons Orange Chiffon Fruit Dressing, page 333	90	
		90

DINNER		
1 cup tossed salad	25	
2 tablespoons French Dressing, page 329	14	
1 cup Bean Soup, page 159	120	
1 serving Bouillabaisse (4 oz. fish), page 182	194	
1/3 cup cooked brown rice	80	
1/2 cup cooked broccoli	25	
2 slices whole-wheat bread	160	
1 cup herb tea	0	
		618

SNACK		
1 oz. Smart Temptations No Oil Tortilla Chips	100	
		100

TOTAL CALORIES		1755

WEIGHT LOSS DIET FOR MEN
1800 CALORIES
DAY 5

BREAKFAST	CALORIES	TOTAL CALORIES
1 cup skim milk	90	
1/2 cup Shredded Wheat cereal	80	
3/4 cup strawberries	60	
1 Breakfast Muffin, page 314	120	
1 tablespoon fruit preserves	42	
1 cup herb tea and lemon wedge	0	
		392
LUNCH		
1 cup Luscious Lentil Soup, page 169	166	
3/4 cup low-fat cottage cheese on bed of lettuce and tomato	250	
1 slice bread	80	
1/8 honeydew melon	60	
		556
SNACK		
1 medium-size kiwifruit	60	
		60
DINNER		
1 cup White Bean & Vegetable Soup, page 180	102	
1 cup tossed salad	25	
3 tablespoons Greek Garlic Dressing, page 330	27	
1 serving Turkey Meatballs in Tomato Wine Sauce, page 234	164	
1 cup cooked linguine	160	
1 slice whole-wheat bread	80	
1 serving Breaded Zucchini, page 281	71	
1 cup herb tea	0	
		629
SNACK		
1 serving Rum Raisin Ice Cream, page 360	122	
		122
TOTAL CALORIES		1759

WEIGHT MAINTENANCE DIET FOR MEN
1800 CALORIES
DAY 6

BREAKFAST	CALORIES	TOTAL CALORIES
1 cup skim milk	90	
3/4 cup oat bran flakes	80	
1/2 banana	60	
1 water bagel	160	
2 tablespoons "Our" Cream Cheese, page 135	18	
1 cup herb tea and lemon wedge	0	
		408
LUNCH		
Chef salad (3 oz. meat, 2 cups vegetables)	275	
3 tablespoons reduced-calorie dressing	67	
1 cup skim milk	90	
2 slices Italian bread	160	
1 baked potato	80	
		672
SNACK		
3/4 cup strawberries	60	
		60
DINNER		
1 cup Egg Drop Soup, page 164	33	
1 serving Vegetable-Topped Baked Fish, page 195	153	
1 serving Winter Squash Medley, page 298	164	
1/3 cup cooked brown rice	80	
1 slice whole-wheat bread	80	
1 cup herb tea	0	
		510
SNACK		
1 serving Pineapple Ice Cream, page 356	139	
		139
TOTAL CALORIES		1789

WEIGHT MAINTENANCE DIET FOR MEN
1800 CALORIES
DAY 7

BREAKFAST	CALORIES	TOTAL CALORIES
1 cup skim milk	90	
1/2 cup Wheatena cereal	80	
1/2 cup raspberries	60	
1 Apple-Cinnamon Muffin, page 313	97	
1 tablespoon fruit preserves	42	
1 cup herb tea and lemon wedge	0	
		369

LUNCH		
1 cup skim milk	90	
1 cup vegetable soup	80	
4 oz. turkey sub sandwich (lettuce, tomato, onion, vegetable (no oil)	465	
		635

SNACK		
1 peach	60	
		60

DINNER		
1 serving Italian Zucchini-Cauliflower Soup, page 167	107	
1 serving Tropical Spinach Salad, page 270	71	
1 serving Cranberry Chicken, page 222	330	
1/3 cup kasha	80	
1 Hawaiian Muffin, page 317	92	
1 cup herb tea	0	
		680

SNACK		
1 oz. Polly-O Lite Mozzarella Stick	60	
		60

TOTAL CALORIES		1804

WEIGHT LOSS DIET FOR WOMEN

The following Weight Loss Diet is prepared with thought for the woman who works away from home or who stays at home. It is nutritionally sound and at the same time void of boredom. I have made this diet with many variables—daily changes of cereals, soups and salads. Feel free to substitute one day for another as long as you keep within the calorie boundary.

Because I have eliminated fats, sugar and salt from the recipes, you will find your portions and amounts larger than the typical diet. This is especially so when you have lost the desired weight and go on "Maintenance." There will actually be times when you feel so full you cannot finish the complete meal!

So enjoy and—remember nutritious can be delicious!

WEIGHT LOSS DIET FOR WOMEN
1200 CALORIES
DAY 1

BREAKFAST	CALORIES	TOTAL CALORIES
1 cup skim milk	90	
1/2 cup oat bran flakes	80	
1/2 cup blueberries	60	
1 slice whole-wheat toast	80	
2 teaspoons fruit preserves	28	
1 cup herb tea and lemon wedge	0	
		338

LUNCH		
1 cup tossed salad	25	
2 tablespoons Creamy Cucumber Artichoke Dressing, page 325	32	
1 cup Minestrone Soup, page 172	108	
1 slice Italian bread	80	
1 cup skim milk	90	
		335

SNACK		
1/2 grapefruit	60	
		60

DINNER		
1 cup tossed salad	25	
2 tablespoons Greek Garlic Dressing, page 330	18	
3/4 cup Curried Carrot Soup, page 162	58	
1 serving King of the Sea Primavera, page 186	275	
1/8 honeydew melon	60	
1 cup herb tea	0	
		436

SNACK		
4 Health Valley Oat Bran Graham Crackers	51	
		51

TOTAL CALORIES		
		1220

WEIGHT LOSS DIET FOR WOMEN
1200 CALORIES
DAY 2

BREAKFAST	CALORIES	TOTAL CALORIES
1 cup skim milk	90	
3 tablespoons Grape-Nuts cereal	80	
1/2 small banana	60	
1 slice rye toast	80	
1 teaspoon fruit preserves	14	
1 cup herb tea and lemon wedge	0	
		324

LUNCH		
8 oz. skim milk	90	
Turkey sandwich (3 oz. meat, lettuce and tomato)	310	
		400

SNACK		
1/2 cup cantaloupe	60	
		60

DINNER		
1 serving Onion Soup, page 165	38	
1 Baked Stuffed Potato with Spinach, page 272	72	
1 serving Marinated Flank Steak, page 203	176	
1 cup herb tea	0	
		286

SNACK		
3 slices whole-wheat melba toast	40	
1 teaspoon fruit preserves	16	
		56

TOTAL CALORIES		1126

WEIGHT LOSS DIET FOR WOMEN
1200 CALORIES
DAY 3

BREAKFAST	CALORIES	TOTAL CALORIES
1 cup skim milk	90	
1/2 cup Shredded Wheat cereal	80	
3/4 cup strawberries	60	
1 cup herb tea and lemon wedge	0	
		230
LUNCH		
Mixed salad with 1/4 cup reduced-calorie dressing	115	
3/4 cup bean soup	160	
1 slice multi-grain bread	80	
1 cup skim milk	90	
		445
SNACK		
1 pear	60	
		60
DINNER		
1 cup tossed salad	25	
2 tablespoons Basic Vinaigrette, page 322	6	
1 cup Delicate Snow Pea Soup, page 163	37	
1 serving Chinese Fish, page 183	180	
1/2 cup cooked broccoli	25	
1 baked potato	88	
2 tablespoons "Our" Sour Cream, page 137	22	
1 cup herb tea	0	
		383
SNACK		
7 Nabisco Snack Well's Wheat Crackers	70	
		70
TOTAL CALORIES		1188

WEIGHT LOSS DIET FOR WOMEN
1200 CALORIES
DAY 4

BREAKFAST	CALORIES	TOTAL CALORIES
1 cup skim milk	90	
3/4 cup oat bran cereal	80	
1 medium peach	60	
1 Breakfast Muffin, page 314	120	
1 teaspoon fruit preserves	14	
1 cup herb tea and lemon wedge	0	
		364

LUNCH		
1/2 cup low-fat cottage cheese	102	
1 cup diced melon	120	
1 slice whole-wheat bread	80	
1 cup skim milk	90	
		392

SNACK		
1/2 cup fresh pineapple	60	
		60

DINNER		
1 cup raw vegetables	25	
2 tablespoons Creamy Artichoke Dressing, page 324	24	
1 serving Cabbage Soup, page 179	42	
1 serving Vegetable-Topped Baked Fish, page 195	153	
1/3 cup cooked brown rice	80	
1 cup herb tea	0	
		324

SNACK		
3 unseasoned rye crisps	40	
		40

TOTAL CALORIES		1180

WEIGHT LOSS DIET FOR WOMEN
1200 CALORIES
DAY 5

BREAKFAST	CALORIES	TOTAL CALORIES
1 cup skim milk	90	
2 pancakes	80	
1/2 cup raspberries	60	
1 slice whole-wheat toast	80	
2 teaspoons fruit preserves	28	
1 cup herb tea and lemon wedge	0	
		338

LUNCH		
1 cup skim milk	90	
1 cup raw vegetables	25	
2 tablespoons French Dressing, page 329	14	
1 serving Mexican Bean Soup, page 171	67	
1 Corn Cake, page 315	34	
		230

SNACK		
1 apple	60	
		60

DINNER		
1 serving Cucumbers in Herbed Yogurt, page 259	43	
1 serving Gingered Sole, page 185	109	
1 serving Natalie's Rice & Black-Eyed Peas, page 311	165	
1/2 cup cooked asparagus	25	
1 slice whole-wheat bread	80	
1 cup herb tea	0	
		422

SNACK		
1 Snyder's Unsalted Sour Dough Pretzel	100	
1 Orange	60	
		160
TOTAL CALORIES		**1210**

WEIGHT LOSS DIET FOR WOMEN
1200 CALORIES
DAY 6

BREAKFAST	CALORIES	TOTAL CALORIES
1 cup skim milk	90	
1/2 cup cooked old-fashioned oats	80	
2 tablespoons raisins	60	
1 Apple-Cinnamon Muffin, page 313	97	
2 teaspoons fruit preserves	28	
1 cup herb tea and lemon wedge	0	
		355

LUNCH		
3 oz. water-packed tuna on a bed of romaine lettuce with tomato	225	
1 slice whole-wheat bread	80	
1 cup herb tea	0	
		305

SNACK		
3/4 cup mandarin orange sections	60	
		60

DINNER		
1 serving Tropical Spinach Salad, page 270	71	
1 serving Clear Mushroom Soup, page 176	40	
1-1/2 servings Casablanca Chicken, page 215	263	
1/3 cup cooked brown rice	80	
1 cup herb tea	0	
		454

SNACK		
1-1/2 cups air-popped popcorn	40	
		40

TOTAL CALORIES		1214

WEIGHT LOSS DIET FOR WOMEN
1200 CALORIES
DAY 7

BREAKFAST	CALORIES	TOTAL CALORIES
1 cup skim milk	90	
1/2 cup Wheatena cereal	80	
2 tablespoons raisins	60	
1/2 water bagel	80	
2 teaspoons fruit preserves	28	
1 cup herb tea and lemon wedge	0	
		338

LUNCH		
1 cup skim milk	90	
1 serving Summer Tomato Salad, page 268	46	
1 serving Soup a la Athens, page 177	29	
2 tablespoons Hummus Party Dip, page 148	58	
1/2 whole-wheat pita pocket (6")	80	
		303

SNACK		
1 medium-size kiwifruit	60	
		60

DINNER		
1 cup tossed salad	25	
2 tablespoons Basic Vinaigrette, page 322	6	
1 cup Spanish Rice Soup, page 178	131	
1 serving Chicken Korma, page 219	175	
1/3 cup kasha	80	
1/2 cup cooked green beans	25	
1 cup herb tea	0	
		442

SNACK		
18 Nabisco Snack Well's Cheese Crackers	60	
		60

TOTAL CALORIES		
		1203

WEIGHT MAINTENANCE DIET FOR WOMEN
1500 CALORIES
DAY 1

BREAKFAST	CALORIES	TOTAL CALORIES
1 cup skim milk	90	
2/3 cup cooked oat bran cereal	80	
2 tablespoons raisins	60	
1 slice whole-wheat toast	80	
2 teaspoons fruit preserves	28	
1 cup herb tea and lemon wedge	0	338

LUNCH		
1 cup skim milk	90	
1 cup raw vegetables	25	
1/4 cup Creamy Garlic Italian Dressing, page 326	32	
1 serving Mexican Bean Soup, page 171	67	
1 serving Mexican Fiesta Omelet, page 252	91	
1 slice whole-wheat bread	80	
1 cup herb tea	0	386

SNACKS		
1 orange	60	
1 serving Creamy Rice Pudding, page 347	196	256

DINNER		
1 cup tossed salad	25	
3 T. Basic Vinaigrette, page 322	9	
1 serving Broccoli Bisque, page 158	86	
1/2 serving Cranberry Chicken, page 222	215	
1/2 cup cooked brown rice	80	
1 serving Green Bean Stir Fry, page 292	37	
1 slice oatmeal bread	80	
1 cup herb tea	0	532
TOTAL CALORIES		1512

WEIGHT MAINTENANCE DIET FOR WOMEN
1500 CALORIES
DAY 2

BREAKFAST	CALORIES	TOTAL CALORIES
1 cup skim milk	90	
1-1/2 cups puffed rice	80	
1/2 banana	60	
1 Apple-Cinnamon Muffin, page 313	97	
2 teaspoons fruit preserves	28	
1 cup herb tea and lemon	0	
LUNCH		**355**
1 cup skim milk	90	
1 serving Summer Tomato Salad, page 268	46	
1 cup Minestrone Soup, page 172	108	
1 slice whole-wheat bread	80	
1 cup herb tea	0	
SNACK		**324**
1 orange	60	
DINNER		**60**
1 serving Tropical Spinach Salad, page 270	71	
1 cup garlic croutons	80	
1 serving Manhattan Clam Chowder, page 170	137	
1 serving Scallops in Lime Sauce, page 192	101	
1 serving Glazed Carrots, page 283	95	
1/3 cup cooked kasha	80	
1 slice multi-grain bread	80	
1 cup herb tea	0	
SNACK		**644**
1 serving Pineapple Cloud Parfait, page 355	126	
		126
TOTAL CALORIES		**1509**

WEIGHT MAINTENANCE DIET FOR WOMEN
1500 CALORIES
DAY 3

BREAKFAST	CALORIES	TOTAL CALORIES
1 cup skim milk	90	
1/2 cup Wheatena cereal	80	
1 cup unsweetened cranberries	60	
1 slice rye toast	80	
2 teaspoons fruit preserves	28	
1 cup herb tea and lemon wedge	0	
		338

LUNCH		
1/2 cup low-fat cottage cheese on a bed of romaine lettuce	102	
1 cup cooked pasta with Marinara Sauce, page 332	185	
1 small whole-wheat roll	80	
		367

SNACK		
1/2 cup cantaloupe	60	
		60

DINNER		
1 serving Lima Bean Soup, page 168	138	
1 cup tossed salad	25	
1 tablespoon Creamy Artichoke Dressing, page 324	12	
1 serving Chicken L'Orange with Mushrooms, page 220	230	
1/3 cup cooked brown rice	80	
2 servings Garlic Basil Green Beans, page 282	38	
1 slice oat bran bread	80	
1 cup herb tea	0	
		603

SNACK		
1 serving Rum Raisin Ice Cream, page 360	122	
		122

TOTAL CALORIES		
		1490

WEIGHT MAINTENANCE DIET FOR WOMEN
1500 CALORIES
DAY 4

BREAKFAST	CALORIES	TOTAL CALORIES
1 cup skim milk	90	
1 tablespoon Grape-Nuts	80	
1/2 small banana	60	
1 Breakfast Muffin, page 314	120	
1 teaspoon fruit preserves	14	
1 cup herb tea and lemon wedge	0	
		364
LUNCH		
1 cup skim milk	90	
1 whole-wheat pita pocket (6")	160	
2 oz. tuna with lettuce and tomato	150	
1 tablespoon reduced-calorie dressing	23	
		423
SNACK		
1/2 grapefruit	60	
		60
DINNER		
1 cup raw broccoli	25	
2 tablespoons Creamy Cucumber Artichoke Dressing, page 325	32	
1 cup Pea, Mushroom & Barley Soup, page 174	79	
1 serving Macaroni Salmon Loaf, page 188	245	
1 serving Winter Squash Medley, page 298	164	
1 slice whole-wheat bread	80	
1 cup herb tea	0	
		625
SNACK		
1/2 cup Orange Gelatin Delight, page 353	30	
		30
TOTAL CALORIES		1502

110

WEIGHT MAINTENANCE DIET FOR WOMEN
1500 CALORIES
DAY 5

BREAKFAST	CALORIES	TOTAL CALORIES
1 cup skim milk	90	
1 waffle (4-1/2" square)	80	
3/4 cup strawberries	60	
1 slice multi-grain bread	80	
2 teaspoons fruit preserves	28	
1 cup herb tea and lemon wedge	0	
		338

LUNCH		
1 cup skim milk	90	
1 serving Pasta e Fagioli Soup, page 175	240	
6 slices whole-wheat melba toast	80	
1 cup tossed salad	25	
2 tablespoons Creamy Garlic Italian Dressing, page 326	16	
		451

SNACK		
1 pear	60	
		60

DINNER		
1 serving Carrot Salad, page 255	205	
4 oz. Fabulous Turkey Breast, page 225	137	
1/2 cup cooked asparagus	25	
1 baked potato	80	
1 slice whole-wheat bread	80	
1 cup herb tea	0	
		527

SNACK		
7 Health Valley Oat Bran Graham Crackers	120	
		120

TOTAL CALORIES		1443

WEIGHT MAINTENANCE DIET FOR WOMEN
1500 CALORIES
DAY 6

BREAKFAST	CALORIES	TOTAL CALORIES
1 cup skim milk	90	
3/4 cup cold oat bran cereal	80	
1/2 cup raspberries	60	
1 slice whole-wheat toast	80	
2 teaspoons fruit preserves	28	
1 cup herb tea and lemon wedge	0	
		338

LUNCH		
1 cup skim milk	90	
3 oz. salmon with lettuce and tomato	250	
1 serving Bean Soup, page 159	120	
1 slice whole-wheat bread	80	
		540

SNACK		
1 medium-size kiwifruit	60	
		60

DINNER		
1 serving Clear Mushroom Soup, page 176	40	
1 cup tossed salad	25	
3 tablespoons Cucumber-Herb Dressing, page 327	34	
1 serving Midweek Meat Surprise, page 205	171	
1/2 cup cooked broccoli	25	
1 small whole-wheat roll	80	
1 cup herb tea	0	
		375

SNACK		
1 oz. Crispini, Sodium Free Flatbreads by Burns & Ricker	98	
2 teaspoons fruit spread	28	126

TOTAL CALORIES		
		1441

WEIGHT MAINTENANCE DIET FOR WOMEN
1500 CALORIES
DAY 7

BREAKFAST	CALORIES	TOTAL CALORIES
1 cup skim milk	90	
1/2 cup Shredded Wheat cereal	80	
1/2 cup blueberries	60	
1/2 water bagel	80	
2 teaspoons fruit preserves	28	
1 cup herb tea and lemon wedge	0	
		338
LUNCH		
1 cup skim milk	90	
1 cup raw vegetables	25	
3 tablespoons Creamy Artichoke Dressing, page 324	36	
1 cup Spanish Rice Soup, page 178	131	
1 Enchilada, page 156	152	
		434
SNACK		
1 large tangerine in sections	60	
2 tablespoons Orange Chiffon Fruit Dressing, page 333	30	
		90
DINNER		
1 cup fresh tossed salad	25	
1 tablespoon Green Goddess Dressing, page 331	15	
1 cup White Bean & Vegetable Soup, page 180	102	
1 serving Stuffed Shells, page 243	278	
1 slice Italian bread	80	
1 cup herb tea	0	
		500
SNACK		
2 servings Banana-Strawberry Sundae, page 341	166	
		166
TOTAL CALORIES		**1528**

THE OVERWEIGHT CHILD

To the parents:

If you have a child over the age of five, whose weight is 20 percent or more than is desirable, as determined by your doctor or other health professional, then this chapter is for you.

It is important for you to remember that most overweight children do not require weight loss as much as they need to improve their eating habits, increase their physical activity and be allowed to "grow into" their present weight. The menus that follow contain approximately 1400 Calories a day. They have been designed to meet the nutritional needs of a growing child. However, we advise you to seek the advice of a physician before beginning any dietary program. If your child has particular preferences or needs which require more precise meal planning, we suggest you consult a registered dietitian.

Here are some tips to help you use the meal plans:

1. Bear in mind that a child will only eat foods that he/she likes— the menu ideas presented here have been chosen carefully. Be sure to follow this advice when you design your own menus for your child.

2. The food you serve your child should not differ from that served to the rest of the family or the child's friends. As you will discover, the meals suggested in this chapter are suitable for everyone.

3. Never force your child to eat something he/she doesn't want. Give your child the opportunity to try something new, but don't force it.

4. Never force your child to "clean his plate" — it would be much better if your taught your child to leave a little something behind.

5. The menus presented here are very low in fat, and moderately low in calories. If your family does not have a strong history of heart disease or high cholesterol, you may want to be more liberal with the fat content of the diet. Additional fat (and calories) may be incorporated into the diet with the use of cooking oils, by using whole milk products instead of skim or low-fat products and also with the use of a corn oil soft spread. The calorie content may be increased with the addition of mid-morning or mid-afternoon snacks.

6. Please see the Approved Products List in the back of this book for our recommendations.

GOOD SNACKS FOR CHILDREN

Do you know what makes a snack good for children to eat? Here are a few hints.

A good snack should:

1. be nutritious
2. taste and look good
3. not spoil a child's appetite for meals
4. vary day by day

Here are some quick and tasty snacks that can be ready in the refrigerator:

Carrot sticks	Cherry tomatoes
Orange sections	Vegetable juice
Pineapple chunks	Watermelon balls
Strawberries	Raisins
Honeydew/cantaloupe balls	Whole-grain bread
Cauliflower pieces	Unsweetened cereal
Broccoli florets	Yogurt
Banana slices	Cottage cheese
Green pepper slices	Skim milk

Are you looking for some healthy snack recipes for your children? Try these—they're guaranteed to please!

1. Banana Pennies—slice 1 banana into 1 cup of orange juice. Chill. Divide mixture into 4 portions and serve in small paper cups with spoons.

2. Monkey Pops—Peel banana, cut in half. Insert flat wooden sticks into one end of each half and freeze. Dip frozen banana in melted orange juice concentrate. Roll in wheat germ, uncooked rolled oats or graham cracker crumbs.

3. Carrot Surprise—Combine 1 cup grated carrot, 1/2 cup unsweetened crushed pineapple and 1/4 cup raisins. Serve chilled. Serves 6.

4. Fruit Slush—Pour fruit juice of choice into undivided ice cube trays. Freeze only until large crystals form and juice is no longer liquid. Remove from freezer and scrape frozen juice with fork into slush. Serve in cups in 1/4-cup portions.

5. Easy Pizza—Spread 1 tablespoon of tomato sauce on 1/2 whole-wheat English muffin, bread or pita. Sprinkle with

oregano and top with 1 tablespoon grated Parmesan cheese. Bake 10 minutes at 400F (205C).

6. Milk-Fruit Frappé—Combine 1 cup milk and one of the following in blender: a pitted and peeled apricot, pear or peach; 1 banana or 2 or 3 tablespoons of frozen fruit concentrate. Whip until smooth. Serves 2.

7. Better-than-a-Banana-Split—Cut banana into 4 pieces. Place 2 side by side on dish. Add 1/4 cup scoop of cottage cheese on top of banana. Repeat with other two. Garnish with wheat germ, raisins or sliced fruit. Use 1 tablespoon frozen fruit juice concentrate as a sauce. Serves 2.

8. Banana Ice Cream—page 342.

DIET PLAN FOR
OVERWEIGHT CHILD

DAY 1	CALORIES	TOTAL CALORIES
3/4 cup dry whole-grain cereal	100	
1 small banana	60	
1 cup skim milk	90	
		250
2 tablespoons peanut butter	180	
1 tablespoon no-sugar preserves	50	
2 slices whole-grain bread	160	
6 dried apricot halves	60	
1 cup skim milk	90	
		540
1 serving of My Favorite Chili, page 206	257	
1 tortilla	80	
Lettuce and tomato	25	
1/2 cup steamed broccoli	25	
1 serving Fruit Medley Gelatin Mold, page 349	62	
1 cup skim milk	90	
		539
1 Health Valley Oatmeal Jumbo Cookie	70	
		70
TOTAL CALORIES		1399

DIET PLAN FOR OVERWEIGHT CHILD

DAY 2	CALORIES	TOTAL CALORIES
1/2 cup cooked oatmeal	100	
1/2 bagel with 1 tablespoon "Our" Cream Cheese, page 135	90	
1/2 cup cantaloupe cubes	60	
1 cup skim milk	90	
		340
1/2 cup tuna (water packed)	110	
2 teaspoons no-cholesterol light mayonnaise	45	
Lettuce and tomato	25	
1 large whole-wheat pita bread	160	
1 pear	60	
1 cup skim milk	90	
		490
1 serving Egg Drop Soup, page 164	33	
1 serving Stir-Fry Chicken, page 230	189	
1/3 cup cooked brown rice	80	
1 apple	60	
1 cup skim milk	90	
		452
18 Nabisco Snack Well's Cheese Crackers	60	
1 cup fresh strawberries	60	
		120
TOTAL CALORIES		1402

DIET PLAN FOR OVERWEIGHT CHILD

DAY 3	CALORIES	TOTAL CALORIES
3 whole-wheat pancakes	150	
with 1 tablespoon no-sugar fruit syrup	50	
1 orange	60	
1 cup skim milk	90	
		350
3 oz. sliced turkey breast, lettuce and mustard	165	
2 slices rye bread	160	
2 fresh plums	60	
1 cup skim milk	90	
		475
1 serving Clear Mushroom Soup, page 176	40	
1 serving Stuffed Shells, page 243	278	
Tossed salad with	25	
2 tablespoons Creamy Garlic Italian Dressing, page 326	16	
1 fresh peach	60	
1 cup skim milk	90	
		509
1 Banana Nut Pop, page 340	89	
		89
TOTAL CALORIES		1423

DIET PLAN FOR OVERWEIGHT CHILD

DAY 4	CALORIES	TOTAL CALORIES
1/2 cup cooked Wheatena cereal	100	
1 slice toast with	80	
2 teaspoons no-sugar preserves	28	
1/4 small honeydew melon	60	
1 cup skim milk	90	
		358
1 cup low-fat yogurt	150	
1/2 cup unsweetened pineapple chunks	70	
3 Glo's Cookies, page 350	159	
1 Ryvita cracker	35	
1 cup iced tea sweetened with 1 teaspoon apple juice concentrate	13	
		427
1 serving Crispy Chicken, page 224	301	
1 Baked Stuffed Potato with Spinach, page 272	144	
1/2 cup unsweetened applesauce	60	
		451
Strawberry Milkshake:		
1 cup skim milk	90	
1 teaspoon apple juice concentrate	13	
1/2 cup frozen strawberries	60	
3 Health Valley Graham Crackers	47	
		210
TOTAL CALORIES		1500

DIET PLAN FOR OVERWEIGHT CHILD

DAY 5	CALORIES	TOTAL CALORIES
2 slices French Toast, page 316	192	
1 tablespoon no-sugar fruit syrup	50	
1 cup skim milk	90	
		332
1 Weekender Sandwich, page 236	266	
1 cup broccoli florets dipped in	25	
2 tablespoons Creamy Garlic Italian Dressing, page 326	16	
1 small banana	60	
1 cup skim milk	90	
		457
1 cup Minestrone Soup, page 172	108	
1 serving "Fried" Fish Fillets, page 184	157	
1 Potato Pancake, page 152	107	
1/2 cup steamed cauliflower	25	
2 tangerines	60	
1 cup skim milk	90	
		547
14 Nabisco Snack Well's Cinnamon Graham Crackers	65	
		65
TOTAL CALORIES		1401

DIET PLAN FOR OVERWEIGHT CHILD

DAY 6	CALORIES	TOTAL CALORIES
1 serving Mexican Fiesta Omelet, page 252	91	
1 cup fresh blueberries	60	
1 slice whole-grain toast with	80	
2 teaspoons no-sugar preserves	28	
1 cup skim milk	90	
		349
2 tablespoons peanut butter	180	
1 tablespoon no-sugar preserves	50	
1 large whole-wheat pita bread	160	
Zucchini spears	25	
1 fresh apple	60	
1 cup skim milk	90	
		565
1 serving Turkey Meatballs in Tomato Wine Sauce, page 234	164	
1/2 cup cooked spaghetti	80	
1 serving Green Bean Stir-Fry, page 292	37	
1/2 cup cantaloupe cubes	60	
		341
1 cup skim milk	90	
12 Nabisco Snack Well's Chocolate Chip Cookies	30	120
TOTAL CALORIES		1465

DIET PLAN FOR
OVERWEIGHT CHILD

DAY 7	CALORIES	TOTAL CALORIES
1 Oat Bran Surprise Muffin Deluxe, page 318	161	
1 nectarine	60	
1 cup skim milk	90	
		311
1 serving Quick Pizza, page 248	103	
Cucumber rounds	25	
1 slice Pineapple-Orange Pie, page 357	120	
1 cup skim milk	90	
		338
1 serving Creamed Corn Chicken, page 223	340	
1 serving Glazed Carrots, page 283	95	
1 cup diced watermelon	60	
1 cup skim milk	90	
		585
2 servings Angel Food Cake, page 337	114	
1 cup fresh raspberries	60	
		174
TOTAL CALORIES		1408

THE PREGNANT WOMAN

The diet during pregnancy should be well-balanced (with particular attention paid to proper calcium, protein and iron intake) and should allow for adequate weight gain. For most women, the rate of weight gain should be approximately 2 to 4 pounds during the first trimester and 3 to 4 pounds per month thereafter. In order to gain this weight, six meals per day are suggested. The menus that follow have been designed to provide a nutritious diet and contain approximately 2000 calories per day.

Those women who are not at ideal body weight at the start of pregnancy or who have particular nutritional needs should seek the advice of a registered dietitian for assistance in modifying the meal plans. Always consult with your physician before beginning any dietary program and follow your physician's advice regarding vitamin/mineral supplementation.

Here are some tips to help you use the meal plans:

1. The menus are very low in fat. While we do recommend limiting all fats, it is important for the pregnant woman to receive adequate fatty acid intake. Therefore, we suggest that you use 2 teaspoons of polyunsaturated fat per day—such as corn oil margarine on bread or corn oil in stir-fry dishes and on salads. Please see Approved Products List in this book for our recommendations.

2. If you work or are away from home and want to have yogurt as suggested in the meal plan, you can stir in some fruit or no-sugar preserves the day before and freeze it. When you take it out the next morning, it will be cold and defrosted by lunch or snack time.

3. Fruits and vegetables provide important nutrients and a variety should be included daily. Avoiding eating the same ones all the time.

4. Many high fiber foods are suggested in the menu plans. This will aid with digestion and may help prevent the common complaint during pregnancy of irregularity. Drinking plenty of fluids (at least 8 glasses per day) is also important—water is the healthiest drink.

5. Some women have a tendency to have high blood sugar during pregnancy (gestational diabetes). These menus contain no added sugars and may help you to avoid or treat this problem. In any case, please follow your physician's advice.

DIET PLAN FOR PREGNANT WOMEN

DAY 1	CALORIES	TOTAL CALORIES
BREAKFAST		
3/4 cup dry whole-grain cereal	100	
1 slice whole-grain bread	80	
2 teaspoons no-sugar preserves	28	
1 cup strawberries	60	
1 cup skim milk	90	
		358
SNACK		
1 serving Delicate Snow Pea Soup, page 163	37	
2 Ryvita crackers	70	
		107
LUNCH		
3/4 cup tuna (water packed)	165	
2 teaspoons no-cholesterol light mayonnaise	45	
Lettuce, tomato	25	
1 large whole-wheat pita bread	160	
1 cup skim milk	90	
		485
SNACK		
1 cup low-fat yogurt	150	
1/2 banana	60	
1 cup strawberries	60	
		270
DINNER		
1 serving Chicken Dijon, page 217	183	
1 serving Glazed Carrots, page 283	95	
1 Stuffed Baked Potato, page 293	122	
1 slice whole-wheat matzo	117	
1 cup fruit salad	60	
2 tablespoons Orange Chiffon Fruit Dressing, page 333	30	
		607
SNACK		
Fruit Milkshake:		
1 cup skim milk	90	
3/4 cup frozen fruit (your choice)	54	
1 teaspoon apple juice concentrate	13	
		157
TOTAL CALORIES		**1984**

DIET PLAN FOR PREGNANT WOMEN

DAY 2	CALORIES	TOTAL CALORIES
BREAKFAST		
1 Oat Bran Muffin Surprise Deluxe, page 318	137	
1/2 cup cooked oatmeal	100	
1 fresh orange	60	
1 cup skim milk	90	
		397
SNACK		
1/2 cup grapefruit juice	60	
2 whole-wheat breadsticks	50	
		110
LUNCH		
2 tablespoons peanut butter	190	
1 tablespoon no-sugar preserves	50	
2 slices whole-grain bread	160	
Carrot and celery sticks	25	
2 figs	60	
1 cup skim milk	90	
		575
SNACK		
1 Health Valley Cinnamon Jumbo Cookie	70	
1 cup skim milk	90	
		160
DINNER		
2 servings Turkey Meatballs in Tomato Wine Sauce, page 234	274	
1 serving sautéed escarole	24	
1 serving Scalloped Potatoes, page 287	116	
1 fresh pear	60	
1 cup herb tea	0	
		474
SNACK		
7 Health Valley Oat Bran Graham Crackers	120	
1 cup skim milk	90	
		210
TOTAL CALORIES		1916

DIET PLAN FOR PREGNANT WOMEN

DAY 3	CALORIES	TOTAL CALORIES
BREAKFAST		
3 whole-wheat pancakes	150	
1 tablespoon no-sugar fruit syrup	50	
1 tangerine	60	
1 cup skim milk	90	
		350
SNACK		
1 Piña Colada Muffin, page 320	94	
1 cup skim milk	90	
		184
LUNCH		
1 serving Microwaved Chili, page 204	225	
1 tortilla	80	
Tossed salad	25	
2 tablespoons Creamy Artichoke Dressing, page 324	24	
1 small banana	60	
1 cup herb tea	0	
		414
SNACK		
1 cup low-fat yogurt	150	
1/2 cup unsweetened pineapple chunks	70	
1 mini whole-wheat pita bread	80	
1 tablespoon "Our" Cream Cheese, page 135	9	
		309
DINNER		
1 serving King of Sea Primavera, page 186	275	
1 2-inch slice Italian bread	160	
1 serving Orange Gelatin Delight, page 353	30	
1 cup skim milk	90	
		555
SNACK		
1/2 cup frozen yogurt	120	
7 Health Valley Graham Crackers	110	
		230
TOTAL CALORIES		**2042**

DIET PLAN FOR PREGNANT WOMEN

DAY 4	CALORIES	TOTAL CALORIES
BREAKFAST		
1/2 cup Crispy Oats cereal	110	
2 teaspoons raisins	20	
1/2 bagel with 1 tablespoon "Our" Cream Cheese, page 135	90	
1/2 cantaloupe	60	
1 cup skim milk	90	
		370
SNACK		
2 plums	60	
2 rice cakes with 2 tablespoons peanut butter	250	
		310
LUNCH		
1 serving Confetti Macaroni Bake, page 239	158	
1 slice whole-wheat matzo	117	
Cucumber rounds	25	
1 cup skim milk	90	
		390
SNACK		
1 serving Angel Cheese Cake, page 336	74	
1 cup skim milk	90	
		164
DINNER		
1 serving Broiled Flank Steak, page 201	175	
1 serving Garlic Basil Green Beans, page 282	19	
1 serving Gourmet Quick Rice Pilaf, page 303	111	
1 slice rye bread	80	
1 fresh apple	60	
1 cup herb tea	0	
		445
SNACK		
2 oz. Snyder's Unsalted Sour Dough Pretzels	200	
1 cup skim milk	90	
		290
TOTAL CALORIES		1969

DIET PLAN FOR PREGNANT WOMEN

DAY 5	CALORIES	TOTAL CALORIES
BREAKFAST		
1/2 cup cooked Wheatena cereal	100	
1 slice whole-wheat toast	80	
2 teaspoons no-sugar preserves	28	
1/2 grapefruit	60	
1 cup skim milk	90	358
SNACK		
1 Hawaiian Muffin, page 317	92	
1 cup skim milk	90	182
LUNCH		
1 serving Creamy Tofu Tomato Soup, page 161	119	
4 small wheat crackers	80	
1 serving Pasta Cheese Bake, page 245	244	
Tossed salad with	25	
2 tablespoons Cucumber-Herb Dressing, page 327	22	
1 serving Fruit Medley Gelatin Mold, page 349	62	
1 cup herb tea	0	552
SNACKS		
1 serving Creamy Rice Pudding, page 347	196	
2 cups skim milk	180	
1 serving Banana Strawberry Sundae, page 341	83	459
DINNER		
2 servings Lime-Broiled Fish, page 187	180	
1 serving Twice Baked Sweet Potato, page 297	100	
Stir-fried zucchini in 2 t. corn oil	115	
1 Corn Cake, page 315	34	
1 fresh pear	60	
1 cup herb tea	0	
		489
TOTAL CALORIES		2040

DIET PLAN FOR PREGNANT WOMEN

DAY 6	CALORIES	TOTAL CALORIES
BREAKFAST		
2 slices French Toast, page 316	192	
1 tablespoon no-sugar fruit syrup	50	
1 cup skim milk	90	
		332
SNACK		
1 popcorn cake	35	
1/2 cup orange juice	60	
		95
LUNCH		
1 serving Grandma's Greek Garbanzo Soup, page 166	140	
1 serving Brown Rice Cheese, page 240	126	
Spinach salad	25	
2 tablespoons Greek Garlic Dressing, page 330	18	
1 fresh peach	60	
1 cup skim milk	90	
		459
SNACK		
2 servings Rich Pound Cake, page 359	198	
1 cup skim milk	90	
		288
DINNER		
2 servings Poached Chicken in Gingered Orange Sauce, page 229	288	
1 serving Glazed Carrots, page 283	95	
1 boiled potato	80	
1 slice whole-grain bread	80	
1 baked apple	60	
1 cup herb tea	0	
		603
SNACK		
2 servings Quick Pizza, page 248	206	
1 cup skim milk	90	
		296
TOTAL CALORIES		2073

DIET PLAN FOR PREGNANT WOMEN

DAY 7	CALORIES	TOTAL CALORIES
BREAKFAST		
1/2 cup cooked oatmeal	100	
1 bagel with 2 tablespoons "Our" Cream Cheese, page 135	180	
6 dried apricot halves	60	
1 cup skim milk	90	
		430
SNACK		
1 Breakfast Muffin, page 314	120	
1 cup skim milk	90	
		210
LUNCH		
3/4 cup tuna (water-packed)	165	
2 teaspoons no-cholesterol light mayonnaise	45	
Lettuce, tomato	25	
1 large whole-wheat pita bread	160	
1 cup fruit salad	60	
1 cup herb tea	0	
		455
SNACK		
2 Health Valley Cinnamon Jumbo Cookies	140	
1 cup skim milk	90	
		230
DINNER		
1 serving Egg Drop Soup, page 164	33	
1 serving Stir-Fry Beef, page 231	230	
1 serving Microwaved Brown Rice, page 306	117	
1 cup watermelon cubes	60	
1 cup herb tea	0	
		440
SNACK		
2 oz. Crispini, Sodium Free Flatbreads by Burns & Ricker	200	
1/2 cup skim milk	45	
1 oz. Polly-O Lite Mozzarella Stick	60	305
TOTAL CALORIES		2070

RECIPES

''OUR'' HOMEMADE BASICS

BARBECUE SAUCE

1/4 cup chopped onion
1/2 cup water
2 tablespoons vinegar
1 tablespoon Worcestershire sauce
1/4 cup fresh lemon juice
2 tablespoons brown rice syrup
1 cup no-salt added ketchup seasoned with chili powder
1/4 teaspoon paprika
1 teaspoon Dijon-style mustard
2 teaspoons garlic powder

METHOD

1. Sauté onion in pan sprayed with No Stick cooking spray.
2. Add remaining ingredients and simmer 20 minutes. Use for barbecued chicken or beef.

Makes 1-1/2 cups.

Variation

For those who prefer more tang, add 1 tablespoon hot salsa.

NUTRITIONAL
BREAKDOWN (Per tablespoon)

- Calories 18
- Protein . . . . tr
- Carbohydrates 4g
- Fat . . . . tr
- Sodium 6mg
- Cholesterol 0mg

"OUR" CREAM CHEESE

1 cup low-fat or non-fat yogurt

METHOD

1. Use a plastic coffee strainer (the type you place in a drip coffee maker). Fill with yogurt and place over a wide mouth jar. Or place a funnel in a container (make sure container opening is smaller than funnel). Place a paper coffee filter in funnel and then fill with yogurt.
2. Cover and refrigerate overnight.
3. The next morning, discard whey in jar. The cream cheese is in the strainer. Place in a small container, cover and refrigerate until needed.

Makes 1/2 cup.

Variations

Add various juice concentrates to the yogurt before straining. Let stand a few hours, then strain overnight. Use as a sweet spread for bagels or bread.

Add salsa (no salt) before straining, let stand a few hours, then strain overnight. Use as a delicious spicy spread for salads, tortillas or main dishes.

NUTRITIONAL
BREAKDOWN (Per tablespoon)
- Calories 9
- Protein 1g
- Carbohydrates. 1g
- Fat . . . . .tr
- Sodium 5mg
- Cholesterol . . . . .tr

"OUR" MAYONNAISE

1-1/2 cups low-fat cottage cheese, drained
1 tablespoon apple juice concentrate
2 tablespoons apple cider vinegar
1 egg white
2 tablespoons fresh lemon juice
1 teaspoon no-salt added Dijon-style mustard
3/4 teaspoon onion powder
1 teaspoon low-sodium soy sauce

METHOD

1. Place all ingredients in a food processor fitted with the metal blade. Process 4 to 5 minutes, until double in volume and very smooth and creamy.
2. Pour into a glass container, cover and refrigerate overnight.

Variations

Season with curry powder, fresh minced garlic, grated horse-radish, crushed pineapple, chives or salsa.

Makes 2-1/2 cups.

NUTRITIONAL
BREAKDOWN (Per tablespoon)

- Calories 18
- Protein 1.5g
- Carbohydrates 1g
- Fat . . . . .tr
- Sodium 58mg
- Cholesterol . . . . .tr

"OUR" SOUR CREAM

1 cup low-fat cottage cheese, drained
2 tablespoons low-fat buttermilk
1/4 teaspoon fresh lemon juice

METHOD

1. Place all ingredients in a blender and blend until smooth and creamy.

Variations

Add 1 tablespoon salsa and use for dips.

Add vanilla or almond extract and/or pureed fruits for dessert toppings (omit lemon juice).

Add no-salt added Dijon-style mustard and 1/2 teaspoon low-sodium soy sauce for meat or fish dishes.

For dips or sauces, add salsa, mustard, parsley or finely chopped spinach, minced jalapeños, etc.

Makes 1 cup.

NUTRITIONAL BREAKDOWN

(Per recipe)		(Per tablespoon)	
• Calories	174	• Calories	11
• Protein	29g	• Protein	1.8g
• Carbohydrates	7.5g	• Carbohydrates	0.5g
• Fat	2g	• Fat	tr
• Sodium	958mg	• Sodium	40mg
• Cholesterol	10mg	• Cholesterol	42mg

BEEF STOCK

4 pounds beef shanks, cut in 2-inch pieces
4 onions, unpeeled, quartered
2 large carrots, quartered
4 celery stalks, quartered
2 tablespoons low-sodium soy sauce
Cheesecloth bag containing 8 parsley sprigs, 1 teaspoon dried
   leaf thyme and 1 large bay leaf, cut in half
5 quarts water

METHOD

1. Preheat oven to 400F (205C). Cook shanks in a baking pan in oven until browned. Drain off and discard fat.
2. Place all ingredients in a large stock pot. Simmer 2 hours, skimming off foam as it rises to surface.
3. Strain through a cheesecloth-lined strainer. Cover and refrigerate overnight.
4. Remove and discard congealed fat from surface. Use within 3 days or freeze. To freeze, pour into containers with airtight lids. Freeze up to 3 months.

Makes 5 quarts.

NUTRITIONAL
BREAKDOWN (Per cup)

- Calories 12
- Protein 1g
- Carbohydrates 2g
- Fat . . . . tr
- Sodium 20mg
- Cholesterol . . . . tr

CHICKEN STOCK

Cold water, to cover chicken 4 inches–about 7 quarts water
5 pounds chicken necks and backs–remove all visible fat
4 carrots cut in thirds
4 stalks celery with leaves–cut in half
1 large parsnip cut in thirds
1 leek–use white part only
Parsley or dill–use your preference
1 large bay leaf
1 large onion–cut in half
6-8 peppercorns

METHOD
1. Place all ingredients in an 8-10 quart stainless steel pot. Cover with cold water. Bring to boil and remove the residue.
2. Lower the heat and simmer for 2-1/2 hours partially covered. Stock should reduce by 1/3 and be gelatinous (fairly thick).
3. Strain through a triple mesh strainer. Cool and place in the refrigerator overnight. Remove congealed fat before using or freezing.
4. Place in plastic containers or ice cube trays. Can remain unused in freezer 3 months.

Makes 2 quarts.

Variation
If you have the need of salt–halfway through cooking add 2 tablespoons Light Miso. This miso resembles peanut butter in texture and color. Mix with 2-3 tablespoons hot stock to liquify miso from its original thick consistency.

Option: Add 5-6 uncooked chicken wings for a stronger sweeter flavor.

NUTRITIONAL
BREAKDOWN (Per cup)

- Calories 12
- Protein 1g
- Carbohydrates 2g
- Fat . . . . tr
- Sodium 17mg
- Cholesterol . . . . tr

FISH STOCK

3 pounds bones, head, etc. of any white fish such as sole, flounder, halibut or whiting
2 cups quartered onions
1 cup coarsely chopped carrots
1 cup coarsely chopped celery
1/2 bunch parsley stems
4 tablespoons fresh lemon juice
9 cups water
3/4 cup white wine

METHOD

1. Combine everything in a large stock pot except water and wine and steam 5 minutes.
2. Add water and wine. Bring to a boil, skimming off foam. Cook stock over medium heat 40 minutes.
3. Strain through a cheesecloth-lined strainer. Cover and refrigerate overnight.
4. Remove and discard any fat from surface.
5. Use within 2 days or freeze. To freeze, pour into containers with airtight lids. Freeze up to 2 months.

Makes 1-1/2 quarts.

NUTRITIONAL
BREAKDOWN (Per cup)

- Calories 12
- Protein 1g
- Carbohydrates 2g
- Fat. . . . . tr
- Sodium . . . . tr
- Cholesterol . . . . tr

VEGETABLE STOCK

8 carrots, cut in thirds
8 celery stalks with leaves, cut in half
2 large onions, cut in quarters
2 medium-size turnips, peeled, cut in quarters
2 teaspoons dried leaf thyme
2 large leeks, white only, cut in half
1/2 bunch Italian parsley sprigs
6 to 8 garlic cloves, coarsely chopped
2 bay leaves, cut in half

METHOD

1. Place all ingredients in a large stock pot and add enough water to cover vegetables by about 3 inches.
2. Bring to a boil, reduce heat and simmer 1 to 1-1/2 hours, skimming off foam.
3. Strain stock through a cheesecloth-lined strainer. Cover and refrigerate until cool. Use within 3 days or freeze. To freeze, pour into containers with airtight lids. Use within 3 months.

Makes 5 quarts.

Variation

Additional vegetables can be added.

NUTRITIONAL BREAKDOWN (Per cup)

- Calories 10
- Protein . . . . tr
- Carbohydrates 0.75g
- Fat 0
- Sodium 5mg
- Cholesterol 0

FROZEN BOUILLON CUBES

2 cups Chicken Stock, page 139, or Beef Stock, page 138
1/2 cup white wine
1 bay leaf, broken in half
1 garlic clove, minced

METHOD

1. Boil all ingredients in a medium-size saucepan until reduced to half the amount.
2. Cool. Pour into ice cube trays and freeze until solid. Remove from trays and place cubes in plastic freezer bags. Freeze up to 3 months.
3. Add 1 cube to a wok or skillet for sautéing or stir-frying.

Makes 16 cubes.

After cubes are frozen, place in plastic bags and close tightly.

NUTRITIONAL
BREAKDOWN (Per cube)

- Calories 8
- Protein 0.5g
- Carbohydrates 0.5g
- Fat . . . . .tr
- Sodium 6mg
- Cholesterol . . . . .tr

ITALIAN CHEESE MIXTURE

4 cups (1 quart) part skim Ricotta, drained
1 egg white
2 tablespoons grated Parmesan cheese
2 tablespoons plus 1 teaspoon parsley, finely chopped
Dash of pepper

METHOD

1. Combine all ingredients in a medium-size bowl.
2. This mixture is enough for one box of jumbo pasta shells.

Makes 4 cups.

NUTRITIONAL
BREAKDOWN (Per 1/2 cup)

- Calories 97
- Protein 16g
- Carbohydrates 3g
- Fat 2g
- Sodium 510mg
- Cholesterol 11mg

CREPES

1/4 cup egg substitute
1/4 cup evaporated skim milk
1/4 cup water plus 2 tablespoons
1 teaspoon Mazola corn oil
1/4 cup all-purpose flour

METHOD

1. Combine all ingredients in a blender on low speed.
2. Heat a 6-inch crepe pan over medium heat. Spray with No Stick cooking spray. Add about 1/4 cup of batter to pan, tilting to cover surface. Cook until bottom of crepe is browned. Turn and cook remaining side. Remove to a flat surface.
3. Repeat with remaining batter, spraying as needed to prevent sticking.
4. Fill crepes with vegetables, meats or fruits. Try filling crepes with chili, chicken salad, tuna or salmon salad.

Makes 8 or 9 crepes.

Note

To season a new crepe pan: Pour oil 1/2 inch deep in pan. Heat until smoking hot. Cool to room temperature. Dispose of oil. Wipe pan clean with paper towels.

NUTRITIONAL
BREAKDOWN (Per crepe)

- Calories 28
- Protein 2g
- Carbohydrates 3.5g
- Fat . . . . tr
- Sodium 20mg
- Cholesterol 0mg

APPETIZERS

VEGETABLE TURNOVERS

12 to 15 whole-wheat bread slices
1 recipe Vegetable Mixture, page 279

METHOD

1. Preheat oven to 375F (190C). Cut crusts off bread. Roll each flat with a rolling pin.
2. Put about 1 tablespoon vegetable mixture in center of 1 bread slice. Fold bread (carefully) corner to corner. Seal edges by pressing with fork dipped in water. Repeat with remaining bread and vegetable mixture.
3. Spray a baking sheet with No Stick cooking spray and place turnovers on sheet. Bake 10 minutes.
4. Spray turnovers lightly with No Stick cooking spray and broil 4 inches from heat 3 or 4 minutes or until slightly crispy.

Makes 12 to 15 turnovers.

Variation

For a complete meal, serve turnovers with a bowl of chili. Great while watching football on TV.

NUTRITIONAL
BREAKDOWN (Per turnover)

- Calories 65
- Protein 2g
- Carbohydrates 12g
- Fat 1g
- Sodium 160mg
- Cholesterol 0mg

146

COTTAGE-CHEESE SPREAD

1 cup low-fat cottage cheese, drained
1 (2-oz.) jar minced pimento
1 tablespoon salsa
1 teaspoon chopped chives

METHOD

1. Combine all ingredients in a small bowl.
2. Cover and refrigerate until chilled.

Makes 1 cup.

NUTRITIONAL
BREAKDOWN   (Per cup)   (Per tablespoon)

- Calories 226
- Protein 30g
- Carbohydrates 18g
- Fat 3g
- Sodium 945mg
- Cholesterol 10mg

- Calories 14
- Protein 2g
- Carbohydrates 1g
- Fat . . . . .tr
- Sodium 59mg
- Cholesterol 0.6mg

CURRY DIP

1 cup low-fat yogurt
2 teaspoons curry powder, or to taste

METHOD

1. Combine yogurt and curry powder in a small bowl.

Makes 1 cup.

NUTRITIONAL
BREAKDOWN   (Per cup)   (Per tablespoon)

- Calories 152
- Protein 13g
- Carbohydrates 16g
- Fat 4g
- Sodium 162mg
- Cholesterol 4mg

- Calories 10
- Protein 1g
- Carbohydrates 3g
- Fat . . . . .tr
- Sodium 10mg
- Cholesterol . . . . .tr

HUMMUS PARTY DIP

1 (16-oz.) can garbanzo beans, drained, liquid reserved
2 tablespoons fresh lemon juice
2 medium-size garlic cloves, minced
1 teaspoon dry minced onion, soaked in 2 tablespoons water,
   or 1 tablespoon finely chopped onion
1/4 teaspoon paprika
Dash of pepper

METHOD

1. In a blender or food processor fitted with the metal blade, combine 1/4 cup reserved bean liquid and remaining ingredients.
2. Process until mixture is a smooth paste. Add more liquid if needed to make desired consistency.
3. Cover and refrigerate until chilled. Serve with crackers or pita bread, use as a dip for crudities or use as a stuffing for celery.

Makes 1 cup.

Variation

Add 2 tablespoons toasted sesame seeds or 1/4 teaspoon toasted sesame oil.

NUTRITIONAL
BREAKDOWN (Per tablespoon)

- Calories 29
- Protein 2g
- Carbohydrates 5g
- Fat . . . . tr
- Sodium 63mg
- Cholesterol 0mg

MEXICAN DIP

1 (16-oz.) can kidney beans
1/8 to 1/4 teaspoon ground cumin
1 garlic clove, minced
1/2 cup no-salt added tomato paste
1/2 small onion, finely chopped
3 tablespoons no-salt added hot salsa or 1/8 teaspoon red
(cayenne) pepper

METHOD

1. In a food processor fitted with the metal blade, process all
ingredients except onion and salsa until pureed.
2. Pour mixture into a bowl, stir in onion and salsa. Cover and
refrigerate until chilled.

Makes 1 cup.

NUTRITIONAL
BREAKDOWN (Per tablespoon)

- Calories 15
- Protein . . . . tr
- Carbohydrates 2.8g
- Fat . . . . tr
- Sodium 20.7mg
- Cholesterol 0mg

MUSHROOM SPREAD

1/2 pound mushrooms, finely chopped
1 small onion, finely chopped
2 hard-cooked egg whites, finely mashed
Chicken Stock, page 139, or Beef Stock, page 138
Tamari
Tabasco sauce

METHOD

1. Spray a medium-size skillet with No Stick cooking spray. Sauté mushrooms and onion in skillet until tender.
2. Add hard-cooked egg whites. Moisten with stock, season with tamari and a dash of tabasco sauce.

Makes 1 cup.

NUTRITIONAL
BREAKDOWN (Per tablespoon)
- Calories 6
- Protein 0.7g
- Carbohydrates 0.8g
- Fat . . . . tr
- Sodium 8mg
- Cholesterol 0mg

ONION DIP

1/2 cup "Our" Sour Cream, page 137
3 green onions, white part only, chopped
1 tablespoon low-fat yogurt
1 teaspoon chopped fresh dill
1 teaspoon chopped chives
1 teaspoon garlic powder

METHOD

1. Place "sour cream" and green onions in a blender; blend 1 minute. Pour into a small bowl.
2. Stir in yogurt, dill, chives and garlic powder.
3. Serve with raw vegetables.

Makes 1/2 cup.

NUTRITIONAL BREAKDOWN

(Per recipe)		(Per tablespoon)	
• Calories	88	• Calories	11
• Protein	.15g	• Protein	2g
• Carbohydrates	4g	• Carbohydrates	tr
• Fat	tr	• Fat	tr
• Sodium	489mg	• Sodium	61mg
• Cholesterol	5mg	• Cholesterol	tr

POTATO PANCAKES

3 pounds potatoes, grated
4 egg whites, beaten
1 large onion, grated
1/4 cup all-purpose flour
1 tablespoon low-sodium soy sauce

METHOD

1. Grate potatoes into cold water so they don't turn brown. Then squeeze water out quickly.
2. Add egg whites, mix well to coat; then add onion, flour and soy sauce.
3. Spray a non-stick skillet with No Stick cooking spray. Drop spoonfuls of potato mixture into skillet; cook until crispy.

Makes 16 pancakes.

NUTRITIONAL
BREAKDOWN (Per pancake)

- Calories 107
- Protein 6g
- Carbohydrates 20g
- Fat 0g
- Sodium 37mg
- Cholesterol 0mg

SALMON DIP WITH TOASTED PITA CHIPS

2 teaspoons low-fat yogurt
2 teaspoons Dijon-style mustard
1/4 teaspoon dried dill weed
1 (17-oz.) can salmon
1/2 cup water-packed artichoke hearts
1 (2-oz.) jar pimentos
1 tablespoon onion powder
1-1/2 teaspoons fresh chopped dill
1 teaspoon paprika
2 cups low-fat cottage cheese
1 cup low-fat yogurt

METHOD

1. Place everything in a blender except the 1 cup yogurt. Blend until smooth.
2. Add yogurt and mix well with a whisk.
3. Serve with brown rice crackers or toasted pita triangles.

Makes about 4 cups.

Variation

Add 1 (1/4-oz.) package unflavored gelatin according to package directions and make a mold.

NUTRITIONAL
BREAKDOWN (Per tablespoon)

- Calories 21
- Protein 3g
- Carbohydrates 1g
- Fat 0.5
- Sodium 35mg
- Cholesterol 3mg

SARDINE DIP

2 (3-3/4-oz.) cans sardines (skinless, boneless in water)
1/2 cup "Our" Sour Cream, page 137
1 large garlic clove, minced
1/4 teaspoon fresh lemon juice

METHOD

1. Blend all ingredients in a medium-size bowl.
2. Cover and refrigerate until chilled.

Makes 1 cup.

NUTRITIONAL
BREAKDOWN (Per tablespoon)

- Calories 36
- Protein 3g
- Carbohydrates 1g
- Fat 2g
- Sodium 64mg
- Cholesterol . . . . tr

MIDDLE EASTERN TUNA SPREAD

1 (6-1/8 oz.) can tuna fish packed with Canola oil, flaked
1 clove garlic, minced
1/2 cup canned chick peas, rinsed well
1/4 cup puréed cottage cheese
1-1/2 tablespoons fresh lemon juice
2 scallions, green part only, chopped
1/2 teaspoon sesame oil
1 teaspoon cumin
1/2 cup chopped flat parsley
1 teaspoon pickle relish (optional)

METHOD

1. Combine tuna, garlic, chick peas, cottage cheese, lemon juice, scallions, sesame oil, and cumin in food processor. Blend until smooth and creamy.
2. Top with parsley.
3. Serve with toasted pita wedges.

Variation

Add 1 teaspoon pickle relish for extra variety.

NUTRITIONAL
BREAKDOWN (Per tablespoon)

- Calories. 31
- Protein 3.5g
- Carbohydrates 2g
- Fat. 1g
- Sodium. 53mg
- Cholesterol. . . . . trace
- Fiber . . . . trace

ENCHILADAS

1/2 (16-oz.) can pinto beans, rinsed, drained
1/2 (16-oz.) can garbanzo beans, rinsed, drained
1/2 cup chopped onion
Mexican spices to taste
8 corn tortillas
1-1/2 cups salsa
Tomato slices

METHOD

1. Preheat oven to 350F (175C). Mash pinto beans and garbanzo beans together in a small bowl.
2. Add onion and spices to beans.
3. Place 2 tablespoons of bean mixture in center of each corn tortilla and roll up.
4. Place rolled tortillas in a small glass baking dish and pour salsa sauce over tortilla. Cover with foil. Bake 20 minutes. Remove foil and bake 5 minutes more or until slightly browned. Garnish with thin slices of tomato.

Note

Tortilla shells can be softened by placing flat in a heated Mexican-flavored tomato sauce 1 or 2 minutes before rolling.

Makes 8 servings.

NUTRITIONAL
BREAKDOWN (per serving—enchilada without rice)
- Calories 152
- Protein 5g
- Carbohydrates 27g
- Fat 2.5g
- Sodium 272mg
- Cholesterol 0

SOUPS

Soups are a very important part of our program. Almost everyone loves soup, which makes things easier for the cook. In addition, soup is a very economical part of the meal, in fact, some of the best soup creations are made from leftovers. Most important it is the simplest as well as the fastest part of the menu to prepare. At our school, I love to show my students how it is possible to make a delicious soup, create a hearty, quick salad and add some fresh bread for a complete meal in less than an hour.

To have a truly "Gourmet" soup, the only basic requirement is a good rich stock. Years ago our grandmothers spent hours cooking up a batch of stock every time soup was made; not so today. Less than one day's preparation will yield substantial amounts of the stock most used in your household. If you are a vegetarian, vegetarian stock will be the only one on your agenda. For most families, the chicken and beef ones will be sufficient. I would recommend making a small amount of fish stock because, like the others in the freezer, it will last at least two months, and it will be a change of pace. The majority of my soups can be made with water if you do not have stock. However, the bisques or creamed soups should be made with stock.

To add interest to your soups, try one of these:

Fresh chile peppers
Fresh jalapeño peppers
Salsa (there are some great, no-salt salsas)
Freshly grated horseradish
Dehydrated onion flakes
Cilantro, or fresh Italian parsley
White wine
Freshly grated Parmesan cheese
Hot pepper sauce
No-salt added Dijon-style mustard
Low-sodium soy sauce
Lemon juice
Prepared horseradish

BROCCOLI BISQUE

3 tablespoons finely diced onion
3 garlic cloves, finely diced
3 cups Chicken Stock, page 139
2 cups broccoli stems, peeled, lightly steamed
2/3 cup non-fat milk powder
1/2 cup skim buttermilk
1-1/2 tablespoons fresh dill
1 tablespoon fresh lemon juice
1 tablespoon low-sodium soy sauce
1 tablespoon dry sherry
2 tablespoons cornstarch mixed with 4 tablespoons water
3/4 cup broccoli flowerets, lightly steamed, chopped

METHOD

1. Sauté onion and garlic in pan sprayed with No Stick cooking spray plus 2 tablespoons stock.
2. Put remaining ingredients except cornstarch mixture and broccoli flowerets in a food processor fitted with the metal blade and puree.
3. Return to pan, add cornstarch mixture and cook over low heat until thickened, stirring constantly.
4. Add broccoli flowerets, heat and serve.

Makes 5 servings.

Variations

Add tofu cubes or crushed toasted pita bread croutons.

Add a dash of black pepper.

NUTRITIONAL
BREAKDOWN (Per serving)

- Calories 86
- Protein 8g
- Carbohydrates 14g
- Fat . . . . tr
- Sodium 142mg
- Cholesterol 2mg

BEAN SOUP

1 medium-size onion, chopped
1 medium-size carrot, sliced
1-1/2 cups Chicken Stock, page 139
1/4 cup white wine (optional)
1/4 teaspoon dried leaf tarragon
2 (16-oz.) cans cannellini beans (white kidney beans), rinsed,
   drained
1/2 cup water
1 teaspoon low-sodium soy sauce
Juice from 1/2 lemon
1-1/2 cups shredded romaine, escarole or spinach
2 or 3 tablespoons minced pimento

METHOD

1. Sauté onion and carrot in 1/4 cup stock and wine, if desired,
   till soft. Add tarragon.
2. Add onion mixture, beans and remaining stock to a food processor fitted with the metal blade; puree till creamy and smooth.
3. Pour into a large saucepan, add water and soy sauce and heat
   thoroughly.
4. Remove from heat; add lemon juice, romaine and pimento.
   Stir to wilt romaine. Serve hot.

Makes 6 servings.

NUTRITIONAL
BREAKDOWN (Per serving)

- Calories 120
- Protein 9g
- Carbohydrates 23g
- Fat 0.1g
- Sodium 278mg
- Cholesterol 0mg

CHICKEN-ESCAROLE SOUP

2 cups Chicken Stock, page 139
2 cups water
1 boneless, skinless chicken breast (about 1/2 pound)
2 medium-size carrots, chopped
2 medium-size celery stalks, chopped
1 medium-size onion, chopped
1/4 cup minced parsley
1/8 teaspoon pepper
1/2 pound escarole, spinach or Swiss chard, trimmed
1 large tomato, peeled, cored, seeded and chopped

METHOD

1. In a large heavy saucepan over medium heat, bring the Chicken Stock and water to a simmer. Add the chicken, carrots, celery, onion, parsley and pepper. Cover and cook until the chicken is tender, about 20 minutes.
2. Remove the chicken and set aside. Stir the escarole and tomato into the saucepan and simmer, uncovered, 5 to 10 minutes or until the escarole is tender.
3. When the chicken is cool enough to handle, cut it into 1/2-inch cubes, return to the saucepan and bring the soup to serving temperature, about 1 minute.

Makes 4 servings.

Variation

For a heartier soup, add 1 cup cooked whole-wheat noodles or rice to make this soup a main course.

NUTRITIONAL BREAKDOWN (Per serving)

- Calories 128
- Protein 18g
- Carbohydrates 13g
- Fat 1g
- Sodium 201mg
- Cholesterol 0mg

CREAMY TOFU TOMATO SOUP

1 onion, diced
1 garlic clove, crushed
1 cup skim milk
Dash of Tabasco sauce
3 tomatoes, diced
12 ounces tofu
2 tablespoons minced parsley

METHOD

1. Spray saucepan with No Stick cooking spray. Sauté onion and garlic over medium heat 3 or 4 minutes, until soft.
2. Add milk, Tabasco sauce and tomatoes, stirring constantly. Cool 10 minutes.
3. Pour into a food processor fitted with the metal blade. Add 10 ounces of the tofu. Process until smooth.
4. Serve hot or cold. Cut remaining tofu into small cubes. Sprinkle with parsley and tofu cubes.

Makes 2 servings.

NUTRITIONAL
BREAKDOWN (Per serving)

- Calories 119
- Protein 10g
- Carbohydrates 12g
- Fat 3g
- Sodium 43mg
- Cholesterol 1mg

CURRIED CARROT SOUP

8 medium-size carrots, cut in thirds
1 medium-size onion, finely chopped
2 large garlic cloves, finely chopped
3 cups Chicken Stock, page 139
2/3 cup non-fat milk powder
About 1 teaspoon curry powder, or to taste
1 teaspoon low-sodium soy sauce
1 carrot, sliced for garnish, or low-fat yogurt

METHOD

1. Steam carrots in a medium-size saucepan until tender.
2. Sauté onion and garlic in a non-stick pan in 1 tablespoon of the stock until soft.
3. Place steamed carrots and 2 cups of the stock in a blender and puree.
4. Add milk powder, curry powder, soy sauce and remaining stock to blender. Puree until creamy.
5. Add onion and garlic mixture to blender; process 30 seconds, until pureed.
6. Return to saucepan to heat before serving.
7. Spoon into 8 bowls; garnish with carrot slices or a dollop of yogurt.

Makes 8 (3/4-cup) servings.

Variations

Add diced tofu in Step 6.

Sprinkle with fresh parsley.

NUTRITIONAL
BREAKDOWN (Per serving)

- Calories 58
- Protein 4g
- Carbohydrates 10g
- Fat . . . . tr
- Sodium 98mg
- Cholesterol 1mg

DELICATE SNOW PEA SOUP

4 cups Chicken Stock, page 139
1 cup finely chopped bok choy (Chinese cabbage)
1/4 cup thinly sliced mushrooms
2 ounces tofu, cut in small cubes
1 garlic cloves, minced
3/4 teaspoon grated gingerroot
1 teaspoon low-sodium soy sauce
1 cup fresh snow peas
1/4 cup diced green onions with tops
1 egg white, lightly beaten (optional)

METHOD

1. Bring all ingredients to a boil except snow peas, green onions and egg white. Simmer 20 minutes.
2. Add snow peas and green onions. Cook 5 minutes; slowly stir in egg white, if desired, to make ribbon effect.

Makes 6 servings.

Variation

For a creamy soup, add 1 heaping teaspoon cornstarch mixed in cold water plus 1/2 teaspoon light soy sauce. Add to soup, heat until thick and bubbly.

NUTRITIONAL
BREAKDOWN (Per serving)

- Calories 37
- Protein 3g
- Carbohydrates 4g
- Fat 0.5g
- Sodium 45mg
- Cholesterol 0mg

EGG DROP SOUP

2 cups Chicken Stock, page 139
1-1/2 tablespoons water
3/4 tablespoon cornstarch
Dash of freshly ground pepper
1 teaspoon dry sherry (optional)
2 green onions, diced
2 teaspoons low-sodium soy sauce diluted with 1 tablespoon
  water
2 egg whites, lightly beaten

METHOD

1. Bring stock to a slow boil.
2. Mix water and cornstarch in a small bowl. Stir into stock and simmer 2 minutes.
3. Add pepper, sherry, if desired, onions and soy sauce mixture.
4. Remove from heat and slowly stir in egg whites. Let stand 1 minute, then serve.

Makes 2 servings.

NUTRITIONAL
BREAKDOWN (Per serving)

- Calories 33
- Protein 4g
- Carbohydrates 3g
- Fat 0g
- Sodium 207mg
- Cholesterol . . . . tr

ONION SOUP

2 large onions, thinly sliced
4 cups Beef Stock, page 138
2 teaspoons low-sodium soy sauce, or tamari
2 tablespoons dry sherry
Dash of pepper
2 teaspoons dried onion flakes
1-1/2 tablespoons onion powder

METHOD

1. Sauté onions in a medium-size saucepan in a small amount of broth and soy sauce until translucent, about 10 minutes.
2. Add remaining ingredients.
3. Cover and simmer 20 minutes.

Makes 4 servings.

Variation

Ladle soup into 4 ovenproof bowls. Place 1 slice of French bread toast in each bowl. Sprinkle 1/2 teaspoon grated Parmesan cheese over each toast slice. Place bowls on a baking sheet and bake at 400F (205C) until cheese melts, about 5 minutes.

NUTRITIONAL
BREAKDOWN (Per serving without bread and cheese)

- Calories 38
- Protein 2g
- Carbohydrates 7g
- Fat 0g
- Sodium 125mg
- Cholesterol 0mg

GRANDMA'S GREEK GARBANZO SOUP

2 medium-size onions, chopped
2 celery stalks, chopped
2 garlic cloves, minced
5 cups Chicken Stock, page 139
2 carrots, chopped
1 red bell pepper, chopped
1 (16-oz.) can no-salt added tomato sauce
1/4 teaspoon black pepper
2 (1-lb.) cans garbanzo beans, drained, rinsed
1 cup cooked white kidney beans, drained, rinsed
1 tablespoon chopped parsley

METHOD

1. Sauté onions, celery and garlic in 1/2 cup of the stock in a large saucepan until soft.
2. Add carrots, bell pepper, tomato sauce, black pepper and remaining stock. Simmer 20 minutes.
3. Add 1 cup garbanzo beans and the kidney beans. Cook 2 or 3 minutes. Puree 1/2 of mixture in a food processor fitted with the metal blade and return to pan.
4. Add remaining garbanzo beans and parsley. Cook 5 minutes. Serve hot.

Makes 12 servings.

NUTRITIONAL
BREAKDOWN (Per serving)

- Calories 140
- Protein 8g
- Carbohydrates 25g
- Fat . . . . tr
- Sodium 125mg
- Cholesterol 0mg

ITALIAN ZUCCHINI-CAULIFLOWER SOUP

2 medium-size onions, finely diced
2 medium-size turnips, finely diced
4 medium-size carrots, finely diced
6 cups Chicken Stock, page 139
1 small cauliflower, cut into tiny florets
1 medium-size zucchini, thinly sliced
3 large tomatoes, or 2 (1-lb.) cans tomatoes, quartered
1/2 cup sliced okra
1-1/2 cups water
1 cup very thin noodles, cooked
2 tablespoons grated Parmesan cheese
1 tablespoon low-sodium soy sauce

METHOD

1. Sauté onions, turnips and carrots in 1 cup of the Chicken Stock in a large saucepan 20 minutes or until tender.
2. Add remaining ingredients except noodles, cheese and soy sauce. Simmer 25 minutes more.
3. Add noodles, cheese and soy sauce. Simmer 10 minutes and serve.

Makes 8 servings.

NUTRITIONAL
BREAKDOWN (Per serving)

- Calories 107
- Protein 6g
- Carbohydrates 18g
- Fat 1g
- Sodium 169mg
- Cholesterol 1mg

LIMA BEAN SOUP

4-1/2 cups Chicken Stock, page 139, or water
3 cups frozen lima beans, thawed
3 celery stalks without leaves, chopped
4 medium-size carrots, chopped
1 medium-size tomato, diced
1 leek, white part only, chopped
2 garlic cloves, chopped
1 medium-size bay leaf
1/2 teaspoon dried leaf sage
1/2 teaspoon dried leaf basil
1 tablespoon dry sherry (optional)
2 tablespoons low-sodium soy sauce
1 tablespoon Italian parsley, chopped

METHOD

1. Combine all ingredients except parsley in a large saucepan and bring to a boil. Reduce heat and simmer until vegetables are tender.
2. Place 3/4 of the mixture in a blender and puree. Return to saucepan and simmer 5 minutes more.
3. Add parsley just before serving.

Makes 6 servings.

Variations

To please children, puree entire recipe—they will love it!

Add cubed chicken or turkey for a one-pot dinner.

Add 1 tablespoon salsa or Tabasco sauce.

NUTRITIONAL
BREAKDOWN (Per serving)

- Calories 138
- Protein 2g
- Carbohydrates 30g
- Fat 0g
- Sodium 139mg
- Cholesterol 0mg

LUSCIOUS LENTIL SOUP

8 cups Chicken Stock, page 139, or water
4 medium-size carrots, sliced
4 celery stalks, sliced
1 medium-size onion, chopped
1 leek, chopped
1 tablespoon fresh parsley, chopped
1-1/2 cups red lentils
1 tomato, chopped
3 garlic cloves, pressed through a garlic press, or minced
1 large bay leaf
1/8 teaspoon freshly ground pepper
1/4 teaspoon ground thyme

METHOD

1. Combine all ingredients in a large saucepan. Cook over medium heat 45 minutes.
2. Puree 2 cups of the soup in a blender. Mix with remaining soup in pot. Heat thoroughly and serve.

Makes 8 servings.

Variations

Serve with lemon wedges for added zest.

Or add 1 tablespoon Miso for extra flavor.

NUTRITIONAL
BREAKDOWN (Per serving)

- Calories 166
- Protein 14g
- Carbohydrates 28g
- Fat 0.5g
- Sodium 38mg
- Cholesterol 0mg

MANHATTAN CLAM CHOWDER

2 cups chopped onions
5 celery stalks, chopped
2 cups chopped carrots
5 cups Fish Stock, page 140
1 cup no-salt added tomato juice
2 medium-size potatoes, cubed
2 cups bottled clam juice
2 (10-oz.) cans baby clams, drained, rinsed
3 cups canned plum tomatoes, chopped, juice reserved
2 teaspoons dried leaf thyme, or to taste
2 tablespoons chopped parsley
2 tablespoons salsa
1 medium-size bay leaf
2 teaspoons Sovez hickory-smoked yeast (available in health food stores)

METHOD

1. Simmer onions, celery and carrots in 1 cup of stock 10 minutes.
2. Add remaining stock, tomato juice and potatoes; cook 5 minutes.
3. Add remaining ingredients and simmer 30 minutes. Serve hot.

Makes 10 servings.

Variations

For a thicker consistency, mix together 1 tablespoon cornstarch, 3 tablespoons water and 1-1/2 tablespoons salsa; add to soup after Step 3. Cook until soup thickens.

To reduce calories, omit potatoes.

To add a delicious taste to all your chowders, make up small packages of 1 medium-size bay leaf, 1/8 teaspoon peppercorns, 1/2 teaspoon dried thyme leaves and 1/4 teaspoon chopped parsley stems; wrap in cheesecloth and tie tightly. Remove before serving.

NUTRITIONAL
BREAKDOWN (Per serving)

- Calories 137
- Protein 12g
- Carbohydrates 18g
- Fat 1g
- Sodium 62mg
- Cholesterol 40mg

MEXICAN BEAN SOUP

1/2 cup navy beans
3 cups cold water
1 garlic clove, minced
3 tablespoons chopped onion
1 tablespoon chopped parsley
1 cup chopped celery
1/2 cup finely shredded cabbage
1/2 teaspoon cumin (optional)
1 cup no-salt added canned tomatoes, crushed
1/2 cup cooked noodles

METHOD

1. Rinse beans and bring to a boil in enough water to cover by 1 inch. Let stand 1 hour; drain. Cook in the 3 cups water until tender, about 2 hours. Puree 1/2 cup of the beans in a blender; reserve.
2. Sauté garlic, onion, parsley, celery and cabbage until wilted in a medium-size saucepan sprayed with No Stick cooking spray.
3. Add beans, reserved puree and cumin, if desired, to above mixture, stir and add tomatoes.
4. Add noodles, heat and serve hot.

Makes 8 servings.

Great High Fiber Dish!

NUTRITIONAL
BREAKDOWN (Per serving)

- Calories 67
- Protein 4g
- Carbohydrates 14g
- Fat 0g
- Sodium 24mg
- Cholesterol 0mg

MINESTRONE SOUP

2 carrots, sliced
1 large onion, chopped
2 celery stalks, sliced
4 garlic cloves, minced
4 cups Chicken Stock, page 139
1 large zucchini, quartered, sliced
1 cup 1-inch pieces green beans or wax beans
1 (6-oz.) can tomato paste
1 (12-oz.) can no-salt added tomato juice
2 large tomatoes, diced
1 tablespoon chopped Italian parsley
2 green onions, white part only
1 tablespoon low-sodium soy sauce
1 teaspoon dried leaf basil
1 teaspoon dried leaf oregano
1 cup cooked or canned garbanzo beans
1 cup cooked or canned white kidney beans
1/3 cup whole-wheat elbow macaroni, cooked
Dash of Tabasco sauce
1 tablespoon grated Parmesan cheese

METHOD

1. Cook carrots, onion, celery and garlic in 1 cup of the stock until tender.
2. Add remaining ingredients except the beans, macaroni, Tabasco sauce and cheese. Cook until vegetables are tender.
3. Meanwhile in a blender or food processor fitted with the metal blade, process half of the garbanzo beans and the white kidney beans until pureed. Set aside.
4. Add remaining ingredients; simmer 10 minutes. Serve hot.

Makes 12 servings.

Variation

If you don't use garbanzo beans, puree 1 cup of the cooked soup. Return to saucepan, mix and serve.

This recipe freezes well. Serve a fresh loaf of Italian bread and a crisp salad with this dish and dinner's made in a flash!

NUTRITIONAL BREAKDOWN (Per serving)

- Calories 108
- Protein 6g
- Carbohydrates 20g
- Fat 0.8g
- Sodium 176mg
- Cholesterol 0mg

MULLIGATAWNY SOUP

1 medium-size acorn squash, halved, cooked
1/2 large apple, chopped
1 medium-size onion, chopped
1 to 2 teaspoons curry powder
1-1/2 cups Chicken Stock, page 139
1/4 cup apple juice
1/2 (16-oz.) can garbanzo beans, drained, rinsed
3/4 to 1 cup skim milk
1 teaspoon low-sodium soy sauce
Snipped chives

METHOD

1. Scrape pulp from squash.
2. Sauté apple, onion, squash and curry powder in 1/4 cup stock in a medium-size saucepan 5 minutes.
3. Add remaining stock and apple juice, bring to a boil, reduce heat to low and cover. Simmer until vegetables are soft, 5 to 10- minutes.
4. Place cooked mixture and beans in a food processor fitted with the metal blade; process until pureed.
5. Return to saucepan and add enough milk to make desired thickness. Add soy sauce.
6. Sprinkle with chives. Serve hot.

Variation

Add diced cooked chicken and/or 1/4 to 1/2 cup cooked brown rice.

Makes 6 servings.

NUTRITIONAL
BREAKDOWN (Per serving without chicken or rice)

- Calories 156
- Protein 8g
- Carbohydrates 30g
- Fat 1g
- Sodium 172mg
- Cholesterol . . . . tr

PEA, MUSHROOM & BARLEY SOUP

2 tablespoons dried mushrooms
3/4 cup dried yellow split peas
3/4 cup dried green split peas
3 cups water
2 large garlic cloves, finely diced
3 celery stalks, diced
3 medium-size carrots, diced
1 medium-size onion, diced
5 cups Chicken Stock, page 139
1/3 cup barley
1/2 teaspoon basil, finely chopped
1 large bay leaf
1/2 teaspoon tarragon, finely chopped
2 teaspoons fresh parsley, finely chopped
Dash of sage
Dash of thyme
2 tablespoons low-sodium soy sauce or 1 to 2 tablespoons light
   miso

METHOD

1. Soak dried mushrooms in very hot water 15 minutes. Then dice.
2. Combine dried yellow and green split peas and enough water
   to cover in a large saucepan and bring to a boil, turn off heat
   and soak 30 minutes.
3. Drain peas and add remaining ingredients to saucepan. Bring
   to a boil and then reduce heat and simmer 2 hours or until
   vegetables are tender. Soup should be fairly thick.
4. Set aside and cool 1/2 hour. Remove 3/4 of the vegetables and
   puree in blender with 1 cup of liquid.
5. Return to saucepan. Heat and serve.

Makes 10 (8-oz.) servings.

NUTRITIONAL
BREAKDOWN (Per serving)

- Calories 79
- Protein 5g
- Carbohydrates 15g
- Fat . . . . tr
- Sodium 62mg
- Cholesterol 0mg

174

PASTA E FAGIOLI

1 large onion, chopped
4 garlic cloves, chopped
1/2 red bell pepper, diced
1/2 green bell pepper, diced
2 tablespoons Chicken Stock, page 139, or water
2 (1-lb.) cans light red kidney beans (puree 1/2 can)
1 (1-lb.) can cannellini beans (white kidney beans)
2 (1-lb.) cans no-salt added whole tomatoes, juice reserved
4 cups water
2 medium-size carrots, sliced
1 teaspoon each dried leaf basil and oregano
1 bay leaf, broken in half
1 tablespoon low-sodium soy sauce
1/3 cup macaroni, Ditalini, if possible
1/4 cup red wine (optional)

METHOD

1. Sauté onion, garlic and bell peppers in stock in a 6-quart saucepan until onion is translucent.
2. Add remaining ingredients except macaroni and wine.
3. Simmer on low heat, stirring constantly, 20 minutes.
4. Add macaroni and wine, if desired, and extra water if soup is too thick and simmer 15 minutes or until macaroni is firm but tender. Serve hot.

Makes 8 to 10 servings.

Variations

For a Northern Italian-style soup, use all white beans.

To freeze, omit macaroni; add when ready to serve.

NUTRITIONAL
BREAKDOWN (Per serving)

- Calories 205
- Protein 10g
- Carbohydrates 41g
- Fat . . . .   tr
- Sodium 149mg
- Cholesterol 0mg

CLEAR MUSHROOM SOUP

3 cups Chicken Stock, page 139
6 fresh mushrooms, sliced
3 green onions with green tops, diced
1 tablespoon dry sherry
1 teaspoon light miso

METHOD

1. Heat stock in a medium-size saucepan, add mushrooms and onions; simmer 3 or 4 minutes just to wilt vegetables.
2. Add sherry.
3. Mix 3 tablespoons of the broth with miso to blend.
4. Add miso mixture to soup. Cook 3 minutes; serve hot.

Makes 3 servings.

NUTRITIONAL
BREAKDOWN (Per serving)

- Calories 40
- Protein 4g
- Carbohydrates 4g
- Fat . . . . tr
- Sodium 276mg
- Cholesterol 0mg

SOUP A LA ATHENS

9 cups Chicken Stock, page 139
2 cups chopped fresh spinach
6 large mushrooms, thinly sliced
1 medium-size onion, thinly sliced
1 tablespoon miso, or 1 tablespoon low-sodium soy sauce
1/4 teaspoon fresh lemon juice
1 egg white

METHOD

1. Bring stock to a boil in a large saucepan. Add remaining ingredients except egg white. Reduce heat and simmer 15 minutes.
2. Beat egg white slightly, and drop in ribbons into stock. Simmer 3 minutes. Serve hot.

Makes 10 servings.

Variation

Eliminate egg white and add 1 poached shredded chicken breast.

NUTRITIONAL
BREAKDOWN (Per serving with egg white)

- Calories 29
- Protein 4g
- Carbohydrates 2g
- Fat 0g
- Sodium 87mg
- Cholesterol 0mg

SPANISH RICE SOUP

5-1/2 cups water
1 (12-oz.) can no-salt added tomato juice
1/3 cup uncooked brown rice
2 cups chopped celery
2 carrots, sliced in 1-inch pieces
1 onion, chopped
2 garlic cloves, chopped
1/2 red bell pepper, diced
1/2 green bell pepper, diced
3 (1-lb.) cans no-salt added tomatoes
1 (4-oz.) can mild green chiles, chopped
1 teaspoon ground cumin, or to taste
1 teaspoon chili powder, or to taste

METHOD

1. In a 5- or 6-quart pot, bring water, tomato juice, rice, celery, carrots, onion and garlic to a boil. Cover, reduce heat and simmer 30 minutes. Check occasionally to make sure there is enough liquid and add as needed, since rice absorbs liquid as it cooks.
2. Add remaining ingredients and simmer 25 minutes more or until rice is tender.

Makes 10 to 12 servings.

Variations

For a one-pot dinner, add 2 cups leftover cubed chicken and reduce rice to 1/3 cup. Soup is also good cold.

NUTRITIONAL
BREAKDOWN (Per 1 cup serving)

- Calories 131
- Protein 4g
- Carbohydrates. 27g
- Fat 0.5g
- Sodium 228mg
- Cholesterol 0mg

CABBAGE SOUP

4 cups Chicken Stock, page 139
1 (8-oz.) can no-salt added tomato sauce
2 cups water
2 carrots, sliced
2 celery stalks, sliced
1/2 head cabbage, shredded
1 leek, white part only, chopped
1 medium-size onion, chopped
2 turnips, sliced
1 garlic clove, minced
1/2 cup cauliflowerets
2 tablespoons chopped fresh dill
2 tablespoons low-sodium soy sauce

METHOD

1. Combine everything except dill and soy sauce in a large saucepan. Cook 1 hour until vegetables are tender.
2. Add dill and soy sauce. Cook 15 minutes. Serve hot.

Makes 10 (1-cup) servings.

Variations

Add 2 cups cooked cubed chicken or 1 cup cubed tofu when adding soy sauce.

For a slightly different taste add 3/4 cup sliced fresh okra to soup with other vegetables.

NUTRITIONAL BREAKDOWN (Per serving)

- Calories 42
- Protein 3g
- Carbohydrates 5g
- Fat 0.2g
- Sodium 177mg
- Cholesterol 0mg

WHITE BEAN & VEGETABLE SOUP

6 cups Chicken Stock, page 139, or water
2 medium-size zucchini
1 large red onion, coarsely chopped
2 small white turnips, diced
1 (16-oz.) can cannellini beans (white kidney beans), rinsed,
    drained
3 medium-size carrots, thinly sliced
1 large celery stalk with leaves, sliced
1 teaspoon dried leaf basil
1 small bay leaf
1 (16-oz.) can no-salt added tomatoes, quartered, liquid reserved
2 tablespoons low-sodium soy sauce
Dash of Tabasco sauce

METHOD

1. Combine all ingredients except Tabasco sauce in a large
   saucepan. Cook until vegetables are tender.
2. In a food processor fitted with the metal blade, process half
   of soup until pureed.
3. Return puree to remaining soup; add Tabasco sauce. Heat and
   serve.

Makes 8 servings.

Variation

Leave tomatoes in soup whole; do not puree.

NUTRITIONAL
BREAKDOWN (Per 8-oz. serving)

- Calories 102
- Protein 5g
- Carbohydrates 20g
- Fat 0g
- Sodium 145mg
- Cholesterol 0mg

SEAFOOD ENTREES

For those who are in good health or those with health problems, both have one thing in common—fish should be an important part of their diet. As you have learned in the earlier part of the book omega-3-rich seafood can lower cholesterol and may be of use in the prevention and treatment of thrombosis, (coagulation of the blood causing clots).

Here are a few facts that are important regarding fish.

FACTS ABOUT FRESH FISH

1. Four ounces of broiled steak has 30 to 45 grams of fat, which is largely saturated. The same amount of broiled fish contains 4 to 12 grams of mostly polyunsaturated fat. The fat in the steak contributes about 70% of its calories, while that in fish is only 35%.

2. Fattier fish such as salmon, tuna and mackerel contain the most omega-3 fatty acids—the fatty acids that may prevent heart attacks.

3. Researchers have shown that men who eat fish once or twice a week are half as likely to die from heart disease as those who eat no fish.

4. To simplify what fish to buy and prepare I suggest one fatty fish such as salmon or halibut and one less fatty fish such as sole or flounder per week.

FACTS ABOUT CANNED FISH

1. Canned salmon and sardines contain more fat than canned tuna but they contain more cholesterol-lowering fish oil.

2. Tuna marked "no salt added" contains 90% less sodium than regular tuna, but to avoid premium prices, buy regular tuna and rinse; this removes much of the sodium.

3. Don't remove bones from sardines or canned salmon, they add calcium.

4. Solid white tuna is slightly lower in fat and calories than chunk white or chunk light.

BOUILLABAISE

1-1/2 cups finely chopped onions
2 tablespoons minced garlic
2 cups finely chopped leeks, white part only
6 cups Fish Stock, page 140
1-1/4 cups finely diced celery
2 cups coarsely chopped red bell pepper
2 teaspoons finely chopped green bell pepper
1/2 teaspoon fennel seeds
2 teaspoons loosely packed saffron
2 tablespoons no-salt added tomato paste
1 large bay leaf
1/2 teaspoon dried leaf thyme
1 teaspoon ground turmeric
1 pound skinned, boned monk fish or snapper fillet
1 pound skinned, boned sword-fish, sea bass or fluke
1 pound skinned, boned tilefish or halibut fillet
2-1/2 cups chopped tomatoes
8 ounces large shrimp, peeled
18 littleneck clams
1/3 cup finely chopped Italian parsley

METHOD

1. Sauté onions, garlic and leeks in 2 tablespoons of the stock in a large saucepan until wilted.
2. Add celery and bell peppers. Cook about 1 minute, stirring, then add fennel, saffron, remaining stock, tomato paste, bay leaf, thyme and turmeric. Cook 10 minutes.
3. Cut all fish into 1- or 2-inch cubes. Add monk fish and tomatoes to vegetable mixture. Stir and cook 3 to 5 minutes, then add swordfish and tilefish. Cook 3 to 5 minutes more; add shrimp and clams. Cook 7 to 10 minutes until shrimp are pink and clams open. Discard any clams that do not open.
4. Sprinkle with parsley and stir. Serve with rice.

Makes 12 servings.

NUTRITIONAL
BREAKDOWN (Per serving without rice)

- Calories 194
- Protein 33g
- Carbohydrates 10g
- Fat 2g
- Sodium 161mg
- Cholesterol 98mg

CHINESE FISH

1 teaspoon grated gingerroot
1 tablespoon dry sherry
1 tablespoon low-sodium soy sauce
2 tablespoons water
1-1/2 teaspoons apple juice concentrate
1 salmon or halibut steak, 9 to 10 ounces (with bone)
4 green onions with green tops, diced
4 or 5 snow peas

METHOD

1. Preheat oven to 375F (190C). Mix gingerroot, sherry, soy sauce, water and apple juice concentrate in a small bowl for sauce; set aside.
2. Spray a baking dish with No Stick cooking spray. Place fish in dish. Combine sauce, green onions and snow peas; pour over fish.
3. Cover and bake 20 to 25 minutes until fish turns from translucent to opaque.
4. Remove sauce from pan; set aside. Broil fish 3 to 4 minutes until crispy.
5. Pour sauce over fish. Serve with rice.

Makes 2 servings.

NUTRITIONAL
BREAKDOWN (Per serving without rice)

- Calories 180
- Protein 29g
- Carbohydrates 7g
- Fat 4g
- Sodium 389mg
- Cholesterol 61mg

"FRIED" FISH FILLETS

4 (4-oz.) fresh fish fillets
3/4 cup dried bread crumbs or matzo meal
2 tablespoons grated Parmesan cheese
2 tablespoons chopped fresh Italian parsley
1 teaspoon paprika
2 egg whites, lightly beaten

METHOD

1. Rinse fish and pat dry.
2. Blend bread crumbs with cheese, parsley and paprika in a flat dish.
3. Dip fillets into beaten egg whites, then bread crumb mixture.
4. Place in a single layer on waxed paper and place in freezer 1 hour.
5. Spray a large skillet with No Stick cooking spray. Place skillet over medium-high heat. Add fillets; cook, carefully turning once, until coating is brown and fish turns from translucent to opaque.

Makes 4 servings.

NUTRITIONAL
BREAKDOWN (Per serving)

- Calories 157
- Protein 20g
- Carbohydrates 12g
- Fat 2g
- Sodium 248mg
- Cholesterol 67mg

184

GINGERED SOLE

1 pound sole fillets (or other similar fish)
1 tablespoon low-sodium soy sauce and 1 tablespoon water
1/2 teaspoon fresh lemon juice or lime juice
1 teaspoon apple juice concentrate or pineapple juice concentrate
1 garlic clove, minced
2 tablespoons slivered gingerroot
2 tablespoons dry sherry
2 green onions with green tops, cut in 1-inch pieces

METHOD

1. Rinse and dry fillets. Place fish on a heatproof plate.
2. Combine soy sauce mixture, lemon juice, apple juice concentrate, garlic, gingerroot, sherry and green onions. Pour 1/2 of this mixture over fish using a brush to coat all fish surfaces. Reserve the rest for sauce.
3. Place plate on a steamer rack in a wok or large steamer in which 2 inches of water has come to a boil.
4. Steam fish until it turns from translucent to opaque, 10 to 15 minutes.
5. Serve with accumulated juice mixed with reserved sauce.
6. Serve over rice or angel hair pasta.

Makes 4 servings.

NUTRITIONAL
BREAKDOWN (Per serving without rice or pasta)

- Calories 109
- Protein 17g
- Carbohydrates 5g
- Fat 0.8g
- Sodium 214mg
- Cholesterol 61mg

KING OF THE SEA PRIMAVERA

12 ounces fresh salmon fillet
About 1 cup water
1/3 cup dry white wine
10 ounces whole-wheat pasta
2 cups broccoli flowerets
1 cup quartered fresh mushrooms
1 red bell pepper, cut in thin strips
1 cup Marinara Sauce, page 332
1/3 cup low-fat buttermilk
2 tablespoons grated Parmesan cheese (optional)

METHOD

1. Poach fish in water in a medium-size skillet until fish turns from translucent to opaque, 7 or 8 minutes depending upon thickness; remove to a bowl.
2. Cover with white wine; set aside.
3. Cook pasta in boiling water in a large saucepan until tender but firm. Drain. Keep warm.
4. Steam broccoli, mushrooms and bell pepper until crisp-tender 3 or 4 minutes.
5. Mix Marinara Sauce with buttermilk in a small saucepan; cook over low heat until hot.
6. Arrange pasta on a large platter. Cover with vegetables. Drain fish and divide into very small pieces and arrange over vegetables. Cover with sauce and cheese, if desired. Lightly toss and serve.

Makes 6 servings.

Note

Even non-fish lovers enjoy this recipe. It's a good dish for a buffet.

NUTRITIONAL
BREAKDOWN (Per serving)

- Calories 275
- Protein 20g
- Carbohydrates 40g
- Fat 3g
- Sodium 72mg
- Cholesterol 25mg

LIME-BROILED FISH

1 teaspoon Dijon-style no-salt added mustard
1/4 cup fresh lime juice
2 teaspoons freshly grated gingerroot
1/8 teaspoon red (cayenne) pepper
1 teaspoon apple juice concentrate
Dash of pepper
4 (4-oz.) boned fish fillets, or 4 (5-1/2- to 6-oz.) fish steaks with
  bone

METHOD

1. Combine all ingredients except fish in a shallow bowl.
2. Add fish to lime mixture; marinate at least 1 hour, turning
   occasionally.
3. Preheat broiler. Place fish on a broiler rack. Broil 5 minutes,
   basting with marinade. Turn fish carefully. Broil 5 to 7 minutes
   more, until fish turns from translucent to opaque.

Makes 4 servings.

NUTRITIONAL
BREAKDOWN (Per serving)

- Calories 89
- Protein 17g
- Carbohydrates 3g
- Fat 1g
- Sodium 80mg
- Cholesterol 67mg

MACARONI SALMON LOAF

4 ounces elbow macaroni, cooked al dente
1 (1-lb.) can pink or red salmon
2 tablespoons onion, finely minced
1 tablespoon chopped parsley
Dash of pepper
1 cup coarse whole-wheat bread crumbs
3 egg whites
3/4 cup skim milk
2 garlic cloves, minced
1 teaspoon dried dill
1/4 teaspoon dried rosemary

METHOD

1. Preheat oven to 350F (175C). Spray a 9-by-5-inch loaf pan with No Stick cooking spray.
2. Combine all ingredients in a medium-size bowl with a fork.
3. Place in loaf pan and bake 35 to 40 minutes.

Makes 4 servings.

Variation

Heat 1/2 cup Marinara Sauce, page 332, with 2 tablespoons low-fat buttermilk. Use as a sauce for salmon loaf.

NUTRITIONAL
BREAKDOWN (Per serving without sauce)

- Calories 245
- Protein 25g
- Carbohydrates 29g
- Fat 5g
- Sodium 444mg
- Cholesterol 36mg

MEXICAN-STYLE SCALLOPS

1 pound sea scallops, cut in half
1-1/2 tablespoons fresh lime juice
Dash of pepper
1 (2-oz.) jar pimentos, rinsed
2 tablespoons red wine vinegar
2 teaspoons dried leaf thyme
1 tomato, finely chopped
1/2 cup white wine
1 teaspoon chopped basil
4 green onions with tops, cut in 1-inch pieces
8 ounces mushrooms, cut in quarters
1 teaspoon chopped green chile

METHOD

1. Combine scallops, lime juice and pepper. Cover and refrigerate until needed.
2. Combine remaining ingredients in a medium-size bowl; let stand 15 minutes.
3. Spray a heavy skillet with No Stick cooking spray. Add vegetable mixture; sauté 10 minutes.
4. Add scallops and cook, stirring frequently, until scallops are opaque, 3 to 5 minutes. Serve over rice.

Makes 4 servings.

NUTRITIONAL
BREAKDOWN (Per serving without rice)

- Calories 135
- Protein 17g
- Carbohydrates 15g
- Fat . . . . tr
- Sodium 155mg
- Cholesterol 30mg

POACHED SALMON IN ORANGE SAUCE

3/4 cup Fish Stock, page 140
1/2 cup white wine
1 teaspoon dried leaf thyme
Dash of pepper
1 tablespoon fresh lemon juice
1 pound salmon fillet
2/3 cup orange juice
1 teaspoon grated orange zest
1 teaspoon cornstarch mixed with 2 tablespoons water

METHOD

1. Preheat oven to 400F (205C). Mix stock, wine, thyme, pepper and lemon juice in a saucepan large enough to hold fish in a single layer. Add fish; poach until fish turns from translucent to opaque, about 8 minutes. Simmer 5 minutes.
2. Remove fish and place in a baking dish.
3. Mix orange juice, zest and cornstarch mixture in a small saucepan. Cook until thickened, stirring. Pour over fish. Heat in oven 5 minutes. Cut in 4 serving pieces.

Makes 4 servings.

NUTRITIONAL
BREAKDOWN (Per serving)

- Calories 183
- Protein 24g
- Carbohydrates 6g
- Fat 8g
- Sodium 79mg
- Cholesterol 40mg

SALMON SURPRISE

6 green lasagna noodles
2 tablespoons low-fat buttermilk or skim milk
6 (3-oz.) salmon fillets
1 cup Marinara Sauce, page 332

METHOD

1. Preheat oven to 350F (175C). Cook lasagna noodles until tender but firm. Drain.
2. Mix milk with Marinara Sauce and pour 1/4 cup on bottom of a baking dish.
3. Place 1 fish fillet in center of 1 cooked noodle and roll up. Place roll in sauce, seam-side down. Repeat with remaining fillets and noodles.
4. Cover rolls with remaining sauce.
5. Bake 20 to 25 minutes, until bubbly and fish is cooked.

Makes 6 servings.

Variation

Add 1 tablespoon chopped spinach to center of lasagna with salmon.

NUTRITIONAL
BREAKDOWN (Per serving)

- Calories 210
- Protein 20g
- Carbohydrates 24g
- Fat 4g
- Sodium 67mg
- Cholesterol 28mg

SCALLOPS IN LIME SAUCE

Juice of 1 large lime
1 teaspoon tamari
2 tablespoons apple juice concentrate
1 pound sea scallops

METHOD

1. Combine lime juice, tamari and apple juice concentrate in a medium-size bowl.
2. Add scallops to lime mixture; cover and refrigerate 1 hour, turning 2 or 3 times. Meanwhile, soak bamboo skewers in water to prevent burning.
3. Preheat broiler. Thread scallops on bamboo skewers and place on a broiler rack. Broil until scallops are opaque, basting with marinade.

Makes 4 servings.

NUTRITIONAL
BREAKDOWN (Per serving)

- Calories 101
- Protein 15g
- Carbohydrates 9g
- Fat . . . . tr
- Sodium 301mg
- Cholesterol 35mg

SKILLET SCALLOPS & PASTA

1 pound sea scallops, halved
3 large garlic cloves, minced
2 tablespoons fresh lemon juice
3 tablespoons Fish Stock, page 140, or Vegetable Stock, page 141
1/2 red bell pepper, cut in strips
1/2 green bell pepper, cut in strips
8 ounces thin spaghetti, cooked until al dente
2 cups Marinara Sauce, page 332

METHOD

1. Sauté scallops, garlic and lemon juice in stock in a large skillet 5 minutes.
2. Add bell peppers. Cook, stirring, 2 or 3 minutes more.
3. Add pasta to skillet; toss to combine. Add Marinara Sauce; toss to combine. Serve hot.

Makes 4 servings.

NUTRITIONAL
BREAKDOWN (Per serving)

- Calories 243
- Protein 18g
- Carbohydrates 38g
- Fat 1g
- Sodium 205mg
- Cholesterol 40mg

SOLE STUFFED WITH SPINACH

1 cup chopped fresh spinach
1/2 cup low-fat cottage cheese
2 garlic cloves, finely minced
2 tablespoons chopped fresh parsley
4 (4-oz.) sole or flounder fillets
Juice of 1/2 lemon
1 cup Marinara Sauce, page 332
3 tablespoons low-fat buttermilk

METHOD

1. Preheat oven to 350F (175C). Spray an ovenproof dish with No Stick cooking spray. Cook spinach in a small saucepan in boiling water just until wilted, 2 to 3 minutes.
2. Mix spinach, cheese, garlic and parsley in a medium-size bowl.
3. Place 2 tablespoons mixture in center of each fillet. Roll fillet and place in dish, seam-side down; pour lemon juice over rolled fillets.
4. Mix sauce and milk together and pour over rolled fillets.
5. Bake about 15 minutes or until fish turns from translucent to opaque.

Makes 4 servings.

Variations

Sprinkle 2 tablespoons grated Parmesan cheese evenly over fish when done and place under broiler, 2 minutes.

Spray No Stick cooking spray lightly over fish before broiling to keep it from becoming dry.

NUTRITIONAL
BREAKDOWN (Per serving)

- Calories 200
- Protein 37g
- Carbohydrates 8g
- Fat 2g
- Sodium 297mg
- Cholesterol 56mg

194

TUNA CROQUETTES
WITH MUSTARD CREAM

Tuna Croquettes
1 cup of mashed potatoes
1 medium onion, finely
  chopped
1 tablespoon plain non-fat
  yogurt
1/4 cup chopped dill, lightly
  packed
2 teaspoons fresh lemon juice

1 (9-1/4 oz.) can tuna fish
  packed with Canola oil,
  lightly flaked with a fork
Fresh ground pepper to taste
2 egg whites, lightly beaten

Mustard Cream
1/4 cup plain non-fat yogurt
1 teaspoon Dijon mustard

METHOD

1. Combine potatoes, onion, and yogurt until smooth. Stir
   in dill, lemon, and pepper. Lightly fold in tuna. Pour in
   egg whites and mix.
2. Divide mixture into 6 croquettes. Spray a large, non-stick
   skillet with butter flavored non-stick vegetable cooking
   spray. Heat skillet over medium heat (30 seconds or until
   hot). Cook 1-1/2 minutes on each side or until nicely
   browned and heated through.
3. Combine yogurt and mustard. Blend until creamy.
4. Place croquettes on whole grain buns and top with 2
   tablespoons of mustard cream on each, lettuce, and
   tomato. Serve.

NUTRITIONAL
BREAKDOWN (Per serving)

- Calories. 94
- Protein 12g
- Carbohydrates 7g
- Fat. 2g
- Sodium. 94mg
- Cholesterol. 18mg
- Fiber . . . . trace

MEAT ENTREES

Medical research has shown us that meat can be one of the culprits in the deaths of 550,000 Americans each year. High blood cholesterol is considered one of the three key heart disease factors along with smoking and high blood pressure. Blood cholesterol levels of 180 and above can be considered elevated. In my schools, students are kept on a regimen of between 100 to 150 mg. of cholesterol per day. Three ounces of beef liver contains 372 mg. of cholesterol and 3 ounces of beef, pork or ham contains 80 mg., they do however, have a high percent of "fat calories." That is why meat takes up little space in this book.

We do use lean flank steak. We suggest a 3-1/2- to 4-ounce serving once a week since it has the least amount of "fat calories" (about 30%) and has approximately 75 mg. cholesterol per 3 ounce serving. When using ground meat, please be sure to use the very leanest available.

APPLE BURGERS

1 pound lean beef flank steak, ground
1 cup whole-wheat bread crumbs
1-1/2 cups unsweetened applesauce
1 small onion, grated
1-1/2 teaspoons dry mustard
1 teaspoon pepper
1 teaspoon low-sodium soy sauce mixed with 2 teaspoons water

METHOD

1. Preheat oven to 350F (175C). Combine all ingredients in a medium-size bowl. Spray 6 muffin cups with No Stick cooking spray.
2. Divide meat among muffin cups. Bake 25 minutes, until cooked through.

Makes 6 servings.

NUTRITIONAL
BREAKDOWN (Per serving)

- Calories 196
- Protein 19g
- Carbohydrates 18g
- Fat 4.5g
- Sodium 178mg
- Cholesterol 47mg

BEANS & BEEF

1 pound ground beef
1 large onion, diced
2 garlic cloves, minced
1/2 green bell pepper, diced
1/2 red bell pepper, diced
2 cups canned no-salt added tomatoes
1 cup cooked kidney beans
1/2 teaspoon chili powder, or to taste

METHOD

1. Preheat oven to 350F (175C). Spray a 1-1/2-quart baking dish with No Stick cooking spray. Brown meat in a medium-size skillet; drain off fat. Add onion, garlic, bell peppers, tomatoes and cook 10 minutes.
2. Add beans and chili powder.
3. Spoon mixture into sprayed baking dish. Cover and bake 1-1/2 hours.
4. Remove cover. Bake 20 minutes more. Serve hot.

Makes 6 servings.

Variation

Serve over cooked rice.

NUTRITIONAL
BREAKDOWN (Per serving without rice)

- Calories 194
- Protein 23g
- Carbohydrates 12g
- Fat 5g
- Sodium 123mg
- Cholesterol 47mg

BEEF & PASTA

Sauce:
2 tablespoons low-sodium soy sauce mixed with 6 tablespoons
  water
1 tablespoon dry sherry
4 teaspoons cornstarch mixed with 1/3 cup water
1/3 cup Beef Stock, page 138

9 ounces lean beef flank steak
2 tablespoons Beef Stock, page 138
1 teaspoon minced garlic
2/3 cup sliced yellow bell pepper
2/3 cup sliced red bell pepper
2/3 cup sliced green bell pepper
3/4 cup cut Italian flat beans, briefly steamed
1 large onion, separated into rings
1-1/2 cups cooked small pasta, such as small shells or macaroni
  (about 1/2 cups uncooked)

METHOD

1. Cook sauce ingredients in a small saucepan, stirring, until
   sauce thickens.
2. Thinly slice steak diagonally across grain. Spray a non-stick
   pan with No Stick cooking spray. Add stock, garlic and meat.
   Cook until meat is tender.
3. Add vegetables, toss and cook 2 minutes or until crisp-tender.
4. Add pasta and sauce. Mix well and serve hot.

Makes 3 servings.

Variation

Substitute green beans or bok choy (Chinese cabbage) for other
above vegetables. If using bok choy, separate stalks.

NUTRITIONAL
BREAKDOWN (Per serving)

- Calories 290
- Protein 34g
- Carbohydrates 25g
- Fat 6g
- Sodium 73mg
- Cholesterol 55mg

BEEF STROGANOFF

1 pound lean beef flank steak, cut in thin strips
1 onion, thinly sliced
1 garlic clove, minced
8 ounces mushrooms, sliced
1/2 (2-oz.) jar pimentos, diced
1/4 cup water
1 cup low-fat yogurt
1 tablespoon low-fat buttermilk
Dash of paprika
Dash of Tabasco sauce
Dash of pepper

METHOD

1. Spray a non-stick skillet with No Stick cooking spray. Sauté meat in sprayed skillet until browned.
2. Add onion, garlic, mushrooms, pimentos and water; cook 10 minutes, stirring frequently.
3. Remove from heat and add yogurt, buttermilk, paprika, Tabasco sauce and pepper. Serve on wide whole-wheat noodles.

Makes 4 servings.

Variation

Add 1 heaping teaspoon cornstarch mixed with 1 tablespoon cold water for a thicker sauce.

NUTRITIONAL
BREAKDOWN (Per serving)

- Calories 256
- Protein 36g
- Carbohydrates 9g
- Fat 7g
- Sodium 120mg
- Cholesterol 70mg

BROILED FLANK STEAK

1 pound lean flank steak
3/4 cup dry red wine
3 garlic cloves, cut in quarters
1 bay leaf, cut in half
1/2 teaspoon onion powder
1/2 teaspoon garlic powder
2 teaspoons Dijon-style no-salt added mustard

METHOD

1. Preheat broiler. Marinate steak in a flat baking dish with wine, garlic and bay leaf 1 hour, turning occasionally.
2. Drain steak. Place steak on a broiler rack; sprinkle with onion powder and garlic powder. Spread a thin layer of mustard over top.
3. Broil to desired doneness, about 5 minutes on each side.

Makes 4 servings.

NUTRITIONAL BREAKDOWN (Per serving)

- Calories 175
- Protein 24g
- Carbohydrates 3g
- Fat 7g
- Sodium 55mg
- Cholesterol 60mg

CHILI CON CARNE

8 ounces very lean ground beef
8 ounces boned, skinned chicken breast, finely chopped
1 large onion, finely chopped
1 medium-size green bell pepper, chopped
2 garlic cloves, minced
1 tablespoon chili powder
1 tablespoon ground cumin
1 (14-1/2-oz.) can no-salt added tomatoes, chopped, juice reserved
1 cup Beef Stock, page 138
1 tablespoon no-salt added tomato paste
1 teaspoon red pepper flakes
1 teaspoon ground coriander
1 teaspoon dried leaf oregano
1 teaspoon dried leaf basil, crumbled
1 bay leaf
1 cup cooked kidney beans
3 tablespoons grated Parmesan cheese (optional)

METHOD

1. Lightly coat a heavy 10-inch skillet with No Stick cooking spray and set over medium heat 30 seconds. Add the ground beef and chicken breast; cook, stirring often, until no longer pink, about 4 to 5 minutes. Push the meat mixture to one side of the skillet.
2. Add the onion, green pepper, garlic, chili powder and cumin; cover and cook until the onion is soft, about 5 minutes. Add the tomatoes, stock, tomato paste, red pepper flakes, coriander, oregano, basil and bay leaf; simmer, uncovered, stirring occasionally, 20 minutes.
3. Add the kidney beans and simmer, uncovered, stirring occasionally, 5 minutes more. Discard bay leaf. Ladle into soup bowls and garnish with cheese, if desired. Serve with rice.

Makes 6 servings.

NUTRITIONAL
BREAKDOWN (Per serving without rice)

- Calories 190
- Protein 24g
- Carbohydrates 10g
- Fat 6g
- Sodium 121mg
- Cholesterol 43mg

MARINATED FLANK STEAK

1-1/2 pounds lean beef flank steak
2 tablespoons low-sodium soy sauce
1 teaspoon ground ginger or grated gingerroot
2 tablespoons pineapple juice concentrate
4 green onions, diced
2 garlic cloves, minced
1 cup pineapple chunks

METHOD

1. Marinate flank steak with next 5 ingredients overnight in the refrigerator. Turn once.
2. Preheat grill or broiler. Broil 5 to 7 minutes each side, or to desired doneness.
3. Slice diagonally. Serve with pineapple.

Makes 6 servings.

NUTRITIONAL
BREAKDOWN (Per serving)

- Calories 192
- Protein 24g
- Carbohydrates 8g
- Fat 7g
- Sodium 200mg
- Cholesterol 60mg

MICROWAVED CHILI

1 pound lean beef flank steak, ground
1 (15-1/2-oz.) can red kidney beans, drained, rinsed
1 (14-1/2-oz.) can no-salt added tomatoes, chopped, juice
  reserved
1 (8-oz.) can no-salt added tomato sauce
1-1/2 tablespoons low-sodium soy sauce
1 tablespoon chili powder, or to taste
1 teaspoon dried minced onion
1/4 teaspoon garlic powder
Tabasco sauce, or 1 tablespoon hot salsa

METHOD

1. Cook flank steak in a non-stick skillet until browned; drain
   off fat. Place beef in a 3-quart microwavable casserole dish.
2. Add all ingredients and cook, covered, on HIGH 5 minutes;
   stir. Cook on MEDIUM 10 minutes; stir. Uncover and cook
   on MEDIUM 10 minutes. Serve on rice.

Makes 4 servings.

NUTRITIONAL
BREAKDOWN (Per serving without rice)

- Calories 225
- Protein 23g
- Carbohydrates 19g
- Fat 5g
- Sodium 338mg
- Cholesterol 47mg

MIDWEEK MEAT SURPRISE

1 pound lean beef flank steak, ground, or very lean ground beef
1/2 onion, chopped
2 tablespoons Beef Stock, page 138, or water
1/3 cup chopped red bell pepper
1/3 cup chopped green bell pepper
Dash of pepper
1/4 teaspoon ground thyme
1 (8-oz.) can no-salt added tomato sauce
1 cup water
2/3 cup uncooked rice

METHOD

1. Sauté meat in a non-stick skillet until browned, drain off fat and place meat in a bowl.
2. Sauté onion in stock or water in same skillet until soft.
3. Add remaining ingredients and meat. Cover and simmer 35 minutes or until rice is tender.

Makes 6 servings.

NUTRITIONAL
BREAKDOWN (Per serving)

- Calories 171
- Protein 18g
- Carbohydrates 18g
- Fat 3g
- Sodium 58mg
- Cholesterol 38mg

MY FAVORITE CHILI

1 large celery stalk, cut in 4 or 5 pieces
1 large onion, cut in quarters
2 large carrots, cut in pieces
2 large garlic cloves
1 cup Chicken Stock, page 139, or Vegetable Stock, page 141
1 (1-lb.) can no-salt added tomatoes
1 (6-oz.) can no-salt added tomato paste
1 red bell pepper, diced
1 (4-oz.) can chopped green chiles
1 cup quartered fresh mushrooms
2 cups no-salt added tomato juice
2 tablespoons salsa
1 tablespoon chili powder
1 teaspoon ground cumin
1 teaspoon dried leaf basil
1 tablespoon minced fresh parsley
2 (1-lb.) cans kidney beans, drained, rinsed
1 pound lean beef flank steak, ground, or very lean ground beef

METHOD

1. Place celery, onion, carrots and garlic in a food processor fitted with the metal blade and coarsely chop.
2. Put chopped vegetables in a large saucepan; sauté in stock until soft.
3. Add tomatoes and tomato paste and bell pepper. Cook 5 minutes.
4. Add chiles, mushrooms, tomato juice and salsa. Simmer 5 minutes.
5. Add remaining ingredients and cook 1 hour. Serve hot.

Makes 6 servings.

Variation

For that hot, hot taste, add 1 tablespoon crushed red pepper.

NUTRITIONAL
BREAKDOWN (Per serving)

- Calories 257
- Protein 17g
- Carbohydrates 42g
- Fat 3g
- Sodium 116mg
- Cholesterol 38mg

206

PINEAPPLE STEAK KABOBS

Marinade:
1 tablespoon tamari or low-sodium soy sauce and 2 tablespoons
   water
1 tablespoon sherry
1 garlic clove, crushed
1 tablespoon apple juice concentrate

1 pound lean beef flank steak, cut in 2-inch squares
1/2 red bell pepper, cut in 1-inch squares
1 (8-oz.) can unsweetened pineapple chunks, juice reserved
8 medium fresh mushrooms

METHOD

1. Combine marinade ingredients in a medium-size bowl. Add
   flank steak; marinate in refrigerator at least 1 to 2 hours, turning every half hour.
2. Preheat grill or broiler. Thread flank steak, bell pepper, pineapple chunks and mushrooms alternately on 14-inch skewers.
3. Grill about 10 minutes or to desired doneness, turning and
   brushing with marinade. Serve on a bed of rice.

Makes 4 servings.

Variation

Substitute hot salsa for above marinade for a spicier flavor.

NUTRITIONAL
BREAKDOWN (Per serving)

- Calories 201
- Protein 26g
- Carbohydrates 13g
- Fat 5g
- Sodium 211mg
- Cholesterol 70mg

SZECHUAN BEEF WITH NOODLES

Marinade:
1 tablespoon low-sodium soy sauce and 1 tablespoon water
2 tablespoons rice vinegar
3/4 teaspoon finely chopped garlic
3/4 teaspoon finely chopped gingerroot
5 green onion tops, finely chopped
2 tablespoons apple juice concentrate

1 pound lean beef flank steak, cut in strips
2 tablespoons Beef Stock, page 138
8 dried mushrooms, soaked in water, then chopped
4 green onions, with tops, thinly sliced
1/2 green bell pepper, cut diagonally
1 pound angel hair pasta, cooked until al dente

METHOD

1. Combine marinade ingredients in a medium-size bowl. Combine beef with 1/3 of marinade mixture. Marinate in refrigerator at least 1 to 2 hours.
2. Drain beef; discard marinade.
3. Add stock to a wok or large skillet over high heat. Add beef and mushrooms. Toss and cook until browned. Add remaining marinade, onions and pepper. Cook until crisp-tender.
4. Serve on bed of pasta.

Makes 4 servings.

Variation

Add 1 teaspoon Chinese hot mustard to remaining marinade for a unique flavor!

NUTRITIONAL
BREAKDOWN (Per serving without pasta)

- Calories 406
- Protein 34g
- Carbohydrates 54g
- Fat 6g
- Sodium 125mg
- Cholesterol 70mg

208

MEXICALI TORTILLAS

6 corn tortillas
1 (8-oz.) jar salsa, mild or hot
12 ounces lean beef flank steak, ground, or very lean ground beef
1 red bell pepper, finely chopped
1/2 lb. mushrooms, finely chopped
1 medium-size onion, finely chopped
1 (1-lb.) can white kidney beans, drained, rinsed
1/2 teaspoon chili powder
1 tablespoon grated Parmesan cheese

METHOD

1. Preheat oven to 350F (175C). Spray an 8-inch-square baking pan with No Stick cooking spray. Soak tortillas in salsa until soft and can be easily rolled.
2. Sauté meat in a non-stick skillet until browned; drain off fat.
3. Add bell pepper, mushrooms and onion. Sauté 10 minutes.
4. Add beans and chili powder; simmer 10 minutes.
5. Spoon some salsa into sprayed pan.
6. Place 2 tablespoons of meat mixture in each tortilla, roll up and place in salsa in dish.
7. Cover with remaining salsa so all sides are covered. Sprinkle with cheese and bake until tortillas are crisp, 15 to 20 minutes.

Makes 3 servings.

NUTRITIONAL
BREAKDOWN (Per serving)

- Calories 471
- Protein 39g
- Carbohydrates 61g
- Fat 7g
- Sodium 360mg
- Cholesterol 70mg

POULTRY ENTREES

Today's variety of chicken products help you to prepare a meal within a very short time. Keep in mind the more the poultry part is cut the more you pay. I therefore advise buying whole chicken breasts, remove the skin, cut them in half, and they are ready. In fact, although the recipe calls for skinless and boneless breasts, leaving the bones on the breast will not change the calories—it will only reduce your cost.

Here are just a few poultry facts that you should keep in mind.

1. Turkey is the leanest poultry.

2. Chicken has two to three times more fat than turkey.

3. Skinless turkey is almost fat-free.

4. White meat has about half the fat as dark meat.

5. In order of leanest: breast, then drumstick, wing and neck.

6. Stay away from self-basting turkeys. Soy, corn or sometimes coconut oil is added, along with salt, artificial coloring and sodium phosphate.

7. Ground turkey from the supermarket is not as lean as turkey you grind yourself since they often grind the turkey with the skin.

8. Last and most important: removing skin cuts fat in half!

KNOW YOUR POULTRY

Chicken Part	Cal.	% Cal. from fat	Chol (mg)
Breast with skin	197	36	84
Breast without skin	165	19	85
Thigh with skin	253	56	91
Thigh without skin	205	43	93
Drumstick with skin	216	46	91
Drumstick without skin	172	30	93

CHICKEN LENTIL CASSEROLE

1 cup lentils
4 cups cold water
2/3 cup minced green onions
1 tablespoon minced parsley
2 garlic cloves, minced
1/2 red bell pepper, diced
1 tablespoon cornstarch mixed with 3 tablespoons water
1/4 cup no-salt added tomato puree
1 cup diced cooked chicken
1/8 teaspoon pepper

METHOD

1. Wash lentils and soak overnight in the cold water.
2. Drain off water, reserving 2 cups. Cook reserved water, lentils, onions, parsley, garlic and bell pepper in a medium-size saucepan, covered, until tender.
3. Add cornstarch mixture, tomato puree, chicken and pepper to cooked lentils. Cook, stirring, until mixture comes a boil and is thickened.

Makes 4 servings.

NUTRITIONAL
BREAKDOWN (Per serving)

- Calories 286
- Protein 28g
- Carbohydrates 38g
- Fat 2g
- Sodium 58mg
- Cholesterol 30mg

LIMA BEAN CASSEROLE

1/4 cup diced onion
1/4 cup diced green bell pepper
2 tablespoons Chicken Stock, page 139
1 cup cream-style corn
3 pimento strips, diced
1 cup no-salt added canned plum tomatoes, diced
1 cup frozen lima beans, thawed
2 cups diced cooked chicken
No-salt added bread crumbs

METHOD

1. Preheat oven to 350F (175C). Spray a 1-1/2-quart casserole dish with No Stick cooking spray. Sauté onion and green pepper in stock in a medium-size saucepan until soft.
2. Stir in corn, pimento strips, tomatoes, lima beans and chicken.
3. Pour into sprayed casserole dish. Cover with bread crumbs.
4. Bake 35 to 40 minutes, until bubbly.

Makes 8 servings.

NUTRITIONAL
BREAKDOWN (Per serving)

- Calories 180
- Protein 20g
- Carbohydrates 19g
- Fat 2g
- Sodium 140mg
- Cholesterol 25mg

GRILLED TARRAGON CHICKEN

2 whole chicken breasts, skinned, boned
2 tablespoons onion, grated
1-1/2 teaspoons dried leaf tarragon
2 teaspoons low-sodium soy sauce
1 large garlic clove, minced
2 tablespoons tarragon vinegar, or 2 tablespoons white rice vinegar

METHOD

1. Cut chicken breasts in half and butterfly or flatten.
2. Combine onion, tarragon, soy sauce, garlic and vinegar in a medium-size bowl. Add chicken. Cover and refrigerate at least 2 to 3 hours.
3. Prepare grill. Spray grill with No Stick cooking spray so chicken doesn't stick.
4. Cook, basting with marinade, about 30 minutes until juices are clear when chicken is pierced.

Makes 4 servings.

Variation

Substitute fresh lime juice and Dijon-style mustard for above marinade.

NUTRITIONAL BREAKDOWN (Per serving)

- Calories 74
- Protein 13g
- Carbohydrates 1g
- Fat 1.5g
- Sodium 202mg
- Cholesterol 37mg

BRAZILIAN HOLIDAY CHICKEN

3 cups chopped chicken (1-inch pieces)
1 large onion, sliced
1-1/2 green bell peppers, diced
1 red bell pepper, diced
3 garlic cloves, chopped
1/2 bay leaf
1 teaspoon garlic powder
1/4 teaspoon ground cumin, or to taste
1/4 teaspoon dried leaf oregano
2 (15-oz.) cans no-salt added tomato sauce
1 (15-oz.) can filled with water
1 tablespoon fresh lemon juice
5 cups chopped celery

METHOD

1. Mix all ingredients except celery in a large saucepan. Cook 1 hour 20 minutes.
2. Add celery and cook 20 to 25 minutes more, until celery is crisp-tender.

Makes 6 servings.

Variation

Serve with cooked brown rice.

NUTRITIONAL
BREAKDOWN (Per serving without rice)

- Calories 233
- Protein 32g
- Carbohydrates 17g
- Fat 4g
- Sodium 126mg
- Cholesterol 77mg

CASABLANCA CHICKEN

2 tablespoons low-fat yogurt
1/2 teaspoon ground cumin
1/2 teaspoon ground cinnamon
2 chicken breasts, skinned and boned, pounded thin
1 large eggplant
1/4 cup Chicken Stock, page 139
3 garlic cloves, finely minced
3 large shallots, finely chopped
12 cherry tomatoes
3/4 teaspoon dried leaf oregano

METHOD

1. Blend yogurt, cumin and cinnamon in a small bowl.
2. Rub 1/2 of the yogurt mixture all over chicken, cover with plastic wrap and marinate in refrigerator 2 hours or overnight.
3. Prick eggplant skin; steam until tender. Peel and chop.
4. Spray a medium-size skillet with No Stick cooking spray. Add stock and sauté garlic and shallots until soft. Add eggplant and stir 2 minutes. Remove from heat, add remaining yogurt mixture and blend well. Keep warm.
5. Spray another medium-size non-stick skillet. Add chicken breasts; cook 3 to 4 minutes on each side, constantly turning so as not to burn or stick.
6. Add tomatoes, chicken and oregano to eggplant mixture. Serve on brown rice.

Makes 4 servings.

NUTRITIONAL
BREAKDOWN (Per serving without rice)

- Calories 175
- Protein 28g
- Carbohydrates 5g
- Fat 3g
- Sodium 70mg
- Cholesterol 75mg

CHICKEN OR TURKEY CURRY

1/2 cup thinly sliced celery
1/2 cup finely chopped onion
2 garlic cloves, minced
3 tablespoons Chicken Stock, page 139
4 tablespoons arrowroot or cornstarch
2 cups skim milk
2 cups water
1 cup unsweetened applesauce
6 tablespoons no-salt added tomato paste
4 teaspoons curry powder
4 Frozen Bouillon Cubes, page 142
6 cups cooked chicken or turkey pieces

METHOD

1. Sauté celery, onion and garlic in stock in a large skillet. Blend in arrowroot, milk, water, applesauce, tomato paste, curry powder and bouillon cubes.
2. Cook and stir until thickened and bubbly. Stir in chicken or turkey and heat thoroughly.

Makes 6 servings.

Variation

Serve over rice and top with raisins, chopped green peppers or chopped hard-cooked egg whites.

NUTRITIONAL
BREAKDOWN (Per serving without rice)
- Calories 258
- Protein 36g
- Carbohydrates 21g
- Fat 4g
- Sodium 130mg
- Cholesterol 62mg

CHICKEN DIJON

2 chicken breasts, skinned, cut in eighths
4 garlic cloves, minced
2 tablespoons low-fat yogurt
1/4 cup dry sherry
1/4 teaspoon ground paprika
1/2 cup fresh orange juice
1 tablespoon cornstarch mixed with 2 tablespoons water

METHOD

1. Preheat oven to 350F (175C). Place chicken in a baking dish.
2. Mix next 4 ingredients and pour over chicken. Cover with foil. Bake 20 to 25 minutes.
3. Combine juice and cornstarch mixture. Pour over chicken and bake, uncovered, until thick and bubbly. Serve hot.

Makes 4 servings.

Variation

Add 2-1/2 teaspoons salt-free Dijon-style mustard for added flavor.

NUTRITIONAL
BREAKDOWN (Per serving)

- Calories 183
- Protein 32g
- Carbohydrates 7g
- Fat 3g
- Sodium 82mg
- Cholesterol 60mg

CHICKEN HAWAIIAN

1 teaspoon freshly grated gingerroot
3 garlic cloves, minced
2 shallots, minced
1 cup Chicken Stock, page 139
3/4 cup chopped onion
6 ounces unsweetened pineapple juice
14 ounces chicken breasts, skinned, boned and cubed
1 cup fresh pineapple, cubed
1/4 teaspoon poultry seasoning
1 tablespoon low-sodium soy sauce or tamari
1/4 cup tomato puree
3/4 cup sliced red bell pepper
3/4 cup sliced green bell pepper
1 tablespoon cornstarch or arrowroot
1/4 cup water
1 tablespoon apple juice concentrate

METHOD

1. Combine gingerroot, garlic, shallots and stock in a large non-stick saucepan. Simmer 10 minutes.
2. Add the onion and cook 5 minutes. Add the pineapple juice. Simmer 1 minute.
3. Add the chicken, pineapple, seasoning, soy sauce, tomato puree and bell peppers. Simmer 15 minutes or until chicken is tender.
4. Dissolve the cornstarch in the water and apple juice concentrate in a small bowl. Blend into the chicken mixture. Cook, stirring constantly, until thickened and clear. Cook 2 minutes more.

Makes 6 servings.

Variation

Serve over cooked brown rice or pasta.

NUTRITIONAL
BREAKDOWN (Per serving without rice or pasta)

- Calories 146
- Protein 18g
- Carbohydrates 17g
- Fat 0.5g
- Sodium 178mg
- Cholesterol 30mg

CHICKEN KORMA

2 (2-1/2- to 3-lb.) chickens, skinned, cut in small pieces
2 cups low-fat yogurt
2 garlic cloves, minced
2 medium-size onions, chopped
1 teaspoon ground paprika
2 teaspoons finely chopped gingerroot
Dash of pepper
2 tablespoons Chicken Stock, page 139
2 teaspoons ground coriander
1/2 teaspoon ground chile
1 teaspoon ground cumin
Small amount of peeled cardamom pods
1 teaspoon poppy seeds
1 tablespoon ground turmeric
1 bay leaf
2 tablespoons chopped cilantro

METHOD

1. Place chicken in a large bowl. Add yogurt, 1 garlic clove, 1/2 onion, paprika, gingerroot and pepper. Cover and refrigerate a few hours.
2. Spray a large heavy saucepan with No Stick cooking spray. Add remaining onions and garlic and 2 tablespoons stock; cook until soft.
3. Add coriander, chile, cumin, cardamom seeds, poppy seeds and turmeric. Sauté 2 to 3 minutes. Add chicken and enough water to cover and add any remaining marinade. Add bay leaf. Simmer about 45 minutes or until chicken is tender. Sprinkle with cilantro. Serve over rice.

Makes 8 servings.

NUTRITIONAL
BREAKDOWN (Per serving without rice)

- Calories 175
- Protein 27g
- Carbohydrates 0g
- Fat 9g
- Sodium 99mg
- Cholesterol 61mg

CHICKEN L'ORANGE WITH MUSHROOMS

1 shallot, minced
4 garlic cloves, minced
1/2 cup dry sherry
1 tablespoon orange juice concentrate
2 cups sliced fresh mushrooms
2 chicken breasts, butterflied, cut in thin strips
2 cups Chicken Stock, page 139
1/4 cup dry sherry
1/2 cup Chicken Stock, page 139
1 teaspoon low-sodium soy sauce
2 teaspoons cornstarch

METHOD

1. Spray a large non-stick skillet with No Stick cooking spray. Add shallot and garlic; sauté until tender, 2 or 3 minutes.
2. Add 1/2 cup sherry; bring to a boil. Reduce heat, then simmer 3 minutes.
3. Add orange juice concentrate; simmer 2 minutes. Add mushrooms; simmer 2 or 3 minutes.
4. Poach chicken in 2 cups stock in a medium-size skillet for 15 minutes or until tender. Strain chicken from poaching liquid and add to mushroom mixture in pan.
5. Combine the 1/4 cup sherry, 1/2 cup stock, soy sauce and cornstarch in a small bowl. Stir into chicken mixture. Simmer until thickened. Serve over rice or wide noodles.

Makes 3 servings.

NUTRITIONAL
BREAKDOWN (per serving without rice or noodles)

- Calories 230
- Protein 20g
- Carbohydrates 18g
- Fat 1g
- Sodium 160mg
- Cholesterol 97mg

CHICKEN TETRAZZINI

1 spaghetti squash (about 3 lbs.)
2 cups plus 2 tablespoons Chicken Stock, page 139
1 medium-size onion, finely chopped
1 large celery stalk, thinly sliced
2/3 cup sliced fresh mushrooms
1/8 teaspoon pepper
3 tablespoons unbleached all-purpose flour
1 cup skim milk
1 bay leaf
2 tablespoons low-fat yogurt
2 tablespoons minced parsley
1 tablespoon fresh lemon juice
2 cups cubed chicken or turkey
2 tablespoons fine dry bread crumbs
1 tablespoon grated Parmesan cheese

METHOD

1. Preheat oven to 350F (175C). Pierce squash in several places with a small knife. Place on an ungreased baking sheet and bake 1 hour or until it can be pierced easily with a fork. Cool.
2. In a medium-size heavy saucepan, heat 2 tablespoons stock over medium heat. Add onion, celery, mushrooms and pepper, and cook until onion is soft, about 5 minutes.
3. Slowly add the flour to the vegetables and stir 1 minute. Add the 2 cups stock, milk and bay leaf, and cook over medium-low heat, stirring occasionally, 20 minutes. Discard the bay leaf; stir in yogurt, parsley and lemon juice. Remove from the heat.
4. Halve squash lengthwise and remove seeds. Using a fork, scrape the flesh into an ungreased shallow 1-1/2-quart casserole dish, smoothing into an even layer; cover with the chicken, then vegetable sauce, and top with bread crumbs and Parmesan cheese. Bake 30 minutes or until bubbly.

Makes 4 servings.

NUTRITIONAL
BREAKDOWN (per serving)

- Calories 245
- Protein 35g
- Carbohydrates 22g
- Fat 2g
- Sodium 174mg
- Cholesterol 77mg

CRANBERRY CHICKEN

4 cups unsweetened cranberry juice
1-1/2 tablespoons dried leaf basil
1 onion, thinly sliced
1 (3- to 3-1/2-lb.) chicken, cut in eighths
8 ounces cranberries
2 tablespoons rice vinegar
4 tablespoons apple juice concentrate
1 teaspoon cornstarch mixed with 2 tablespoons cold water

METHOD

1. In a medium-size saucepan, simmer 3 cups cranberry juice, basil and onion 10 minutes. Let cool, add chicken and marinate overnight in refrigerator.
2. The following day poach chicken in same marinade until tender. Keep warm.
3. Simmer cranberries, vinegar, apple juice concentrate and the 1 cup cranberry juice in a medium-size saucepan until berries are tender, about 20 minutes.
4. Stir in cornstarch mixture; cook until thickened. Pour over chicken and serve.

Makes 4 servings.

This is a great Christmas week dish for a buffet. The same cranberry sauce can be served over sliced turkey.

NUTRITIONAL
BREAKDOWN (Per serving)

- Calories 330
- Protein 30g
- Carbohydrates 43g
- Fat 4g
- Sodium 125mg
- Cholesterol 77mg

CREAMED CORN CHICKEN

1 (1-lb.) can no-salt added creamed corn
1 bunch green onions, chopped with tops
1 cup skim milk
1 egg white
2 tablespoons unbleached all-purpose flour
1 (3- to 4-lb.) chicken, skinned and cut into eighths
1 teaspoon poultry seasoning
Paprika
Dry whole-wheat bread crumbs

METHOD

1. Preheat oven to 350F (175C). Mix corn, green onions, milk, egg white and flour in a 13" x 9" baking dish.
2. Place chicken over mixture and sprinkle with seasoning and paprika.
3. Cover with bread crumbs and bake 1 hour 20 minutes until chicken is tender.

Makes 4 servings.

Variation

Add a few pimento strips for color.

NUTRITIONAL
BREAKDOWN (Per serving)

- Calories 340
- Protein 38g
- Carbohydrates 33g
- Fat 5g
- Sodium 125mg
- Cholesterol 60mg

CRISPY CHICKEN

1 (2-1/2- to 3-lb.) chicken, skinned, cut into eighths
1-1/2 cups French Dressing, page 329, or a no-oil diet French
  dressing
2 cups oat bran flakes

METHOD

1. Preheat oven to 375F (190C). Marinate chicken in French dressing at least 1 hour in refrigerator, turning a few times.
2. Crush oat bran flakes in a blender or food processor fitted with the metal blade. Coat the chicken in the crumbs.
3. Spray a baking sheet with No Stick cooking spray. Arrange chicken on sprayed baking sheet. Bake at least 1 hour. If you like it very crisp, it may take 1 hour and 15 minutes.

Makes 4 servings.

NUTRITIONAL
BREAKDOWN (Per serving)

- Calories 301
- Protein 30g
- Carbohydrates 34g
- Fat 5g
- Sodium 71mg
- Cholesterol 66mg

FABULOUS TURKEY BREAST

3 ounces frozen orange juice concentrate, do not dilute
3 garlic cloves, minced
1/4 teaspoon paprika
1 tablespoon no-sugar added orange marmalade
1/2 teaspoon tamari or low-sodium soy sauce
1 (3-lb.) turkey breast, fresh or if frozen, completely thawed
2 teaspoons cornstarch mixed with 2 tablespoons cold water

METHOD

1. Combine orange juice concentrate, garlic, paprika, marmalade and tamari in a small bowl.
2. Cut two pieces of plastic wrap at least 18 inches long and overlap them about 2 inches to create a very large piece of plastic wrap.
3. Place turkey in center of this sheet and cover turkey completely on all sides with orange mixture.
4. Wrap turkey very, very tightly with wrap. Use extra piece if you think it needs it.
5. Repeat Step 4 with foil.
6. Place in oven on a baking sheet and bake 3 hours at 350F (175C). Don't open, don't look until time is up.
7. Drain juice from turkey into saucepan, stir in cornstarch mixture; cook until thick and bubbly.

Makes 9 servings.

This may sound crazy, but it is the best, juiciest turkey you've ever tasted. Leftovers are great for salads or sandwiches.

NUTRITIONAL
BREAKDOWN (Per serving)

- Calories 119
- Protein 19g
- Carbohydrates 5g
- Fat 3g
- Sodium 23mg
- Cholesterol 55mg

HOT & SPICY CHICKEN

2 chicken breasts
1/2 cup Chicken Stock, page 139
1 teaspoon minced gingerroot
1 garlic clove, minced
3 dried red Szechuan peppers, finely chopped
1/2 lb. snow peas, stems removed
1 tablespoon low-sodium soy sauce
1 tablespoon dry sherry
10 shiitake mushrooms
1 teaspoon cornstarch or arrowroot
3 tablespoons cold water
2 green onions, cut in 1-inch pieces

METHOD

1. Trim and cut chicken in strips.
2. Put stock in a wok; add gingerroot, garlic and Szechuan peppers. Cook over medium heat.
3. Add chicken and cook 3 or 4 minutes, stirring constantly.
4. Add snow peas, soy sauce, sherry and mushrooms; cook, stirring, 2 or 3 minutes.
5. Mix cornstarch and cold water in a small bowl; add to mixture in wok. Cook, stirring, until mixture thickens. Add green onions, reduce heat and cook 1 minute. Serve over brown rice.

Makes 4 servings.

NUTRITIONAL
BREAKDOWN (per serving without rice)

- Calories 181
- Protein 27g
- Carbohydrates 14g
- Fat 3g
- Sodium 253mg
- Cholesterol 60mg

LIME CHICKEN SHISH KABOB

2 chicken breasts, cut in cubes
Juice of 2 limes
2 garlic cloves, minced
1 tablespoon low-sodium soy sauce
1 tablespoon apple juice concentrate
8 ounces medium-size mushrooms
1 red bell pepper, cut in 1-inch pieces
16 white pearl onions
1 green bell pepper, cut in 1-inch pieces
2 small zucchini, cubed

METHOD

1. Marinate chicken in lime juice, garlic, soy sauce and apple juice concentrate in a medium-size bowl at least 2 hours in the refrigerator, turning at least once.
2. On skewers, alternate chicken, mushrooms, red pepper, onions, green pepper and zucchini.
3. Prepare grill. Grill about 10 minutes, turning and basting often with marinade.

Makes 4 servings.

NUTRITIONAL
BREAKDOWN (Per serving)

- Calories 132
- Protein 17g
- Carbohydrates 17g
- Fat 1g
- Sodium 192mg
- Cholesterol 30mg

ORANGE CHICKEN

1 (2- to 3-lb.) chicken, skinned, cut in eighths
3 tablespoons no-sugar added orange marmalade, apricot jam
  or pineapple jam
3 tablespoons orange juice concentrate
1/4 teaspoon grated gingerroot
1/2 teaspoon fresh lemon juice
2 teaspoons fresh garlic, crushed
1/4 teaspoon paprika
1 tablespoon low-sodium soy sauce
2 teaspoons cornstarch mixed with 1 tablespoon cold water

METHOD

1. Preheat oven to 350F (175C). Place chicken in a baking dish.
2. Mix all ingredients except cornstarch mixture together in a medium-size bowl; pour over chicken.
3. Cover with foil, pierce holes in foil and bake 30 minutes, basting once.
4. Remove foil cover. Drain juices into a small saucepan. Add cornstarch mixture; cook until thickened, stirring.
5. Place chicken on bed of brown rice and pour gravy over. Serve.

Makes 4 servings.

NUTRITIONAL
BREAKDOWN (Per serving without rice)

- Calories 187
- Protein 28g
- Carbohydrates 12g
- Fat 3g
- Sodium 225mg
- Cholesterol 60mg

228

POACHED CHICKEN IN GINGERED ORANGE SAUCE

4 chicken breasts, skinned, cut in strips
3 cups Chicken Stock, page 139
1 (1-inch) piece gingerroot
1 teaspoon grated orange zest
1 cup fresh orange juice
2 tablespoons sherry
1/2 teaspoon low-sodium soy sauce
2 navel oranges, skinned and sectioned
2 teaspoons cornstarch mixed with 3 tablespoons water

METHOD

1. Poach chicken strips in 2 cups of the Chicken Stock in a medium-size saucepan with gingerroot. After 5 minutes, discard gingerroot and cook until chicken is cooked, about 15 minutes. Remove from heat, let stand 5 minutes, covered.
2. In a small saucepan, combine zest, orange juice and sherry. Let stand 5 minutes. Add remaining 1 cup Chicken Stock and simmer until half the liquid has evaporated.
3. Add soy sauce and orange sections. Cook 5 minutes.
4. Stir in cornstarch mixture; cook until thickened. Drain chicken and add to orange mixture. Heat and serve.

Makes 6 servings.

NUTRITIONAL
BREAKDOWN (Per serving)

- Calories 144
- Protein 19g
- Carbohydrates 12g
- Fat 2g
- Sodium 77mg
- Cholesterol 97mg

STIR-FRY CHICKEN

Marinade:
2 tablespoons low-sodium soy sauce
1 tablespoon rice vinegar
3 tablespoons water
1 tablespoon apple juice concentrate
1 tablespoon dry sherry

Sauce:
2 tablespoons Chicken Stock, page 139
1 tablespoon apple juice concentrate
1 tablespoon low-sodium soy sauce
2 tablespoons water
1 tablespoon dry sherry
1-1/2 tablespoons cornstarch
1/4 teaspoon toasted sesame oil

1-1/4 pounds chicken breasts, skinned, thinly sliced
1/2 cup Chicken Stock, page 139
1 piece gingerroot
2 garlic cloves, minced
1 cup broccoli flowerets
1 cup cauliflowerets
4 green onions, diced
1/2 cup snow peas
1/2 red bell pepper, cut in strips
1/2 cup fresh mushrooms
1/2 cup bean sprouts

METHOD

1. Combine marinade ingredients in a medium-size bowl. Add chicken, cover and refrigerate at least 1 hour. Drain.
2. Combine sauce ingredients in a small bowl; set aside.
3. Spray a wok or large skillet with No Stick cooking spray. Add 2 tablespoons of the stock, gingerroot and garlic. Cook on high heat, 2 minutes; remove gingerroot.
4. Add chicken and remaining stock; stir-fry until tender. Remove from pan. Add more stock, if needed, and vegetables. Stir-fry until crisp-tender.
5. Add sauce and chicken; cook until thick, 1 to 2 minutes. Serve over rice.

Makes 6 servings.

Variations

Stir-Fry Beef: Substitute 1-1/4 pounds thinly sliced flank steak for chicken.

Vegetarian Stir-Fry: Substitute 30 ounces cubed tofu for chicken.

For extra zing, add Chinese mustard to sauce or add 1/4 teaspoon Chinese hot chili oil for Szechuan flavor.

NUTRITIONAL
BREAKDOWN (per serving without rice)

	With Chicken	With Beef	Vegetarian
• Calories	189	230	162
• Protein	23g	30g	13g
• Carbohydrates	12g	12g	16g
• Fat	3g	6g	5g
• Sodium	280mg	272mg	275mg
• Cholesterol	51mg	60mg	0mg

QUICKIE CHICKEN L'ORANGE

1 chicken, skinned, cut in eighths
3 ounces orange juice concentrate
1 tablespoon low-sodium soy sauce
2 tablespoons no-sugar added orange marmalade
1 tablespoon minced garlic

METHOD

1. Preheat oven to 325F (165C). Put chicken pieces in a baking dish. Combine the other ingredients in a small bowl and pour over chicken.
2. Cover and bake until chicken is tender.

Makes 4 servings.

Variation

If a thicker sauce is desired, drain sauce after cooking and quickly stir in 1 tablespoon cornstarch mixed with 2 tablespoons cold water. Cook until thickened, pour over chicken and serve.

NUTRITIONAL
BREAKDOWN (Per serving)

- Calories 208
- Protein 28g
- Carbohydrates 16g
- Fat 3g
- Sodium 163mg
- Cholesterol 51mg

TURKEY MEATBALLS

1 pound ground turkey (no skin)
1-1/2 cups bread crumbs
1 cup chopped onions
1 cup chopped carrots
1 cup no-salt added tomato sauce
3/4 teaspoon rubbed sage
1/4 teaspoon garlic powder
Dash of poultry seasoning

METHOD

1. Preheat oven to 375F (190C). Combine all ingredients in a medium-size bowl and mix well.
2. Shape into balls and place on a non-stick baking sheet.
3. Bake 35 minutes until browned.

Makes 4 servings.

Variation

Add oregano for an Italian flavor.

NUTRITIONAL
BREAKDOWN (Per serving)

- Calories 315
- Protein 30g
- Carbohydrates 40g
- Fat 4g
- Sodium 346mg
- Cholesterol 82mg

TURKEY MEATBALLS IN TOMATO WINE SAUCE

Sauce:
1 medium-size onion, sliced
2 garlic cloves, minced
2 cups Chicken Stock, page 139
1-1/2 tablespoons cornstarch
1 (8-oz.) can no-salt added tomatoes, drained, chopped
1 bay leaf
1 teaspoon low-sodium soy sauce
1-1/2 teaspoons dried leaf thyme
1/4 cup dry sherry
2 tablespoons no-salt added tomato paste

1 pound ground turkey
2 slices soft whole-wheat bread, torn in pieces
1/4 cup dry whole-wheat bread crumbs
1 teaspoon onion powder
1 teaspoon garlic powder
1 teaspoon low-sodium soy sauce
1 egg white
1/2 teaspoon dried leaf thyme
1/2 teaspoon dried leaf basil
1/4 cup Chicken Stock, page 139
1/4 cup tomato sauce
Dash of pepper
1/2 medium-size onion, minced

METHOD

1. To make sauce, sauté onion and garlic in small amount of stock until translucent.
2. Mix cornstarch with 2 tablespoons of the stock and set aside.
3. Combine remaining sauce ingredients with onion and garlic. Bring to a boil, reduce heat to low and simmer, 5 to 7 minutes.
4. Stir in cornstarch mixture, cook, stirring until thickened.
5. To make meatballs, combine turkey and all ingredients thoroughly. Shape into balls.
6. Drop into simmering sauce. Cook on low heat, partially covered, 30 to 45 minutes. Serve over noodles or rice.

Makes 8 servings.

NUTRITIONAL BREAKDOWN (Per serving without noodles or rice)

- Calories 137
- Protein 18g
- Carbohydrates. 12g
- Fat 2g
- Sodium 246mg
- Cholesterol 45mg

CHICKEN WINGS CACCIATORE

24 chicken wings
1 onion, finely chopped
1 carrot, thinly sliced
1 celery stalk, thinly sliced
1 red bell pepper, diced
1 green bell pepper, diced
6 garlic cloves, finely chopped
3 tablespoons Chicken Stock, page 139
3/4 teaspoon dried leaf oregano
1/4 teaspoon dried leaf basil or thyme
1 (28-oz.) can no-salt added plum tomatoes, quartered, liquid
   reserved
1/2 cup dry white wine
2 tablespoons chopped fresh parsley

METHOD

1. Cut out skin from each wing between drumette and middle wing part. The part you cut out will look like a V.
2. Sauté onion, carrot, celery, peppers and garlic in stock in a large saucepan until slightly soft.
3. Add remaining ingredients except wine and parsley; cook 15 minutes.
4. Add wings and simmer 30 minutes.
5. Add wine and parsley; cook 25 minutes more. Serve hot.

NUTRITIONAL
BREAKDOWN (Per serving—3 pieces)

- Calories 215
- Protein 20g
- Carbohydrates 10g
- Fat 8g
- Sodium 84mg
- Cholesterol 60mg

WEEKENDER SANDWICH

1 garlic clove, minced
1/2 small onion, chopped
1/4 green bell pepper, chopped
4 ounces ground turkey
1 (8-oz.) can no-salt added tomato sauce
1/2 teaspoon chili powder
1 tablespoon salsa
2 large whole-wheat pita breads, cut in half crosswise
Thinly sliced tomato
Shredded lettuce

METHOD

1. Spray a non-stick skillet with No Stick cooking spray. Sauté garlic and onion 2 minutes.
2. Add pepper, turkey, tomato sauce, chili powder and salsa. Simmer 10 to 15 minutes, mixture should be thick.
3. Spoon evenly into two warmed pita breads sliced in half. Top with sliced tomato and lettuce.

Makes 2 servings.

NUTRITIONAL
BREAKDOWN (Per sandwich)

- Calories 239
- Protein 22g
- Carbohydrates 28g
- Fat 3g
- Sodium 268mg
- Cholesterol 85mg

WEEKENDER ON WEEKDAYS

1 recipe Weekender Sandwich, opposite
1/2 cup frozen baby peas, thawed
1 cup cooked elbow macaroni

METHOD

1. Make first two steps of Weekender recipe but use 1/2 pound ground turkey.
2. Add peas and macaroni. Heat 2 minutes.

Makes 2 servings.

Enjoy this with a tossed salad and you will have a dinner that's less than 400 calories.

NUTRITIONAL
BREAKDOWN (Per serving)

- Calories 340
- Protein 25g
- Carbohydrates 44g
- Fat 6g
- Sodium 370mg
- Cholesterol 85mg

VEGETARIAN ENTREES

CONFETTI MACARONI BAKE

3 cups uncooked whole-wheat elbow macaroni
2 cups boiling water
1 pound low-fat cottage cheese
1/2 red bell pepper, diced
1/2 green bell pepper, diced
1 cup sliced yellow squash
1 cup sliced zucchini
1 medium-size onion, sliced
1/2 teaspoon garlic powder
1 teaspoon dried leaf oregano
1/2 teaspoon dried leaf basil
2 tablespoons chopped fresh parsley
1 (6-oz.) can no-salt added tomato paste
1 (16-oz.) can tomatoes, quartered, reserved juice
3 tablespoons grated Parmesan cheese

METHOD

1. Preheat oven to 300F (150C). Arrange macaroni evenly on bottom of a large baking dish. Pour water over macaroni.
2. Spread cottage cheese over macaroni.
3. Next layer peppers, squash, zucchini and onion over cottage cheese.
4. Sprinkle with seasonings, then top with tomato paste, tomatoes and juice.
5. Sprinkle with Parmesan cheese and bake, uncovered, 1-1/2 hours.

Makes 12 servings.

NUTRITIONAL
BREAKDOWN (Per serving)

- Calories 158
- Protein 10g
- Carbohydrates 27g
- Fat 1g
- Sodium 189mg
- Cholesterol 3mg

BROWN RICE CHEESE

2-1/2 cups cooked brown rice
3 green onions with tops, diced
1 cup low-fat cottage cheese, lightly drained
1 teaspoon dried dill weed
1/4 cup grated Parmesan cheese
2 tablespoons skim milk
1 teaspoon low-sodium soy sauce

METHOD

1. Preheat oven to 350F (175C). Spray a 1-quart baking dish with No Stick cooking spray. Combine all ingredients in a medium-size bowl.
2. Pour into sprayed baking dish. Bake 20 minutes.

Makes 6 servings.

Variation

Substitute cooked ditalini or other small pasta for rice.

NUTRITIONAL BREAKDOWN (Per serving)

- Calories 126
- Protein 8g
- Carbohydrates 18g
- Fat 2g
- Sodium 252mg
- Cholesterol 4mg

MEATLESS MOUSSAKA

1 eggplant (about 1-1/4 lb.), peeled, cut in 1/4-inch slices
3 egg whites
1 cup cooked brown rice
2 cups low-fat cottage cheese
1/2 cup instant non-fat milk powder
1/2 cup finely chopped onion
1/4 teaspoon crushed or ground sage
1-3/4 cups Marinara Sauce, page 332
3 tablespoons grated Parmesan cheese

METHOD

1. Preheat oven to 375F (190C). Drop eggplant in unsalted boiling water 4 minutes. Drain on paper towels.
2. Lightly beat egg whites. Add rice, cottage cheese, milk, onion and sage. Mix well.
3. Spread 1/2 cup sauce on bottom of an 11" x 7" baking dish. Alternate layers of eggplant, cottage cheese mixture and sauce until all is used.
4. Finish with sauce and cover with cheese. Bake 30 to 40 minutes, until bubbly.

Makes 5 servings.

NUTRITIONAL
BREAKDOWN (Per serving)

- Calories 226
- Protein 18g
- Carbohydrates 34g
- Fat 2g
- Sodium 500mg
- Cholesterol 5mg

VEGETABLE LASAGNA CURLS

12 lasagna noodles
1 pound low-fat cottage cheese
1 to 2 cups broccoli flowerets
1 cup chopped fresh mushrooms
2 green onions, diced
2 tablespoons chopped fresh basil
1 teaspoon chopped fresh oregano
2 tablespoons finely chopped fresh parsley
2 cups Marinara Sauce, page 332
2 tablespoons grated Parmesan cheese

METHOD

1. Preheat oven to 375F (190C). Cook lasagna noodles in a large saucepan until tender but firm, 8 to 10 minutes. Drain, rinse and keep in cold water until ready to use.
2. Mix remaining ingredients in a medium-size bowl. Place one-twelfth of mixture on each lasagna noodle and roll up to enclose filling.
3. Spray baking dish with No Stick cooking spray and place rolls seam-side down in dish.
4. Cover with Marinara Sauce and bake 20 minutes, covered. Remove cover and bake 20 minutes more. Sprinkle with Parmesan cheese; broil 1 minute.

Makes 6 servings.

NUTRITIONAL
BREAKDOWN (Per serving)

- Calories 320
- Protein 21g
- Carbohydrates 53g
- Fat 3g
- Sodium 371mg
- Cholesterol 4mg

STUFFED SHELLS

1 (12-oz.) box of large pasta shells (30 to 35 shells)
2 tablespoons grated Parmesan cheese
4 cups low-fat cottage cheese
2 garlic cloves, minced
2 tablespoons chopped fresh parsley, or fresh basil
1 egg white
2 cups Marinara Sauce, page 332

METHOD

1. Preheat oven to 350F (175C). Cook shells in boiling water in a large saucepan 5 to 7 minutes, until tender but firm. Rinse under cold water.
2. Mix 1 tablespoon Parmesan cheese and remaining ingredients except Marinara Sauce together in a medium-size bowl until fairly smooth.
3. Place 1 heaping tablespoon of cheese mixture into each shell.
4. Thinly spread 1/2 cup of Marinara Sauce on bottom of a baking pan. Arrange shells in sauce. Cover with remaining 1-1/2 cups sauce and bake 25 to 30 minutes.
5. Sprinkle remaining 1 tablespoon Parmesan cheese on top and broil until cheese melts. Serve hot.

Makes 8 servings.

Variations

For a thicker filling consistency, drain cottage cheese in strainer 1 hour in refrigerator.

Substitute lean chopped beef for cheese mixture.

NUTRITIONAL
BREAKDOWN (Per serving)

- Calories 278
- Protein 19g
- Carbohydrates 45g
- Fat 2g
- Sodium 366mg
- Cholesterol 4mg

SPINACH MUSHROOM LASAGNA

6 lasagna noodles
1-1/2 cups skim milk
3 tablespoons unbleached all-purpose flour
2 garlic cloves, minced
1 pound fresh spinach, chopped without stems, or 1 (10-oz.)
  package frozen chopped spinach, thawed, drained
3 or 4 tablespoons grated Parmesan cheese
2 cups Marinara Sauce, page 332
8 ounces fresh mushrooms, sliced

METHOD

1. Preheat oven to 400F (205C). Cook lasagna noodles in boiling water in a large saucepan until tender but firm, 8 to 10 minutes. Drain, rinse and keep in cold water until ready to use.
2. In a medium-size saucepan, blend milk, flour and garlic. Cook over medium heat, stirring, until thick. Reduce heat and simmer 2 to 3 minutes.
3. Remove from heat, add spinach and 2 tablespoons Parmesan cheese.
4. Spread 2 or 3 tablespoons sauce on bottom of an 8-inch-square baking dish. Place lasagna strips on bottom and trim edges. Spread 2 tablespoons sauce over noodles and add half of spinach mixture with half of mushrooms. Pour 1/4 cup of sauce over mushrooms and sprinkle with half of remaining cheese. Repeat for second layer ending with remaining sauce and cheese.
5. Bake in preheated oven 30 minutes. Let stand about 10 to 15 minutes to make cutting easier.

Makes 4 servings.

For perfect slices, place first layer of lasagna noodles horizontally and second layer at right angle to first layer. Slices won't fall apart.

NUTRITIONAL
BREAKDOWN (Per serving)

- Calories 300
- Protein 16g
- Carbohydrates 53g
- Fat 3g
- Sodium 173mg
- Cholesterol 5mg

PASTA CHEESE BAKE

1 cup Marinara Sauce, page 332
1/2 cup low-fat cottage cheese
8 ounces cooked pasta of your choice
1 tablespoon grated Parmesan cheese

METHOD

1. Preheat oven to 350F (175C). Spray a 1-1/2-quart casserole dish with No Stick cooking spray. Mix Marinara Sauce, cottage cheese and pasta in a large bowl.
2. Pour mixture into sprayed casserole dish.
3. Sprinkle Parmesan cheese on top. Bake 15 minutes, until bubbly.

Makes 4 servings.

NUTRITIONAL
BREAKDOWN (per serving)

- Calories 244
- Protein 11g
- Carbohydrates 45g
- Fat 2.5g
- Sodium 130mg
- Cholesterol 2mg

MANICOTTI WITH VEGETABLES & CHEESE

3 large shallots, chopped finely
2 large garlic cloves, minced
1 medium-size carrot, grated
1 medium-size zucchini, grated (1 cup), or 1 (10-oz.) package
  of chopped spinach
3 tablespoons Chicken Stock, page 139
1 (28-oz.) can no-salt added tomatoes, coarsely chopped, juice
  reserved
1/4 cup no-salt added tomato paste
1/2 tablespoon dried leaf oregano
1 tablespoon dried leaf basil
2 tablespoons apple juice concentrate
12 ounces low-fat cottage cheese
3 egg whites
3 tablespoons chopped parsley
3 tablespoons grated Parmesan cheese
12 manicotti tubes, cooked al dente

METHOD

1. Sauté shallots, garlic, carrot and zucchini in stock in a large
   saucepan.
2. Add tomatoes and juice, tomato paste, oregano, basil and apple
   juice concentrate. Cook 12 to 15 minutes, stirring. Set aside.
3. Combine cottage cheese, egg whites, parsley and 2 tablespoons
   Parmesan cheese in a medium-size bowl. Add vegetable
   mixture.
4. Fill manicotti tubes with vegetable mixture.
5. Pour 1/4 cup of the reserved sauce in a baking dish. Arrange
   manicotti in sauce. Cover with remaining sauce. Sprinkle with
   remaining 1 tablespoon Parmesan cheese.
6. Bake 35 minutes, until bubbly.

Makes 4 servings.

NUTRITIONAL
BREAKDOWN (Per serving—3 manicotti)

- Calories 404
- Protein 25g
- Carbohydrates 68g
- Fat 2g
- Sodium 391mg
- Cholesterol 7mg

HUMMUS SANDWICH FILLING

1/4 cup sesame seeds
2 cups cooked or canned garbanzo beans, if canned, rinse well and drain
3 tablespoons fresh lemon juice
1/2 teaspoon ground cumin, or to taste
3 garlic cloves, minced
1/4 teaspoon low-sodium soy sauce mixed with 1/2 teaspoon water
Dash of red (cayenne) pepper

METHOD

1. Roast sesame seeds in a dry skillet until slightly toasted. Set aside.
2. Combine ingredients in a food processor fitted with the metal blade; turn on-and-off until well chopped.
3. Process until light and fluffy. Add 1 tablespoon water at a time if consistency is too thick.

Makes 8 servings.

Variation

Add 1/4 teaspoon sesame oil.

NUTRITIONAL
BREAKDOWN (per 1/4 cup serving without bread)

- Calories 211
- Protein 11g
- Carbohydrates 32g
- Fat 5g
- Sodium 80mg
- Cholesterol 0mg

QUICK PIZZA

1 large pita bread
4 tablespoons Marinara Sauce, page 332
4 tablespoons low-fat cottage cheese
1/4 teaspoon dried leaf oregano
1 teaspoon Parmesan cheese

METHOD

1. Split pita bread in half horizontally; place on a baking sheet. Broil until lightly toasted (not crisp).
2. Cover each half with half of the Marinara Sauce, followed by half of the cottage cheese.
3. Sprinkle each half with oregano, then with Parmesan cheese.
4. Broil until cheese melts.

Makes 2 servings.

Variation

Substitute an English muffin for pita.

NUTRITIONAL
BREAKDOWN (Per serving)

- Calories 103
- Protein 7g
- Carbohydrates 15g
- Fat 1g
- Sodium 166mg
- Cholesterol 2mg

CAN OPENER CHILI

1 (16-oz.) can dark red kidney beans, drained, rinsed
1 (16-oz.) can pink beans, drained, rinsed
1 (16-oz.) can pinto beans, drained, rinsed
1 (16-oz.) can no-salt added tomatoes, chopped, juice reserved
2 (8-oz.) cans no-salt added tomato sauce
1 green bell pepper, chopped
1 red bell pepper, chopped
1 large onion, chopped
1 (4-oz.) can chopped green chiles
3 garlic cloves, minced
2 tablespoons chili powder, or to taste
1 tablespoon cumin powder, or to taste
1 teaspoon dried leaf basil
1 teaspoon garlic powder
Few dashes Tabasco sauce, if desired
Dash of pepper

METHOD

1. Put all ingredients except spices in a 4- to 5-quart saucepan and bring to a boil.
2. Add spices, stir, cover partially and simmer, stirring occasionally, 30 to 45 minutes.
3. Serve hot.

Makes 8 servings.

Variations

Cook in a crock pot. Add everything at once and cook on low 4 hours.

One or two cups diced cooked chicken may be added. Use chili for tacos or burritos. Serve with shredded lettuce, chopped tomatoes and onions. Or serve over cooked brown rice.

Cook in a microwave. Combine all ingredients in a 2-1/2-quart microwavable casserole dish. Microwave on MEDIUM-LOW 10 minutes, then MEDIUM 5 minutes, then HIGH 5 minutes. Stir once between each setting.

NUTRITIONAL BREAKDOWN (Per serving)

- Calories 233
- Protein 13g
- Carbohydrates 42g
- Fat 1.5g
- Sodium 425mg
- Cholesterol 0mg

LENTIL & MUSHROOM CURRY

1 cup lentils
3 cups water
3 medium-size onions, chopped
2 tablespoons Vegetable Stock, page 141, or Chicken Stock, page 139
1 teaspoon tamari
8 ounces mushrooms, sliced
1 teaspoon curry powder, or to taste
1 cup low-fat yogurt
1 cup chopped green onions

METHOD

1. Rinse lentils, combine with water in a medium-size saucepan. Bring to a boil, reduce heat to low and simmer 40 minutes. Most water should be absorbed by end of cooking time.
2. Preheat oven to 350F (175C).
3. Sauté onions in stock in a large saucepan. When soft add tamari, mushrooms and curry powder. Cook 5 minutes.
4. Combine lentils, mushroom mixture and yogurt, reserving 4 teaspoons, and place in a 2-quart baking dish.
5. Bake, covered, 25 minutes. Remove from oven and serve. Top each serving with 1 teaspoon yogurt and 1/4 cup green onions.

Makes 4 servings.

NUTRITIONAL
BREAKDOWN (Per serving)

- Calories 249
- Protein 17g
- Carbohydrates 44g
- Fat 0.5g
- Sodium 129mg
- Cholesterol 1mg

LENTIL STEW CREOLE

2 carrots, sliced crosswise
1 large celery stalk, chopped
1 large onion, chopped
8 ounces fresh okra, sliced
4 ounces fresh green beans, cut in 1-inch pieces
1 teaspoon low-sodium soy sauce
1 teaspoon apple juice concentrate
1/2 green bell pepper, chopped
1 (16-oz.) can no-salt added tomatoes, quartered, juice reserved
1 large garlic clove, minced
1 tablespoon red wine (optional)
1 cup cooked lentils (about 1/2 cup uncooked)
Tabasco sauce (optional)

METHOD

1. Mix all ingredients except lentils and Tabasco sauce, if using, in a large saucepan. Heat partly covered until mixture boils. Reduce heat to low; simmer 10 minutes.
2. Add lentils and simmer 15 to 20 minutes more.
3. Add a few drops Tabasco sauce, if desired.

Makes 6 servings.

Variation

For a complete meal, serve over brown rice.

NUTRITIONAL
BREAKDOWN (per serving without rice)

- Calories 81
- Protein 4g
- Carbohydrates 14g
- Fat 1g
- Sodium 78mg
- Cholesterol 0mg

MEXICAN FIESTA OMELET

1/4 cup diced red bell pepper
1/4 cup diced green bell pepper
1 small onion, finely diced
1 small tomato, diced
1/4 teaspoon dried leaf basil
1 cup egg substitute (equals 4 eggs)
1 tablespoon hot or medium salsa

METHOD

1. Spray a skillet with No Stick cooking spray. Add bell peppers and onion; sauté until onion is translucent. Add tomato and basil and mix well. Sauté another minute. Remove from pan and keep warm.
2. Spray skillet again with No Stick cooking spray and add egg substitute. Lift edge of omelet so center cooks well. Spoon vegetables over one-half and fold other half of omelet over vegetables.
3. Top with salsa.

Makes 2 servings.

NUTRITIONAL
BREAKDOWN (Per serving)

- Calories 91
- Protein 12g
- Carbohydrates 11g
- Fat . . . . tr
- Sodium 173mg
- Cholesterol 0mg

252

SHEPHERD'S PIE

Mashed Potatoes:
2 large potatoes, peeled, cooked
1/2 cup low-fat yogurt
1 teaspoon low-sodium soy sauce
1/4 cup minced chives
1/4 cup minced parsley
Dash of pepper

1 medium-size onion, diced
2 large garlic cloves, minced
3 tablespoons Chicken Stock, page 139

1 celery stalk, minced
12 ounces mushrooms, chopped
1 (1-lb.) eggplant, peeled, cut in small cubes
1 green bell pepper, diced
1 cup fresh or frozen green peas
3 tablespoons grated Parmesan cheese
1/4 teaspoon dried leaf thyme
1/2 teaspoon each dried leaf basil and oregano
1 tablespoon cider vinegar

METHOD

1. Place potatoes, yogurt and soy sauce in a blender. Pulse/blend until smooth and creamy. Spoon into a bowl and stir in chives, parsley and pepper.
2. Preheat oven to 350F (175C). Spray a 2- to 3-quart casserole dish with No Stick cooking spray. In a large heavy skillet, sauté onion and garlic in stock until tender.
3. Add celery, mushrooms and eggplant. Cover and cook until eggplant is tender.
4. Add green pepper and peas. Cook 5 minutes more.
5. Remove from heat. Toss in cheese, thyme, basil, oregano and vinegar. Pour into sprayed casserole dish. Cover with mashed potatoes. Bake 20 minutes.

Makes 6 servings.

NUTRITIONAL
BREAKDOWN (Per serving)

- Calories 106
- Protein 7g
- Carbohydrates 18g
- Fat 1g
- Sodium 82mg
- Cholesterol . . . . tr

SALADS

CARROT SALAD

9 carrots, shredded in processor
1 (8-oz.) can unsweetened crushed pineapple, drained
1/2 cup raisins
1/2 cup "Our" Mayonnaise, page 136, or "Our" Sour Cream, page 137

METHOD

1. Mix shredded carrots with pineapple and raisins in a medium-size bowl.
2. Toss with mayonnaise.

Makes 4 servings.

NUTRITIONAL
BREAKDOWN (Per serving)

- Calories 205
- Protein 5g
- Carbohydrates 43g
- Fat . . . . tr
- Sodium 209mg
- Cholesterol . . . . tr

CHICKEN ORANGE SALAD

8 ounces chicken, cooked
1 ounce dried shiitake mushrooms, soaked 20 minutes
4 navel oranges, sectioned
4 green onions, minced
3 garlic cloves, minced
1 teaspoon dried red pepper flakes
6 tablespoons fresh lime juice
1/4 cup fresh lemon juice

METHOD

1. Slice chicken diagonally into thin strips.
2. Combine chicken and remaining ingredients in a medium-size bowl.

Makes 2 servings.

NUTRITIONAL
BREAKDOWN (Per serving)

- Calories 379
- Protein 40g
- Carbohydrates 50g
- Fat 4.5g
- Sodium 81mg
- Cholesterol 70mg

CORN RELISH

1 (8-oz.) can no-salt added whole-kernel corn
1 large tomato, peeled, diced
1 small cucumber, peeled, seeded and diced
1 celery stalk, diced
1 large garlic clove, minced
1 jalapeño pepper, minced
3 tablespoons fresh lime juice
1/4 teaspoon ground cumin
3 tablespoons chopped cilantro

METHOD

1. Combine all ingredients in a medium-size bowl.
2. Cover and refrigerate until chilled.

Makes 1-1/2 cups.

NUTRITIONAL
BREAKDOWN (Per tablespoon)

- Calories 8
- Protein . . . . tr
- Carbohydrates 2g
- Fat . . . . tr
- Sodium 3mg
- Cholesterol 0mg

CRANBERRY RELISH

1 cup whole raw cranberries
1 large red apple, diced
1/2 cup apple juice concentrate
1 teaspoon ground cinnamon
1/2 teaspoon ground allspice
3 tablespoons fresh lemon juice
2 tablespoons grated gingerroot
2 tablespoons grated orange peel
1/4 cup raisins

METHOD

1. Combine all ingredients in a medium-size saucepan. Simmer over low heat 1 hour.
2. Serve hot or cold.

Makes 1-1/2 cups.

NUTRITIONAL
BREAKDOWN (Per tablespoon)

- Calories 18
- Protein . . . . tr
- Carbohydrates 4g
- Fat . . . . tr
- Sodium 1mg
- Cholesterol 0mg

CUCUMBERS IN HERBED YOGURT

1 large cucumber, sliced lengthwise in 1/8-inch slices
2 cups low-fat yogurt
3 tablespoons minced fresh basil
2 tablespoons minced fresh mint
1 tablespoon minced green onion
1 garlic clove, minced
1/4 teaspoon freshly ground pepper

METHOD

1. Pour boiling water over cucumber, then drain. Pat dry.
2. Combine yogurt, basil, mint, onion, garlic and pepper in a medium-size bowl. Blend well.
3. Add cucumbers and stir until cucumber is coated with yogurt mixture.
4. Cover and refrigerate at least 1 to 2 hours or up to 24 hours.

Makes 8 servings.

NUTRITIONAL
BREAKDOWN (Per serving)

- Calories 43
- Protein 3g
- Carbohydrates 5g
- Fat 1g
- Sodium 41mg
- Cholesterol 1mg

DILLED POTATO SALAD

4 small potoates, cooked whole, cubed
1 cup seeded, chopped cucumber
8 radishes, sliced
1/2 red bell pepper, chopped
1/2 green bell pepper, chopped
1 teaspoon dried dill weed or 2 teaspoons fresh dill

Creamy Dressing:
8 tablespoons low-fat cottage cheese
1/4 teaspoon fresh lemon juice
About 2 tablespoons low-fat buttermilk

METHOD

1. Mix all ingredients except those for dressing in a medium-size bowl.
2. To make dressing, combine all ingredients in a blender. Process until thick and creamy. Add additional buttermilk to make desired consistency, if necessary. Add dressing to salad. Toss until combined. Cover and chill before serving.

Makes 4 servings.

NUTRITIONAL
BREAKDOWN (Per serving)

- Calories 133
- Protein 9g
- Carbohydrates 25g
- Fat . . . . .tr
- Sodium 138mg
- Cholesterol 2mg

MEXICAN BEAN SALAD

1/2 cup uncooked ditalini (or other small pasta)
1 (16-oz.) can kidney beans, rinsed, drained
1/2 (16-oz.) can garbanzo beans, rinsed, drained
2 celery stalks, coarsely chopped
1/2 red bell pepper, chopped
1/2 large red onion, coarsely chopped
1/2 green bell pepper, chopped
1/2 cup diced jicama (optional)

Tomato Vinaigrette:
1/2 cup Basic Vinaigrette, page 322
1 tablespoon no-salt tomato paste
1 teaspoon low-sodium soy sauce
1/2 teaspoon ground cumin
1 teaspoon chili powder
1 garlic clove, minced
2 teaspoons cider vinegar
1 teaspoon fresh lime juice

METHOD

1. Cook ditalini in boiling water in a medium-size saucepan until tender but firm. Drain. Rinse with cool water.
2. Combine cooked pasta and remaining ingredients except those for dressing.
3. To make dressing, whisk all ingredients in a small bowl until combined.
4. Pour over bean salad.
5. Cover and refrigerate until chilled.

Makes 4 servings.

NUTRITIONAL
BREAKDOWN (Per serving)

- Calories 220
- Protein 12g
- Carbohydrates 40g
- Fat 1g
- Sodium 286mg
- Cholesterol 0mg

MUSHROOM-CHICKEN SALAD

3/4 pound fresh mushrooms, sliced
2 cups cubed cooked chicken
1 cup diced celery

Tarragon Dressing:
1/2 cup low-fat yogurt
2 tablespoons fresh orange juice
1 teaspoon chopped fresh tarragon, diced
1/4 to 1/2 teaspoon Dijon-style no-salt added mustard
1/8 teaspoon pepper

METHOD

1. Toss mushrooms, chicken and celery in a medium-size bowl.
2. To make dressing, combine all ingredients in a small bowl.
3. Add dressing to chicken mixture. Toss to combine.

Makes 4 servings.

NUTRITIONAL
BREAKDOWN (Per serving)

- Calories 157
- Protein 26g
- Carbohydrates 5g
- Fat 2.5g
- Sodium 105mg
- Cholesterol 37mg

ORIENTAL PASTA SALAD

8 ounces spaghetti, broken in half

1 to 2 cups broccoli flowerets, steamed until crisp-tender

2 green onions, sliced

1 cup snow peas, steamed until crisp-tender

1 carrot julienned, steamed until crisp-tender

1/2 cucumber, peeled, seeded, sliced

Oriental Dressing:

1 teaspoon cornstarch

2 tablespoons plus 1 teaspoon Chicken Stock, page 139

1 tablespoon low-sodium soy sauce

3 tablespoons rice vinegar

1 tablespoon fresh lemon juice

3 garlic cloves, minced

1 teaspoon grated gingerroot

2 green onions, sliced

1/4 teaspoon five-spice powder

1 teaspoon apple juice concentrate

2 drops Oriental sesame oil

METHOD

1. Cook pasta in boiling water in a large saucepan until tender but firm. Drain. Rinse with cool water. Mix pasta with vegetables. Spray with No Stick cooking spray.
2. Mix dressing ingredients in a small saucepan. Bring to a boil. Boil 1 minute, stirring constantly.
3. Pour warm dressing over salad and toss to coat. Serve at room temperature.

Makes 4 servings.

Variation

Add 1 cup shredded chicken or tuna.

Note

Spraying cooked pasta with No Stick cooking spray keeps it from becoming gummy and herbs and spices adhere better to pasta.

NUTRITIONAL
BREAKDOWN (Per serving without chicken)

- Calories 262
- Protein 10g
- Carbohydrates 52g
- Fat. . . . . tr
- Sodium 173mg
- Cholesterol 0mg

PINEAPPLE CHICKEN SALAD

1-1/2 cups diced poached chicken
1 (8-oz.) can unsweetened crushed pineapple, lightly drained
3/4 cup low-fat yogurt
1/4 cup sliced celery
1/4 cup sliced green onions
1/4 teaspoon ground ginger
1/4 to 1/2 teaspoon curry powder
Shredded lettuce

METHOD

1. Combine all ingredients except lettuce in a medium-size bowl.
2. Serve salad on shredded lettuce.

Makes 4 servings.

NUTRITIONAL
BREAKDOWN (Per serving)

- Calories 197
- Protein 24g
- Carbohydrates 15g
- Fat 3g
- Sodium 105mg
- Cholesterol 28mg

PINEAPPLE TURKEY SALAD

3 cups diced cooked turkey
1 cup thinly sliced celery
1 cup unsweetened crushed pineapple, juice reserved
1/2 cup green onions with green tops, diced
1/2 cup sliced water chestnuts
Lettuce leaves

Pineapple Dressing:
3 tablespoons reserved pineapple juice
1 teaspoon dried leaf tarragon
1 tablespoon unsweetened orange marmalade
1/2 cup low-fat yogurt

METHOD

1. Combine all ingredients except lettuce and those for dressing in a medium-size bowl.
2. To make dressing, combine all dressing ingredients in a small bowl.
3. Toss salad with dressing. Cover and refrigerate until chilled.
4. Serve on a bed of lettuce.

Makes 6 servings.

NUTRITIONAL
BREAKDOWN (Per serving)

- Calories 125
- Protein 13g
- Carbohydrates 10g
- Fat 2g
- Sodium 87mg
- Cholesterol 23mg

SALMON SALAD

1 (15-1/2-oz.) can salmon, drained
1/2 cup "Our" Sour Cream, page 137
3 water-packed artichokes, rinsed, drained
1 green onion
3 tablespoons finely chopped fresh dill
3 drops Tabasco sauce
1 teaspoon Dijon-style no-salt added mustard
1 tablespoon fresh lemon juice or lime juice
1 tablespoon chopped chives
3 tablespoons finely chopped parsley
1 (2-oz.) jar pimento, chopped

METHOD

1. Combine salmon, Sour Cream, artichokes, green onion, dill, Tabasco sauce, mustard and lemon juice in a blender. Process until finely chopped.
2. Add remaining ingredients; process 1/2 minute.
3. Cover and refrigerate overnight before serving.

Makes 4 servings.

Variation

Add 1 (1/4-oz.) package unflavored gelatin according to package directions for a great mold.

NUTRITIONAL
BREAKDOWN (Per serving)

- Calories 201
- Protein 26g
- Carbohydrates 10g
- Fat 6g
- Sodium 553mg
- Cholesterol 42mg

SPRING GARDEN PASTA SALAD

8 ounces whole-wheat pasta or tri-colored pasta
1-1/2 pounds broccoli flowerets
8 ounces small fresh mushrooms, quartered
1 large red bell pepper, diced
1 tablespoon plus 1 teaspoon grated Parmesan cheese
1/2 cup Creamy Garlic Italian Dressing, page 326

METHOD

1. Cook pasta in boiling water in a large saucepan until tender but firm. Drain. Rinse in cool water. Spray with Mazola No Stick cooking spray.
2. Combine pasta and remaining ingredients except dressing in a medium-size bowl.
3. Pour dressing over salad. Toss and serve.

Makes 8 servings.

NUTRITIONAL
BREAKDOWN (Per serving)

- Calories 130
- Protein 6g
- Carbohydrates 25g
- Fat 0.5g
- Sodium 25mg
- Cholesterol 0mg

SUMMER TOMATO SALAD

2 large tomatoes, thickly sliced
2 large purple or other sweet onions, thickly sliced
1/2 cup rice vinegar
1 large fresh basil leaf, chopped, or 1 tablespoon chopped fresh
  Italian parsley

METHOD

1. Alternate slices of tomato and onion on a large dish.
2. Pour rice vinegar over top, covering each slice well.
3. Sprinkle basil or parsley on top. Cover and refrigerate 1/2 hour
   before serving.

Makes 4 servings.

NUTRITIONAL
BREAKDOWN (Per serving)

- Calories 46
- Protein 1g
- Carbohydrates 11g
- Fat . . . . tr
- Sodium 9mg
- Cholesterol 0mg

TEX-MEX TACO SALAD

1 head shredded iceberg lettuce
2 large tomatoes, chopped
1 small onion, diced
4 cups Can Opener Chili, page 249, heated

METHOD

1. Divide lettuce, tomatoes and onion among 6 plates.
2. Cover with 3/4 cup hot chili.

Makes 6 servings.

Variation

Serve with baked corn chips. To make, place a soft corn tortilla in oven and bake at 375F (190C) until crispy, about 10 minutes.

NUTRITIONAL
BREAKDOWN (Per serving—without chips)

- Calories 275
- Protein 15g
- Carbohydrates 40g
- Fat 6g
- Sodium 443mg
- Cholesterol . . . . tr

TROPICAL SPINACH SALAD

1 or 2 navel oranges, cut in chunks
1/2 medium-size red onion, sliced
1 large bunch spinach, stems removed, torn in bite-size pieces

Buttermilk Dressing:
1 cup low-fat buttermilk
1/4 cup fresh orange juice
1 small clove garlic, minced

METHOD

1. To make salad, toss orange pieces, onion and spinach in a medium-size bowl.
2. To make dressing, whisk dressing ingredients together in a small bowl. Pour over salad and toss.

Makes 4 servings.

Variation

Add Garlic Croutons. To make croutons, cut French bread in cubes. Place in a bowl and spray with No Stick cooking spray. Sprinkle with garlic powder and toss. Arrange on a baking sheet; bake until golden.

NUTRITIONAL
BREAKDOWN (Per serving without croutons)

- Calories 71
- Protein 4g
- Carbohydrates 17g
- Fat 0g
- Sodium 101mg
- Cholesterol 2mg

VEGETABLES

BAKED STUFFED POTATOES
WITH SPINACH

2 baking potatoes
3 tablespoons skim milk
1 egg white
1/2 (10-oz.) package frozen chopped spinach, thawed, drained
2 tablespoons low-sodium soy sauce
1 tablespoon grated Parmesan cheese (optional)

METHOD

1. Preheat oven to 425F (220C). Bake potatoes about 45 minutes or until potatoes are tender. Cut in half lengthwise, scoop out center and puree in a food processor fitted with the metal blade with milk and egg white.
2. Add spinach and soy sauce.
3. Replace in shells; sprinkle with cheese, if desired. Broil until browned.

Makes 4 servings.

Variation

Mexican Potatoes: Add 2 tablespoons salsa with spinach and soy sauce.

NUTRITIONAL
BREAKDOWN (Per 1/2 potato)

- Calories 72
- Protein 4g
- Carbohydrates 14g
- Fat 0
- Sodium 33mg
- Cholesterol 1mg

SPINACH CASSEROLE
WITH MUSHROOMS

1 pound fresh mushrooms, sliced
2 tablespoons Chicken Stock, page 139
2 (10-oz.) packages frozen chopped spinach, thawed, drained
2 teaspoons dried minced onion
1/8 teaspoon pepper
2/3 cup "Our" Sour Cream, page 137
2 tablespoons skim milk

METHOD

1. Preheat oven to 325F (165C). Spray a 1-quart casserole dish with No Stick cooking spray.
2. Sauté mushrooms in stock in a large skillet.
3. Combine mushrooms and remaining ingredients. Pour into casserole dish. Cover and bake 1 hour.

Makes 8 servings.

NUTRITIONAL
BREAKDOWN (Per serving)

- Calories 37
- Protein 4g
- Carbohydrates 4g
- Fat . . . . tr
- Sodium 77mg
- Cholesterol . . . . tr

BAKED ZUCCHINI, EGGPLANT & TOMATOES

1 medium-size eggplant, thinly sliced
1 medium-size zucchini, thinly sliced
2 tomatoes, thinly sliced
6 fresh mushrooms, thinly sliced
1 medium-size onion, thinly sliced
1/4 teaspoon dried leaf thyme
1/4 cup Chicken Stock, page 139
3 garlic cloves, minced
1 tablespoon low-sodium soy sauce
Dash of pepper

METHOD

1. Preheat oven to 400F (205C). Spray a casserole dish with No Stick cooking spray. Arrange vegetables in rows in baking dish, alternating colors. (Place onion slices over mushrooms so they don't dry out.)
2. Mix remaining ingredients and spoon over vegetables.
3. Cover with foil and bake 30 minutes. Serve over rice.

Makes 4 servings.

NUTRITIONAL
BREAKDOWN (Per serving without rice)

- Calories 82
- Protein 4.5g
- Carbohydrates 17g
- Fat . . . . tr
- Sodium 165mg
- Cholesterol 0mg

STIR-FRY SNOW PEAS & RED PEPPER

Sauce:
1 tablespoon low-sodium soy sauce
2 teaspoons cornstarch
2 tablespoons cold water
1 tablespoon dry sherry
1 tablespoon apple juice concentrate

1 garlic clove, minced
3 tablespoons Chicken Stock, page 139
1 (8-oz.) can bamboo shoots, drained
1 (8-oz.) can water chestnuts, drained, sliced
1/2 pound fresh mushrooms, sliced
1 red bell pepper, cut julienne style
3 green onions, diced with tops
12 ounces fresh or thawed frozen snow peas

METHOD

1. Combine sauce ingredients in a small bowl.
2. Stir-fry garlic in stock in a wok or large skillet 1 minute; add bamboo shoots, water chestnuts, mushrooms, bell pepper, green onions and snow peas. Stir-fry 3 or 4 minutes.
3. Add sauce and stir until thickened. Serve at once over rice or angel hair pasta.

Makes 6 servings.

NUTRITIONAL
BREAKDOWN (Per serving without rice or pasta)

- Calories 63
- Protein 3g
- Carbohydrates 13g
- Fat 0
- Sodium 114mg
- Cholesterol . . . . tr

SUMMER RATATOUILLE

1 large onion, thinly sliced
2 garlic cloves, minced
3 tablespoons Chicken Stock, page 139
1 (16-oz.) can no-salt added tomatoes, quartered, drained
1-1/2 teaspoons dried leaf thyme
1 bay leaf, cut in half
1 medium-size unpeeled eggplant, diced
2 medium-size zucchini, diced
1 green bell pepper, sliced in strips
1 red bell pepper, sliced in strips
Dash Tabasco sauce
2 teaspoons cornstarch mixed with 2 tablespoons water (optional)

METHOD

1. Sauté onion and garlic in stock in a dutch oven until soft.
2. Add tomatoes, thyme and bay leaf. Cover and simmer 10 to 20 minutes.
3. Remove bay leaf. Add remaining ingredients. Cover and cook 20 minutes.
4. If thicker consistency is desired, add cornstarch mixture. Cook, stirring, until thick and bubbly.
5. Serve over hot rice.

Makes 8 servings.

Variation

Add 2 tablespoons hot or mild salsa.

NUTRITIONAL
BREAKDOWN (per serving without rice)

- Calories 50
- Protein 1g
- Carbohydrates 11g
- Fat . . . . tr
- Sodium 13mg
- Cholesterol 0mg

276

SWEET POTATO & CARROT GNOCCHI

3/4 pound sweet potatoes, baked, peeled
3 young tender carrots, steamed
1/4 cup low-fat yogurt
7 or 8 tablespoons all-purpose flour
Dash of pepper
1/4 teaspoon grated nutmeg
1/8 teaspoon ground cumin
3 egg whites
4 tablespoons grated Parmesan cheese
1 cup Chicken Stock, page 139
Parsley, chopped, for garnish

METHOD

1. Add potatoes and carrots to a food processor fitted with the metal blade. Process until pureed. Add yogurt and flour to processor. Process to combine. Add pepper, nutmeg, cumin, egg whites and cheese; process to combine.
2. Wet your hands and shape small amounts of mixture into miniature egg shapes.
3. Drop in boiling water. When pieces come to top, boil 3 to 4 minutes.
4. Heat stock; pour over gnocchi, sprinkle with parsley.

Makes 4 servings.

NUTRITIONAL
BREAKDOWN (Per serving)

- Calories 213
- Protein 10g
- Carbohydrates 38g
- Fat 2g
- Sodium 165mg
- Cholesterol 1mg

VEGETABLE CURRY

1 lb. eggplant, peeled, cut in cubes
3/4 cup Chicken Stock, page 139
1 teaspoon low-sodium soy sauce or tamari
2 tablespoons mild curry powder
1 teaspoon ground cumin
2 large garlic cloves, crushed
2 medium-size carrots, thinly sliced
2 cups diced potatoes
1 green bell pepper, thinly sliced
1 large onion, chopped
2 cups small cauliflowerets
1 medium-size zucchini, sliced
2 cups peeled tomatoes
1/4 cup tomato juice
1 (16-oz.) can garbanzo beans, drained, rinsed
1/4 cup raisins
Low-fat yogurt for garnish

METHOD

1. Put eggplant in a colander; rinse, then let drain 30 minutes. Wipe dry.
2. Sauté eggplant in 2 tablespoons stock in a large saucepan, stirring often, about 5 minutes.
3. Remove eggplant from pan and set aside.
4. Add 1 more tablespoon of stock, soy sauce, curry powder, cumin and garlic. Stir in remaining stock; cook 2 minutes.
5. Add carrots, potatoes, pepper, onion and cauliflower. Cover and simmer 5 to 7 minutes or until vegetables are crisp-tender.
6. Add reserved eggplant, zucchini, tomatoes, tomato juice, garbanzo beans and raisins. Cover and simmer 10 minutes. Serve with a dollop of yogurt.

Makes 12 servings.

NUTRITIONAL
BREAKDOWN (Per serving)

- Calories 94
- Protein 4g
- Carbohydrates 19g
- Fat 1g
- Sodium 122mg
- Cholesterol . . . . tr

VEGETABLE MIXTURE

2 zucchini, shredded
4 carrots, shredded
1 onion, finely chopped
2 cups finely chopped broccoli
2 cups finely chopped cauliflower
2 plum tomatoes, chopped
1 green bell pepper, chopped
4 garlic cloves, minced
1/2 cup Chicken Stock, page 139, or Vegetable Stock, page 141
2 teaspoons dried leaf basil
1/2 teaspoon garlic powder
1/2 teaspoon onion powder
1 tablespoon low-sodium soy sauce

METHOD

1. Sauté vegetables in stock in a large skillet, until soft.
2. Add basil, garlic powder, onion powder and soy sauce.
3. Cook 5 to 10 minutes over medium heat.

Makes about 1-1/2 quarts cooked vegetables.

Note

This is a very adaptable recipe. Vary the ingredients and amounts to suit your own needs. The vegetables used here are suggestions only. Use what you have on hand.

NUTRITIONAL
BREAKDOWN (Per tablespoon)

- Calories 5
- Protein . . . . tr
- Carbohydrates 1g
- Fat 0g
- Sodium 9mg
- Cholesterol 0mg

VEGETABLE PAELLA

2 cups sliced onions
1 garlic clove, crushed
1-1/2 cups Chicken Stock, page 139
1 cup uncooked white rice
1/2 teaspoon ground turmeric
Dash of pepper
1-1/2 cups cold water
4 medium-size carrots, diced
1 large red bell pepper, diced
1 (10-oz.) package frozen green peas, thawed
1-1/2 cups boiling water
2 tomatoes, cut in eighths
Grated Parmesan cheese (optional)

METHOD

1. Sauté onions and garlic in a small amount of stock in a 6-quart dutch oven.
2. When onions and garlic are softened, add rice, turmeric and pepper. Mix well. Add remaining broth and cold water. Bring to a boil, reduce heat and simmer, covered, 20 minutes.
3. Combine carrots, bell pepper and peas with boiling water in a large skillet. Simmer until carrots are tender. Add cooked rice to vegetable mixture. Cover with tomatoes and simmer, covered, 5 minutes. Place in a serving dish. Sprinkle with Parmesan cheese, if desired.

Makes 8 servings.

Variation

Serve over cooked kashka or couscous.

NUTRITIONAL
BREAKDOWN (Per serving)

- Calories 99
- Protein 4g
- Carbohydrates 19g
- Fat . . . . tr
- Sodium 118mg
- Cholesterol 0mg

280

BREADED ZUCCHINI

3/4 cup dry bread crumbs
1 teaspoon dried leaf oregano
1 teaspoon dried leaf parsley
2 tablespoons grated Parmesan cheese
3 to 4 medium-size zucchini, cut in 1/4-inch slices
3 egg whites, beat until foamy
Dash of pepper

METHOD

1. Preheat oven to 325F (165C). Mix bread crumbs, oregano, parsley and cheese in a flat dish.
2. Dip zucchini slices in egg whites, then in bread crumbs; spray with No Stick cooking spray.
3. Spray a baking sheet with No Stick cooking spray. Arrange coated zucchini on sprayed baking sheet. Bake 5 to 7 minutes; turn. Spray zucchini again, bake another 5 to 7 minutes or until golden brown.
4. Serve hot.

Makes 6 servings.

Variation

Substitute cauliflower, whole mushrooms or whole green beans for zucchini.

NUTRITIONAL
BREAKDOWN (3 or 4 pieces)

- Calories 71
- Protein 4g
- Carbohydrates 11g
- Fat. . . . . .tr
- Sodium 137mg
- Cholesterol 1mg

GARLIC BASIL GREEN BEANS

1 pound fresh green beans
1/2 cup Chicken Stock, page 139
2 teaspoons dried leaf basil
2 garlic cloves, minced
Dash of Tabasco sauce (optional)
1 teaspoon cornstarch

METHOD

1. Rinse and trim beans.
2. Steam until crisp-tender, 7 to 8 minutes.
3. While beans cook, combine remaining ingredients in a small saucepan. Bring to a boil, reduce heat and simmer 2 to 3 minutes, until thickened. Or combine in a glass dish; microwave on HIGH 2 to 3 minutes, stirring at 30-second intervals.
4. Arrange beans in a serving dish.
5. Pour sauce over beans. Serve hot.

Makes 5 servings.

Variations

Use sauce with cooked broccoli, peas or zucchini.

Sprinkle 1/2 teaspoon toasted sesame seeds over sauced beans.

Add a squeeze of lemon juice for extra flavor.

NUTRITIONAL
BREAKDOWN (Per serving)

- Calories 19
- Protein 1g
- Carbohydrates 4g
- Fat 0g
- Sodium 8mg
- Cholesterol 0mg

GLAZED CARROTS

8 medium-size carrots, cut diagonally in thin slices
4 tablespoons apple juice concentrate
1/2 teaspoon ground cinnamon
1/8 teaspoon ground allspice
2 teaspoons grated orange peel
1-3/4 cups water
2 teaspoons cornstarch mixed with 3 tablespoons water

METHOD

1. Put carrots and remaining ingredients except cornstarch mixture in a medium-size saucepan.
2. Bring to a boil, reduce heat and simmer 20 minutes or until carrots are tender, but not soft.
3. Add cornstarch mixture; cook, stirring constantly, until mixture thickens.

Makes 4 servings.

NUTRITIONAL
BREAKDOWN (Per serving)

- Calories 95
- Protein 2g
- Carbohydrates 23g
- Fat 0g
- Sodium 76mg
- Cholesterol 0mg

GOLDEN HASH BROWN POTATOES & ZUCCHINI

2 large all-purpose potatoes, peeled
1 medium-size zucchini
1 medium-size onion
2 egg whites, or 1/3 cup egg substitute
1/3 cup matzo meal
1 tablespoon plus 1 teaspoon low-sodium soy sauce

METHOD

1. Shred potatoes and zucchini in a food processor. Drain well.
2. Grate onion and drain well.
3. Combine vegetables and remaining ingredients in a medium-size bowl.
4. Spray a large skillet generously with No Stick cooking spray; add mixture. Cook until brown and crusty.

Makes 4 servings.

NUTRITIONAL
BREAKDOWN (Per serving)

- Calories 66
- Protein 4g
- Carbohydrates 9g
- Fat. . . . . tr
- Sodium 217mg
- Cholesterol 0mg

GREEN PEAS WITH CURRIED MUSHROOMS

2 pounds unshelled green peas
6 ounces fresh mushrooms, thinly sliced
1 medium-size onion, finely chopped
1 teaspoon curry powder
1/2 cup Chicken Stock, page 139
1/2 cup low-fat yogurt

METHOD

1. Boil peas in water in a medium-size saucepan until crisp-tender, about 4 minutes. Rinse in cool water. Drain.
2. In same saucepan, sauté mushrooms, onion and curry powder in stock over medium heat 10 to 15 minutes, until onion is softened. Add peas. Cook 2 or 3 minutes.
3. Remove from heat and add yogurt. Stir to combine and serve.

Makes 8 servings.

Variation

Use pearl onions instead of chopped onion.

NUTRITIONAL BREAKDOWN (Per serving)

- Calories 40
- Protein 3g
- Carbohydrates 6g
- Fat 0g
- Sodium 30mg
- Cholesterol . . . . tr

MUSHROOMS IN WINE

1 pound fresh small mushrooms, stems removed
1 cup red wine
1 teaspoon dried rosemary
8 garlic cloves, diced
1 cup water
6 green onions with green tops, cut in 1-inch pieces
Chopped fresh parsley
Dash of pepper

METHOD

1. Combine mushrooms with wine, rosemary, garlic and 1 cup water in a medium-size saucepan. Bring to a boil, reduce heat and simmer 10 minutes.
2. Add green onions; cook until liquid is reduced by one-third.
3. Sprinkle with parsley and pepper; serve warm or cold.

Makes 4 servings.

NUTRITIONAL
BREAKDOWN (Per serving)

- Calories 72
- Protein 2g
- Carbohydrates 7g
- Fat 0g
- Sodium 12mg
- Cholesterol 0mg

SCALLOPED POTATOES

2 tablespoons and 1 teaspoon cornstarch
2 cups skim milk
1/2 medium-size onion, minced
1 teaspoon low-sodium soy sauce
1/4 teaspoon garlic powder
1/4 teaspoon onion powder
2 teaspoons dried parsley
1 to 2 tablespoons snipped chives
2 tablespoons Parmesan cheese
5 medium-size potatoes, peeled, sliced and parboiled 10 minutes

METHOD

1. Preheat oven to 375F (190C). Spray a 1-1/2-quart baking dish with No Stick cooking spray. Combine cornstarch and a little milk in a medium-size saucepan until smooth. Add remaining ingredients except potatoes.
2. Cook over medium-high heat, stirring constantly, until smooth and thick.
3. Combine with parboiled potatoes in a baking dish. Bake 35 to 40 minutes, until bubbly and browned on top. Serve hot.

Makes 6 servings.

NUTRITIONAL
BREAKDOWN (Per serving)

- Calories 116
- Protein 5g
- Carbohydrates 22g
- Fat . . . . tr
- Sodium 80mg
- Cholesterol 4mg

SPAGHETTI SQUASH PRIMAVERA

1 large spaghetti squash
2 tablespoons cornstarch
1 cup cold skim milk
1 large garlic clove, minced
1-1/4 teaspoons dried leaf basil
1 cup low-fat cottage cheese
3 cups of a combination of 4 of the following: sliced fresh mushrooms; sliced zucchini; water chestnuts, cut in half; red/green bell pepper strips; broccoli flowerets; green beans or sliced carrots
2-1/2 tablespoons grated Parmesan cheese

METHOD

1. Cut squash in half lengthwise, remove seeds and place in water in a large saucepan, steam until crisp-tender.
2. Meanwhile, mix cornstarch with 1/4 cup cold milk, garlic and basil. Stir in remaining milk.
3. Cook over medium heat until thickened, stirring.
4. Place with cottage cheese in a food processor fitted with the metal blade; process until smooth.
5. Steam vegetables 5 to 8 minutes, until crisp-tender.
6. Remove cooked squash and shred pulp into a bowl. Separate strands with two forks. Put in a large platter, cover with vegetables. Spoon sauce on top; sprinkle with Parmesan cheese. Mix and serve.

Makes 6 servings.

Variations

Substitute cooked angel hair pasta or thin spaghetti for spaghetti squash. Substitute Marinara Sauce, page 332, for cheese sauce.

NUTRITIONAL
BREAKDOWN (Per serving)

- Calories 92
- Protein 8g
- Carbohydrates 12g
- Fat 1g
- Sodium 231mg
- Cholesterol 1mg

288

SPINACH GNOCCHI

1 medium-size onion, finely chopped
2 tablespoons Chicken Stock, page 139
1 (10-oz.) package frozen chopped spinach, thawed, drained
2/3 cup low-fat cottage cheese
6 tablespoons grated Parmesan cheese
2 egg whites
1/8 teaspoon grated nutmeg
1/2 cup unbleached all-purpose flour

METHOD

1. Sauté onion in stock and place in a medium-size bowl with spinach. Mix well.
2. Add remaining ingredients and drop by spoonfuls into boiling water.
3. When gnocchi float to the top, boil 3 minutes.
4. Drain, cover with Marinara Sauce, page 332, and serve.

Makes 4 servings.

NUTRITIONAL
BREAKDOWN (Per serving without sauce)

- Calories 128
- Protein 9g
- Carbohydrates 21g
- Fat . . . . tr
- Sodium 204mg
- Cholesterol 2mg

SPINACH PUFF

1 (10-oz.) package frozen spinach, cooked, squeezed dry
1 cup low-fat cottage cheese
1 tablespoon grated Parmesan cheese
1 small onion, minced
.1 garlic clove, minced
1 teaspoon fresh lemon juice
1 teaspoon low-sodium soy sauce
3/4 cup egg substitute
2 tablespoons toasted bread crumbs
1 tablespoon grated Parmesan cheese

METHOD

1. Preheat oven to 350F (175C). Spray a 9-inch pie pan with No Stick cooking spray. Mix all ingredients except bread crumbs and 1 tablespoon Parmesan cheese in a medium-size bowl.
2. Pour into sprayed pie plate.
3. Sprinkle with bread crumbs and remaining cheese.
4. Bake 20 to 25 minutes, until set. Serve immediately.

Makes 6 servings.

Variation

Top with seasoned tomato sauce.

NUTRITIONAL
BREAKDOWN (per serving)

- Calories 110
- Protein 10g
- Carbohydrates 6g
- Fat 5g
- Sodium 307mg
- Cholesterol 1.5mg

SPINACH SOUFFLÉ

3 medium-size potatoes, boiled
2 egg whites
2 tablespoons skim milk
2 tablespoons low-sodium soy sauce
1 (10-oz.) package chopped spinach, thawed, drained

METHOD

1. Preheat oven to 375F (190C). Spray a 1-1/2-quart baking dish with No Stick cooking spray. Place all ingredients in a blender except spinach. Blend until smooth.
2. Add spinach; blend until smooth.
3. Pour into sprayed baking dish. Cover and bake 15 to 20 minutes until puffed and golden brown.

Makes 4 to 5 servings.

NUTRITIONAL
BREAKDOWN (Per serving)

- Calories 71
- Protein 5g
- Carbohydrates 13g
- Fat 0g
- Sodium 320mg
- Cholesterol . . . . tr

GREEN BEANS STIR-FRY

1 teaspoon cornstarch
2 teaspoons low-sodium soy sauce
1/4 cup water
1 tablespoon apple juice concentrate
1 pound green beans, trimmed
Grated peel and juice of 1/2 lemon or lime
1 pimento, julienne cut
1 (4-oz.) can water chestnuts, drained
2 tablespoons Chicken Stock, page 139

METHOD

1. Combine cornstarch, soy sauce, water and apple juice concentrate in a small bowl; set aside.
2. Boil or steam green beans with lemon juice and peel 6 to 8 minutes, until crisp-tender. Drain.
3. In a large skillet or wok, stir-fry beans, pimento and water chestnuts with stock.
4. Add cornstarch mixture; cook until thickened, stirring.

Makes 6 servings.

Variations

Sprinkle with toasted sesame seeds when served.

Substitute asparagus or your favorite vegetable for beans.

NUTRITIONAL
BREAKDOWN (Per serving)

- Calories 37
- Protein 1g
- Carbohydrates 8g
- Fat 0g
- Sodium 73mg
- Cholesterol 0mg

STUFFED BAKED POTATOES

4 medium-size baking potatoes
1 medium-size onion, finely chopped
2 garlic cloves, finely chopped
1/2 cup Chicken Stock, page 139
1 teaspoon low-sodium soy sauce
1 teaspoon paprika
1/4 cup low-fat yogurt

METHOD

1. Preheat oven to 400F (205C). Bake potatoes 1 hour or until tender when pricked with a fork.
2. Sauté onion and garlic in stock in a small saucepan.
3. When potatoes are done, scoop out and place in a food processor fitted with the metal blade. Add onion mixture, soy sauce and paprika; process until combined.
4. Stir in yogurt. Spoon mixture into potato shells.
5. Bake until hot.

Makes 8 servings.

NUTRITIONAL
BREAKDOWN (Per serving)

- Calories 61
- Protein 2g
- Carbohydrates 13g
- Fat 0g
- Sodium 49mg
- Cholesterol . . . . tr

STUFFED MUSHROOMS

1 pound fresh mushrooms
1 small onion, minced
1 garlic clove, minced
2 tablespoons Chicken Stock, page 139, or water
1 (10-oz.) package frozen cauliflower, cooked, mashed
3 tablespoons grated Parmesan cheese
1 teaspoon low-sodium soy sauce
Dash of paprika and pepper

METHOD

1. Preheat oven to 350F (175C). Remove mushroom stems and finely chop stems.
2. Sauté onion and garlic in stock or water in a small saucepan.
3. Combine mushrooms stems, cauliflower, 2 tablespoons Parmesan cheese, soy sauce and onion mixture in a medium-size bowl.
4. Stuff mushrooms with mixture, sprinkle with remaining cheese, the paprika and pepper. Arrange stuffed mushrooms in a baking pan.
5. Bake 20 minutes. Broil 1 minute until cheese browns. Serve hot.

Makes 4 servings.

Variation

Omit cauliflower and add 1/4 pound cooked lean ground beef.

NUTRITIONAL
BREAKDOWN (Per serving)

- Calories 60
- Protein 6g
- Carbohydrates 7g
- Fat 1g
- Sodium 137mg
- Cholesterol 3mg

STUFFED TOMATOES

1 onion, diced
1/2 pound mushrooms, chopped
2 tablespoons Chicken Stock, page 139
2 to 3 tablespoons matzo meal or bread crumbs
2 egg whites, slightly beaten
1/2 teaspoon dried leaf basil
1/2 teaspoon dried leaf oregano
Grated Parmesan cheese
Chopped parsley
3 tomatoes, cut in half, pulp removed

METHOD

1. Preheat oven to 350F (175C). Sauté onion and mushrooms in stock in a medium-size skillet.
2. Place in a bowl and mix with remaining ingredients except cheese, parsley and tomatoes.
3. Stuff tomatoes with mushroom mixture; sprinkle with parsley and cheese. Arrange in a baking dish. Bake 20 minutes or until hot.

Makes 6 servings.

NUTRITIONAL
BREAKDOWN (Per serving—half tomato)

- Calories 27
- Protein 2g
- Carbohydrates 4g
- Fat 0g
- Sodium 35mg
- Cholesterol . . . . tr

SWEET & SOUR RED CABBAGE

1 medium-size red cabbage, shredded
1-1/2 cups water
2 tablespoons apple juice concentrate
2 whole garlic cloves
2 tablespoons fresh lemon juice
1 tablespoon white wine vinegar
1/2 teaspoon ground ginger

METHOD

1. Place cabbage in a deep saucepan. Add remaining ingredients and simmer 35 minutes, stirring occasionally, until tender.
2. Remove garlic.
3. Serve hot or cold.

Makes 8 servings.

NUTRITIONAL
BREAKDOWN (Per serving)

- Calories 17
- Protein 1g
- Carbohydrates 4g
- Fat 0g
- Sodium 8mg
- Cholesterol 0mg

TWICE BAKED SWEET POTATOES

2 large sweet potatoes, scrubbed
1 egg white
1/2 cup crushed pineapple, drained, juice reserved
1/4 to 1/2 cup skim milk
Paprika
Chopped parsley

METHOD

1. Preheat oven to 400F (205C). Make a 1/4 inch deep slit all the way around potatoes, and prick with a fork. Bake 45 to 60 minutes, until tender.
2. Cool slightly, then cut in half at slit.
3. Scoop out insides and put in a bowl.
4. Mash; add egg white, 4 tablespoons reserved juice and enough milk to make a good consistency for stuffing. Stir in pineapple.
5. Stuff potato skins with potato mixture; sprinkle with paprika.
6. Bake 15 minutes, until hot. Sprinkle with chopped parsley.

Makes 4 servings.

Sweet potatoes are one of the best sources of fiber—4 grams per potato.

NUTRITIONAL
BREAKDOWN (Per serving—half potato)

- Calories 100
- Protein 3g
- Carbohydrates 22g
- Fat 0g
- Sodium 44mg
- Cholesterol 1mg

WINTER SQUASH MEDLEY

4 medium-size acorn squash
2 Granny Smith apples, or any hard, slightly tart apples
1/4 cup apple juice concentrate
2 tablespoons cornstarch mixed with 4 tablespoons water
1/2 cup unsweetened canned crushed pineapple
1/8 teaspoon ground cinnamon, nutmeg or allspice
1/4 cup raisins (optional)
2 teaspoons cereal nuggets

METHOD

1. Preheat oven to 350F (175C). Cut acorn squash in half. Scoop out all seeds. Scoop out meat from squash with a paring knife or melon ball scooper. Take out as much squash as possible but do not break bottom of cavity.
2. Peel and core apples and cut into slices.
3. Combine apple juice concentrate and cornstarch mixture.
4. Combine pineapple, cinnamon and raisins, if using; mix with squash and apples. Pour concentrate mixture over squash and apples; mix well.
5. With a tablespoon, fill squash cavity with mixture. Arrange squash in a baking dish.
6. Cover with foil and bake about 35 minutes, until tender but not mushy.
7. Sprinkle cereal nuggets over squash and broil 2 minutes.

Makes 8 servings.

Variation

To cook in a microwave: Follow recipe but place in a glass dish, add 5 tablespoons water to bottom of dish and cover with plastic wrap. Cook on HIGH 16 to 18 minutes.

NUTRITIONAL
BREAKDOWN (Per serving—1/2 acorn squash)

- Calories 164
- Protein 4g
- Carbohydrates 42g
- Fat 0.5g
- Sodium 10mg
- Cholesterol 0mg

ZUCCHINI PUDDING

1 medium-size onion, diced
3 garlic cloves, diced
3 zucchini, shredded
1 cup egg substitute
1 cup low-fat cottage cheese
2 cups cooked rice
2 egg whites, beaten until fluffy
3/4 teaspoon dried leaf thyme
1/4 teaspoon pepper

METHOD

1. Preheat oven to 375F (190C). Spray a large glass dish with No Stick cooking spray. Sauté onion and garlic in a non-stick pan sprayed with No Stick cooking spray. (Add a few drops of water or broth if necessary).
2. Add onion and garlic to remaining ingredients in a medium-size bowl and mix well.
3. Put in sprayed dish; cover with foil and make holes for steam to escape. Bake 1 hour.
4. Remove foil and broil top until crisp.

Makes 6 servings.

Variations

Substitute broccoli for the zucchini.

Add 1 tablespoon low-sodium soy sauce (diluted with 2 table-spoons water).

NUTRITIONAL
BREAKDOWN (Per serving)

- Calories 176
- Protein 12g
- Carbohydrates 19g
- Fat 5g
- Sodium 245mg
- Cholesterol . . . . tr

PASTA, RICE & GRAINS

Kasha, brown rice, bulgur and millet will probably be new additions to your kitchen shelf. These plus many more grains will now become an integral part of your diet since we regard "high fiber" to be a necessary part of retaining good health. It is now a medical fact that a high fiber diet will help decrease high cholesterol and is a deterrent for various types of cancer.

Our use of whole-wheat pasta, whole grains and brown rice is essential. Please keep in mind that when we mention pasta or rice in our recipes, we refer to whole-wheat pasta and brown rice, if possible. If your family isn't happy with brown rice, mix half white and half brown rice together. Although wild rice is more expensive than regular rice, use it on special occasions for its delicious taste.

Always start on a high fiber diet slowly. Elevating your fiber intake too rapidly can cause bloating, and excessive fiber intake can interfere with the absorption of minerals like calcium and zinc.

BROCCOLI & PASTA

1 medium-size onion, chopped
2 teaspoons minced garlic
2 teaspoons dried leaf basil
3 tablespoons Chicken Stock, page 139
1/4 cup white wine
8 ounces shells or tri-colored corkscrew pasta
4 cups broccoli flowerets
2 tablespoons low-fat yogurt
3 tablespoons grated Parmesan cheese

METHOD

1. Sauté onion, garlic and basil in stock and wine in a small skillet until soft.
2. Cook pasta in boiling water in a large saucepan until firm but tender. Drain.
3. Steam broccoli until crunchy. Add broccoli to onion mixture.
4. Combine pasta, yogurt, broccoli mixture and cheese. Toss and serve.

Makes 4 servings.

NUTRITIONAL
BREAKDOWN (Per serving)

- Calories 267
- Protein 11g
- Carbohydrates 46g
- Fat 4g
- Sodium 119mg
- Cholesterol 4mg

GLORIA'S RAVIOLI

Semolina Pasta Dough:
1 cup unbleached all-purpose flour
1 cup semolina flour
1/2 cup water

1 cup low-fat cottage cheese
2 cups parsley leaves, finely chopped
1/4 cup grated Parmesan cheese
1/4 teaspoon grated nutmeg
Dash of pepper
1/2 cup skim milk

METHOD

1. To make pasta dough, mix flours in a medium-size bowl. In center of bowl, make a well in flour. Pour water in middle, slowly adding water to flour. Dough should be soft not sticky.
2. When you can form a ball transfer to a lightly floured surface. Knead a few minutes. Wrap dough in waxed paper. Let rest 15 minutes.
3. Blend cottage cheese, parsley, Parmesan cheese, nutmeg, pepper and milk in a medium-size bowl.
4. Roll out dough to 1/8 inch thick. Drop filling by teaspoonfuls about 2 inches apart over half of dough. Fold over remaining dough, cut in squares and seal.
5. Boil in unsalted water until tender, about 5 minutes.
6. Cover with favorite sauce and serve.

Makes 6 servings.

NUTRITIONAL
BREAKDOWN (Per serving without sauce)

- Calories 210
- Protein 11g
- Carbohydrates 37g
- Fat 2g
- Sodium 2276mg
- Cholesterol 3mg

GOURMET QUICK RICE PILAF

1 small onion, finely chopped
1 garlic clove, minced
2 tablespoons water, or stock
1/4 red bell pepper, diced
1/4 green bell pepper, diced
3 green onions, with green tops, chopped
1 tablespoon low-sodium soy sauce mixed with 2 tablespoons water
2 cups cooked brown rice (cooked according to package directions—using chicken stock instead of water—2/3 cup uncooked rice)

METHOD

1. Sauté onion and garlic in a non-stick pan sprayed with No Stick cooking spray. Add 2 tablespoons of water or stock and cook until tender.
2. Add peppers, green onions and soy sauce and cook 3 minutes.
3. Pour over rice and toss until well mixed. Serve hot.

Makes 4 servings.

Variation

Add 8 ounces fresh sliced mushrooms and 1 tablespoon dry sherry.

NUTRITIONAL
BREAKDOWN (Per serving)

- Calories 111
- Protein 3g
- Carbohydrates 23g
- Fat . . . . tr
- Sodium 116mg
- Cholesterol 0mg

GRANDMA'S PASTA WITH KALE

1 large bunch fresh kale, cleaned and stems removed
1 pound ziti or rigatoni
3 cups Marinara Sauce, page 332, heated
Grated Parmesan cheese
Toasted bread crumbs

METHOD

1. Bring water to a boil in a large (10-quart) pot. Add kale, part-ly cover and cook 5 minutes.
2. Add pasta and cook about 12 minutes until pasta is tender but firm.
3. Drain well and return to pot. Add sauce as desired and mix.
4. To serve, place on plate, add a little extra sauce if desired, then sprinkle with a little cheese and bread crumbs.

Makes 6 servings.

NUTRITIONAL
BREAKDOWN (Per serving)

- Calories 337
- Protein 13g
- Carbohydrates 65g
- Fat 2g
- Sodium 76mg
- Cholesterol . . . . tr

MEXICAN KASHA

1 cup chopped onion
1/2 cup chopped celery
1/2 green bell pepper, chopped
1/2 red bell pepper, chopped
2 garlic cloves, minced
1/4 cup Chicken Stock, page 139
1 teaspoon dried leaf oregano
1/2 teaspoon ground cumin
1 teaspoon mild chili powder
2 (16-oz.) cans no-salt added tomatoes, coarsely chopped,
liquid reserved
3/4 cup uncooked kasha

METHOD

1. Sauté onion, celery, peppers and garlic in stock 5 minutes or
   until soft.
2. Add oregano, cumin, chili powder and tomatoes with liquid
   and kasha.
3. Bring to a boil, cover and simmer 15 minutes or until kasha
   is tender and liquid is absorbed.

Makes 6 servings.

NUTRITIONAL
BREAKDOWN (Per serving)

- Calories 101
- Protein 4g
- Carbohydrates 20g
- Fat . . . . tr
- Sodium 38mg
- Cholesterol 0mg

SIRENA'S SPRING PASTA

1/2 lb. bow tie pasta
1/2 lb. low-fat (1%) cottage cheese
2 teaspoons non-fat sour cream
1 teaspoon parmesan cheese
1 teaspoon dried basil, crumbled
1 cup frozen peas, thawed
1 (6-1/8 oz.) can tuna fish packed with Canola oil,
  drained and flaked
Fresh grated black pepper

METHOD

1. Prepare pasta according to package directions reserving 1/4 cup cooking water for sauce.
2. Purée cottage cheese in processor with sour cream, parmesan cheese, and basil. Add reserved cooking water.
3. Toss pasta with sauce. Add peas and tuna and toss lightly. Add black pepper. Serve.

NUTRITIONAL
BREAKDOWN (Per serving)

- Calories. 300
- Protein 29g
- Carbohydrates 33g
- Fat. 4.7g
- Sodium. 436mg
- Cholesterol. 18mg
- Fiber 3g

PASTA, ROMAN STYLE

1 cup parsley sprigs
2 garlic cloves
1 large onion
3 green onions, diced
2 radishes, thinly sliced
2 medium-sized carrots, chopped
3 tablespoons fresh basil leaves
1 cup Chicken Stock, page 139
3 large tomatoes, coarsely chopped
3 cups shredded cabbage
2 medium-size zucchini, chopped
2 cups cooked or canned cannellini beans (white kidney beans), drain and rinse if canned
1/2 to 1 pound rigatoni (depending upon thickness of stew desired), cooked until al dente
1/4 cup grated Parmesan cheese

METHOD

1. Mince together parsley, garlic, onion, green onions, radishes, carrots and basil.
2. Heat 1/4 cup stock in a deep pot and add parsley mixture. Cook until soft.
3. Add tomatoes, remaining stock, cabbage, zucchini and beans. Cook 5 minutes more.
4. Toss rigatoni with Parmesan cheese. Combine with vegetables, mix and serve.

Makes 8 side-dish servings.

NUTRITIONAL
BREAKDOWN (Per serving)

- Calories 262
- Protein 13g
- Carbohydrates 51g
- Fat 2g
- Sodium 83mg
- Cholesterol 2mg

SLIM ZUCCHINI PASTA

1 large zucchini, shredded
1/2 cup green onions with tops, chopped
2 cups angel hair pasta, cooked until al dente
1 tablespoon fresh parsley
1/2 cup Chicken Stock, page 139
1/2 teaspoon dried leaf basil
1/2 teaspoon dried leaf oregano
2 tablespoons fresh lemon juice
2 tablespoons grated Parmesan cheese

METHOD

1. Steam or cook zucchini and green onions until crisp-tender, 3 minutes.
2. Place all ingredients except cheese in a large pot. Toss well over low heat. Add Parmesan cheese and toss again. Serve hot.

Makes 4 servings.

NUTRITIONAL
BREAKDOWN (Per serving)

- Calories 146
- Protein 6g
- Carbohydrates 28g
- Fat 0.8g
- Sodium 67mg
- Cholesterol 2mg

SPANISH RICE

1/2 cup green bell pepper, chopped
1/2 cup onion, chopped
2 garlic cloves, minced
1/2 teaspoon dried leaf basil
1/2 teaspoon dried rosemary
3 tablespoons Chicken Stock, page 139, or water
1 cup uncooked brown rice or white long grain rice
2 cups water
1 cup chopped, peeled tomatoes
1/8 teaspoon pepper
Dash of Tabasco sauce

METHOD

1. Cook bell pepper, onion, garlic, basil and rosemary in stock in a medium-size saucepan until tender.
2. Stir in rice, water, tomatoes, pepper and Tabasco sauce. Cover and cook over low heat about 20 minutes or until rice is done. Serve hot.

Makes 6 servings.

NUTRITIONAL
BREAKDOWN (Per serving)

- Calories 136
- Protein 3g
- Carbohydrates 30g
- Fat . . . . tr
- Sodium 8mg
- Cholesterol 0mg

TABBOULEH

4 cups boiling water, or Chicken Stock, page 139
1-1/4 cups bulgur (cracked wheat)
3/4 cup cooked or canned garbanzo beans, rinsed, drained
1/2 cup fresh mint, minced
3/4 cup fresh parsley, minced
2 or 3 chopped fresh tomatoes
3/4 cup green onions, chopped
1/4 cup fresh lemon juice
2 teaspoons low-sodium soy sauce
Sprouts or lettuce

METHOD

1. Pour boiling water over bulgur in a large bowl. Cover and let stand 1 to 2 hours until fluffy and most of water is absorbed.
2. Pour bulgur into a strainer and squeeze out excess water.
3. Combine all ingredients except sprouts or lettuce together in a medium-size bowl, cover and refrigerate until chilled. Serve with sprouts or lettuce.

Makes 6 servings.

NUTRITIONAL
BREAKDOWN (Per serving)

- Calories 157
- Protein 5g
- Carbohydrates 34g
- Fat . . . . tr
- Sodium 100mg
- Cholesterol 0mg

NATALIE'S RICE & BLACK-EYED PEAS

2 tablespoons Chicken Stock, page 139
1 medium-size onion, diced
1 large tomato, diced
1 cup uncooked brown rice
2 cups water
1 (16-oz.) can black-eyed peas, rinsed, drained

METHOD

1. Spray a medium-size saucepan with No Stick cooking spray. Add stock and sauté onions until tender.
2. Add tomato and cook 5 minutes more.
3. Add rice and water, cover and cook until rice is tender.
4. Add beans and cook 5 minutes more.

Makes 4 servings.

Thank you to Natalie Lopes, our most capable computer programmer, for her recipe contribution!

NUTRITIONAL
BREAKDOWN (per serving)

- Calories 165
- Protein 8g
- Carbohydrates 32g
- Fat 1g
- Sodium 125mg
- Cholesterol 0mg

BREADS

APPLE-CINNAMON MUFFINS

1/2 cup low-fat yogurt
2 egg whites, lightly beaten
1/2 cup oat bran flakes
1/2 cup (rounded) chopped apples
3-1/2 tablespoons apple juice concentrate
1/2 cup all-purpose flour
1/2 teaspoon ground cinnamon
1/2 teaspoon baking soda

METHOD

1. Preheat oven to 375F (190C). Spray 6 muffin cups with No Stick cooking spray. Mix first 5 ingredients in a medium-size bowl and set aside until flakes are soft.
2. Combine flour, cinnamon and baking soda in a small bowl; add to yogurt mixture. Mix until combined.
3. Spoon immediately into sprayed muffin cups. Bake about 25 minutes, until golden brown and a wooden pick inserted in center comes out clean.

Makes 6 muffins.

NUTRITIONAL BREAKDOWN (Per muffin)

- Calories 97
- Protein 4g
- Carbohydrates 20g
- Fat 1g
- Sodium 100mg
- Cholesterol . . . . tr

BREAKFAST MUFFINS

1/2 cup low-fat yogurt
2 egg whites, lightly beaten
3-1/2 tablespoons orange juice concentrate
1/2 cup soaked raisins (soaked in hot water to plump, drained)
1/2 cup rolled oats
1/2 cup all-purpose flour
1/2 teaspoon ground cinnamon
1/2 teaspoon baking soda

METHOD

1. Mix first 5 ingredients in a medium-size bowl and set aside to soak 10 minutes.
2. Preheat oven to 375F (190C). Spray 6 muffin cups with No Stick cooking spray. Combine flour, cinnamon and baking soda in a small bowl, then add to yogurt mixture. Mix until combined.
3. Spoon immediately into sprayed muffin cups.
4. Bake about 25 minutes, until golden brown and a wooden pick inserted in center comes out clean.

Makes 6 muffins.

NUTRITIONAL
BREAKDOWN (per muffin)

- Calories 120
- Protein 5g
- Carbohydrates 24g
- Fat 1g
- Sodium 101mg
- Cholesterol . . . . tr

CORN CAKES

1/2 cup yellow cornmeal
1 cup boiling water
3 tablespoons apple juice concentrate
1 cup whole-kernel corn
2 egg whites

METHOD

1. Combine cornmeal, water and apple juice concentrate in a medium-size bowl. Blend well. Add corn.
2. Beat egg whites until stiff peaks form.
3. Fold egg whites into cornmeal mixture.
4. Spray a large skillet with No Stick cooking spray. Heat skillet over medium heat until hot. Spoon out batter, 1 tablespoon at a time. Cook 3 minutes on each side until golden brown.

Makes 15 cakes.

NUTRITIONAL
BREAKDOWN (Per cake)

- Calories 34
- Protein 1g
- Carbohydrates 7g
- Fat 0.5g
- Sodium 33mg
- Cholesterol 0mg

FRENCH TOAST

1/2 cup egg substitute
1/4 cup skim milk
1 teaspoon vanilla extract
Dash of grated nutmeg
6 slices whole-grain bread

METHOD

1. Combine all ingredients except bread in a shallow bowl. Mix well.
2. Generously spray a non-stick skillet with No Stick cooking spray. Dip bread slices in egg mixture. Cook in sprayed skillet until golden brown, turning once.
3. Serve warm.

Makes 3 servings (2 slices per serving).

Variation

Sprinkle with cinnamon before serving, or serve with no-sugar added fruit syrup.

NUTRITIONAL
BREAKDOWN (Per slice—1/2 serving)

- Calories 96
- Protein 5g
- Carbohydrates 12g
- Fat 3g
- Sodium 122mg
- Cholesterol . . . . tr

HAWAIIAN MUFFINS

1/4 cup mashed bananas
1/4 cup unsweetened crushed drained pineapple
3-1/2 tablespoons orange juice concentrate
1/2 cup low-fat yogurt
2 egg whites, lightly beaten
1/2 cup oat bran flakes
1/2 cup all-purpose flour
1/2 teaspoon baking soda

METHOD

1. Preheat oven to 375F (190C). Spray 6 muffin cups with No Stick cooking spray. Mix first 6 ingredients in a medium-size bowl and set aside until flakes are soft.
2. Combine flour and baking soda in a small bowl. Add yogurt mixture. Mix until combined.
3. Immediately spoon into sprayed muffin cups.
4. Bake about 25 minutes, until golden brown and a wooden pick inserted in center comes out clean.

Makes 6 muffins.

NUTRITIONAL
BREAKDOWN (Per muffin)

- Calories 92
- Protein 3g
- Carbohydrates 19g
- Fat . . . . tr
- Sodium 101mg
- Cholesterol . . . . tr

OAT BRAN MUFFIN SURPRISE DELUXE

1 cup whole-wheat flour
2/3 cup wheat bran
3 tablespoons oat bran
1/2 teaspoon baking powder
1/2 teaspoon baking soda
1 teaspoon ground cinnamon
1/2 cup low-fat buttermilk
1/2 cup egg substitute
1/2 cup brown rice syrup
2 tablespoons unsweetened crushed pineapple
1/3 cup grated carrot
1-1/2 tablespoons canola oil
No-sugar added jam or jelly

METHOD

1. Preheat oven to 375F (190C). Place cupcake liners in 12 muffin cups. Combine all dry ingredients in a medium-size bowl.
2. Combine all liquid ingredients except jam or jelly in another bowl.
3. Mix dry ingredients with liquid ingredients until combined.
4. Spoon one-half of batter into muffin cups.
5. Drop 1/4 teaspoon of jam or jelly in each muffin cup. Spoon remaining batter over jam.
6. Bake about 25 minutes, until golden brown and a wooden pick inserted in center comes out clean.

Makes 12 muffins.

Variation

For those not diabetic or overweight, add golden raisins, carob chips or diced green apple.

NUTRITIONAL
BREAKDOWN (Per muffin)

- Calories 147
- Protein 5g
- Carbohydrates 28g
- Fat 2g
- Sodium 85mg
- Cholesterol . . . . .tr

OAT BRAN MUFFINS
(FOR WEIGHT REDUCTION ONLY)

1/3 cup low-fat buttermilk
1/4 cup water
1/4 cup egg substitute
2 tablespoons barley malt syrup or brown rice syrup
2 tablespoons apple juice concentrate
2 tablespoons unsweetened crushed pineapple
1/3 cup finely grated carrot
1/2 teaspoon orange or lemon extract
1/2 cup whole-wheat flour
2/3 cup wheat bran
2 tablespoons oat bran
1/2 teaspoon baking powder
1/2 teaspoon baking soda
1/2 teaspoon ground cinnamon

METHOD

1. Preheat oven to 375F (190C). Spray 12 muffin cups with No Stick cooking spray.
2. Mix liquid ingredients in a medium-size bowl. Mix dry ingredients in another bowl.
3. Mix dry ingredients with liquid ingredients until combined. Spoon into muffin cups.
4. Bake about 20 minutes, until golden brown and a wooden pick inserted in center comes out clean.

Makes 12 muffins.

NUTRITIONAL
BREAKDOWN (Per muffin)

- Calories 77
- Protein 3g
- Carbohydrates 15g
- Fat 0.5g
- Sodium 64mg
- Cholesterol . . . . tr

PIÑA COLADA MUFFINS

1/2 cup low-fat yogurt
1/2 cup drained unsweetened crushed pineapple
3-1/2 tablespoons pineapple juice concentrate
2 egg whites, lightly beaten
1/2 teaspoon coconut extract
1/2 cup all-purpose flour
1/2 teaspoon baking soda

METHOD

1. Preheat oven to 375F (190C). Spray 6 muffin cups with No Stick cooking spray. Mix first 5 ingredients in a medium-size bowl.
2. Combine flour and baking soda, then add to yogurt mixture. Mix to combine.
3. Immediately spoon into sprayed muffin cups.
4. Bake about 25 minutes, until golden brown and a wooden pick inserted in center comes out clean.

Makes 6 muffins.

NUTRITIONAL
BREAKDOWN (Per muffin)

- Calories 94
- Protein 4g
- Carbohydrates 18g
- Fat 1g
- Sodium 102mg
- Cholesterol 1mg

DRESSINGS, SPREADS & SAUCES

BASIC VINAIGRETTE

1/4 cup red wine vinegar or rice vinegar
1/2 cup water
1 tablespoon plus 1 teaspoon apple juice concentrate
1/4 teaspoon garlic powder
1/4 teaspoon onion powder
1 teaspoon fresh lemon juice
1 teaspoon tamari or low-sodium soy sauce
1/2 teaspoon Dijon-style no-salt added mustard
Dash of red (cayenne) pepper (optional)

METHOD

1. Place all ingredients in jar with a tight-fitting lid and shake well.
2. When mixture is well blended, place in refrigerator until served.

Makes 1 cup.

NUTRITIONAL
BREAKDOWN (Per tablespoon)

- Calories 5
- Protein . . . . .tr
- Carbohydrates 1g
- Fat . . . . .tr
- Sodium 8mg
- Cholesterol 0mg

COCKTAIL SAUCE

3/4 cup chili sauce or mild salsa
1/4 cup finely chopped celery
Dash of red (cayenne) pepper
1 tablespoon fresh lemon juice or rice vinegar

METHOD

1. Mix in a small bowl and serve.

Makes 1 cup.

Variation

Add 1/4 teaspoon grated horseradish.

NUTRITIONAL
BREAKDOWN (Per tablespoon)

- Calories 13
- Protein 0g
- Carbohydrates 3g
- Fat 0g
- Sodium 173mg
- Cholesterol 0mg

CREAMY ARTICHOKE DRESSING

1/2 cup low-fat cottage cheese
1/2 cup low-fat buttermilk or skim milk
1/2 (14-oz.) can water-packed artichokes, rinsed, drained and
  chopped
1 tablespoon apple juice concentrate
1 tablespoon chopped green chiles
1 tablespoon chopped fresh dill
1/2 onion, finely chopped
1 teaspoon dried leaf basil

METHOD

1. Combine cottage cheese and buttermilk in a blender; process
   until combined.
2. Add artichokes and apple juice concentrate; blend until
   smooth.
3. Add remaining ingredients. Process just to combine.
4. Pour into a bowl, cover and refrigerate until chilled.

Makes about 1-1/2 cups.

NUTRITIONAL
BREAKDOWN (Per tablespoon)

- Calories 12
- Protein 1.5g
- Carbohydrates 2g
- Fat . . . . tr
- Sodium 34mg
- Cholesterol . . . . tr

CREAMY CUCUMBER ARTICHOKE DRESSING

1/2 medium-size cucumber, peeled, seeded and chopped
3 water-packed artichokes, rinsed, chopped
1/2 teaspoon garlic powder, or 1 garlic clove, minced
1 or 2 green onions, white part only
1 teaspoon fresh lemon juice
1 teaspoon low-sodium soy sauce
1/2 cup low-fat buttermilk
1/4 teaspoon dried dill weed

METHOD

1. Combine all ingredients in a blender or food processor fitted with the metal blade. Process until smooth.
2. Pour into a serving dish.

Makes 1 cup.

NUTRITIONAL BREAKDOWN (Per tablespoon)

- Calories 16
- Protein 1g
- Carbohydrates 3g
- Fat . . . . tr
- Sodium 31mg
- Cholesterol . . . . tr

CREAMY GARLIC ITALIAN DRESSING

1/2 cup low-fat buttermilk
1/2 cup low-fat cottage cheese
1 medium-size garlic clove, minced
2 water-packed artichoke hearts, rinsed, chopped
1/4 small onion, minced
2 teaspoons fresh lemon juice
1 teaspoon tamari
1 teaspoon cider or wine vinegar
1/4 teaspoon dried leaf oregano
1/4 teaspoon grated Parmesan cheese
1 generous teaspoon minced fresh parsley

METHOD

1. Place all ingredients except parsley in a food processor fitted with the metal blade. Process until smooth.
2. Add parsley. Pour into a bowl, cover and refrigerate until chilled. Dressing can be refrigerated up to 3 days.

Makes 1 cup.

NUTRITIONAL
BREAKDOWN (Per tablespoon)

- Calories 8
- Protein 1g
- Carbohydrates 1g
- Fat . . . . .tr
- Sodium 32mg
- Cholesterol . . . . .tr

CUCUMBER-HERB DRESSING

1/2 cup chopped parsley
1 tablespoon minced fresh dill
1 teaspoon minced fresh tarragon
2 tablespoons apple juice concentrate
1 medium-size cucumber, peeled, seeded and chopped
1 large garlic clove, minced
2 green onions, cut in 1-inch pieces
1-1/2 teaspoons white wine vinegar
1/2 cup low-fat yogurt
1/4 teaspoon Dijon-style no-salt added mustard

METHOD

1. Combine all ingredients except yogurt and mustard in a blender; process until smooth. Stir in yogurt and mustard.
2. Cover and refrigerate until chilled.

Makes 3/4 cup.

NUTRITIONAL BREAKDOWN (Per tablespoon)

- Calories 11
- Protein 0.5g
- Carbohydrates 1g
- Fat . . . . tr
- Sodium 6mg
- Cholesterol . . . . tr

MARINADE SAUCE

2 tablespoons tamari or low-sodium soy sauce
5 tablespoons water
1 tablespoon dry sherry, or to taste
2 tablespoons apple juice concentrate

METHOD
1. Combine ingredients in a small bowl.
2. Use as a marinade.

Makes 3/4 cup.

Variations

Add 1 teaspoon fresh grated gingerroot, 1/2 to 1 teaspoon fresh minced garlic, 1/2 to 1 teaspoon grated orange rind, 1/2 teaspoon Dijon-style no-salt added mustard, 1/4 teaspoon sesame oil or 1/4 teaspoon hot chili oil.

To thicken marinade to be used as gravy, combine 1 tablespoon cornstarch or arrowroot and 2 tablespoons cold water. Combine marinade and cornstarch mixture in a small saucepan and heat until bubbly.

NUTRITIONAL
BREAKDOWN (Per recipe)
- Calories 115
- Protein 3g
- Carbohydrates 25g
- Fat 0g
- Sodium 858mg
- Cholesterol 0mg

FRENCH DRESSING

3/4 cup water
1/2 cup rice vinegar
2 tablespoons no-salt added tomato paste
1 tablespoon apple juice concentrate
1 tablespoon tamari or low-sodium soy sauce
2 tablespoons fresh lemon juice
1 cup cubed cooked yams, peeled (about 1 medium-size yam)
1/4 teaspoon garlic powder
1/2 teaspoon dry mustard
1/4 teaspoon onion powder
Dash red (cayenne) powder (optional)

METHOD

1. Combine water, vinegar, tomato paste, apple juice concentrate, tamari and lemon juice in a food processor fitted with the metal blade; process until combined.
2. Add yams and process until smooth. Add spices and more water if too thick. Pour into a container with a tight-fitting lid. Refrigerate up to 3 days.

Makes about 2-1/2 cups.

NUTRITIONAL
BREAKDOWN (Per tablespoon)

- Calories 7
- Protein . . . . tr
- Carbohydrates 2g
- Fat . . . . tr
- Sodium 10mg
- Cholesterol 0mg

GREEK GARLIC DRESSING

4 cups (1 quart) low-fat yogurt
2 medium-size cucumbers, peeled, seeded and diced
2 garlic cloves, minced
3 tablespoons finely chopped fresh dill weed

METHOD

1. Combine all ingredients in a glass bowl. Cover and refrigerate several hours.
2. Use as a dip or salad dressing.

Makes 4 cups.

- Calories 9
- Protein 1g
- Carbohydrates 1g
- Fat . . . . tr
- Sodium 10mg
- Cholesterol 1mg

GREEN GODDESS DRESSING

3 garlic cloves, minced
2 tablespoons chopped parsley leaves
1/2 cup rice vinegar
1 teaspoon Dijon-style no-salt added mustard
3 tablespoons low-fat cottage cheese
1 cup skim buttermilk
1-1/2 tablespoons apple juice concentrate
1 tablespoon grated Parmesan cheese
1/2 cucumber, seeded, peeled and chopped
Juice from 1/2 fresh lime
Dash of pepper

METHOD

1. Combine all ingredients in a food processor fitted with the metal blade. Process until smooth.

Makes 2-1/2 cups dressing.

NUTRITIONAL
BREAKDOWN (Per serving)

- Calories 20
- Protein 3g
- Carbohydrates 2g
- Fat . . . . tr
- Sodium 12mg
- Cholesterol 2mg

MARINARA SAUCE

1/2 cup onions, diced
16 oz. tomato sauce
20 oz. (1 lb. 13 oz.) can tomato puree
1 lb. can crushed plum tomatoes undrained
2 tablespoons tomato paste
1/4 cup red bell pepper (optional)
4 large garlic cloves, diced
1 tablespoon apple juice concentrate
2 tablespoons fresh Italian parsley, chopped
1 large bay leaf, break in half
1 teaspoon oregano, crushed
1/3 cup dry red wine
1/2 teaspoon dried thyme
1/2 teaspoon basil, if fresh basil, use 4 leaves
Pinch black pepper

METHOD

1. Sauté onion just until soft.
2. Mix all remaining ingredients in large 6 or 8 quart stockpot.
   Bring to boil. Lower heat immediately and simmer for 1-1/4
   hours.
3. If extra thickness is desired either cook longer or add a little
   more tomato paste.

Makes 7-3/4 cups.

Variation

For a very delicate and less tomato taste, add 2 to 3 tablespoons
skim buttermilk to entire recipe—A secret from a famous four-
star restaurant!

NUTRITIONAL
BREAKDOWN (Per 1/2-cup serving)

- Calories 40
- Protein 2g
- Carbohydrates 6g
- Fat 1g
- Sodium 29mg
- Cholesterol 0mg

ORANGE CHIFFON FRUIT DRESSING

1/2 cup evaporated skim milk
1/2 cup low-fat cottage cheese
2 or 3 tablespoons orange juice concentrate

METHOD

1. Combine all ingredients in a blender. Process until smooth.
2. Serve with fresh fruit.

Makes 1 cup.

NUTRITIONAL
BREAKDOWN (Per tablespoon)

- Calories 15
- Protein 1g
- Carbohydrates 2g
- Fat . . . . tr
- Sodium 37mg
- Cholesterol . . . . tr

SWEET & SOUR SAUCE

1/2 cup Vegetable Stock, page 141, or Chicken Stock, page 139
1 garlic clove, minced
1/2 teaspoon minced gingerroot
1 medium-size onion, diced
1/2 medium-size green bell pepper, diced
1/2 medium-size red bell pepper, diced
2 tomatoes, chopped
2 tablespoons fresh lemon juice
6 tablespoons pineapple juice concentrate
4 teaspoons arrowroot or cornstarch
1 tablespoon low-sodium soy sauce
Freshly ground pepper to taste
2 green onions, chopped
1/2 cup unsweetened pineapple chunks

METHOD

1. Heat 1/2 of broth in a wok or large skillet. Add garlic and gingerroot. Cook 2 minutes.
2. Add onion, peppers and tomatoes. Cook 5 minutes.
3. Add lemon juice, pineapple juice concentrate and remaining broth except 2 tablespoons.
4. Mix arrowroot and remaining broth. Add to skillet mixture; cook, stirring, until mixture thickens.
5. Add remaining ingredients. Serve over rice, noodles or pieces of cubed chicken.

Makes 1-1/2 cups.

NUTRITIONAL
BREAKDOWN (Per 1/2 cup sauce only)

- Calories 109
- Protein 2g
- Carbohydrates 24g
- Fat . . . . tr
- Sodium 168mg
- Cholesterol 0mg

DESSERTS & SNACKS

No oils or fats are used in any recipes in this book except in this chapter. You will find a few dessert recipes which contain no more than two teaspoons of oil. This is necessary since oil becomes the binding agent. The quantity is 80% less than that used in the average recipe and enables the dessert to retain a soft texture. When oil is called for, I prefer to use canola oil in my recipes.

Because we use a liquid sweetener (i.e. brown rice syrup and barley malt syrup), it is necessary to use more flour. This makes cakes slightly heavier than usual, but does not alter the taste.

ANGEL CHEESE CAKE

3 cups low-fat cottage cheese
3/4 cup egg substitute
8 to 10 tablespoons no-sugar added pineapple preserves
3 tablespoons apple juice concentrate
1/3 cup low-fat yogurt
1/3 cup cornstarch
1 teaspoon baking powder
2 teaspoons vanilla extract
2 tablespoons all-purpose flour
1 tablespoon fresh lemon juice

Glaze:
1 (20-oz.) can unsweetened crushed pineapple
1 pint fresh blueberries
1 tablespoon cornstarch
1 tablespoon apple juice concentrate

METHOD

1. Preheat oven to 325F (165C). Spray an 8-inch springform pan with No Stick cooking spray.
2. Blend all ingredients except those for glaze in a food processor fitted with the metal blade until smooth. Taste for sweetness. Add 1 tablespoon more preserves if more sweetness is desired.
3. Bake 1 hour 40 minutes.
4. Turn oven off and leave cake in oven to cool, about 1 hour.
5. Combine all glaze ingredients in a medium-size saucepan; cook over medium heat, stirring constantly, until sauce thickens. Spoon over cooled cake and refrigerate.
6. Cut cake with a knife dipped in water.

Makes 14 servings.

NUTRITIONAL
BREAKDOWN (Per serving)

- Calories 74
- Protein 8g
- Carbohydrates 9g
- Fat 0.5g
- Sodium 230mg
- Cholesterol 2mg

ANGEL FOOD CAKE

1/2 cup egg whites
1/2 cup brown rice syrup
1/2 teaspoon vanilla extract
3/4 cup cake flour, sifted
1 teaspoon baking powder

METHOD

1. Preheat oven to 325F (165C).
2. Line the bottom of a 6-inch round cake pan with waxed paper.
3. Beat egg whites until stiff peaks form. Add brown rice syrup and beat until thoroughly mixed. Add vanilla.
4. Carefully fold in sifted flour and baking powder with a spatula. Work carefully with this, so as not to break down the air in the egg whites. Pour into pan.
5. Bake about 30 minutes, or until wooden pick inserted into the center of cake comes out clean.
6. Cool slightly. Run knife around edges, and turn out while still warm.
7. Cool and serve.

Makes 12 to 14 servings.

Note

Due to the type of sweetening agent used this cake is not as light as a traditional angel food cake. More flour has to be used in this recipe and as a result the cake is slightly heavier.

NUTRITIONAL
BREAKDOWN (Per serving)

- Calories 57
- Protein 2g
- Carbohydrates 11g
- Fat . . . . tr
- Sodium 65mg
- Cholesterol 0mg

APPLE CINNAMON RAISIN COOKIES

3/4 cup all-purpose flour
1 teaspoon all-purpose baking powder
1/2 teaspoon ground cinnamon
2 tablespoons egg substitute
1/3 cup apple juice concentrate
2 tablespoons brown rice syrup
1 teaspoon vanilla extract
1 teaspoon canola oil
2 tablespoons raisins
1 small apple, peeled, diced in 1/2-inch pieces
2 tablespoons cereal nuggets

METHOD

1. Preheat oven to 375F (190C). Spray a baking sheet with No Stick cooking spray.
2. Combine flour, baking powder and cinnamon in a medium-size bowl.
3. Add egg substitute, apple juice concentrate, brown rice syrup, vanilla and oil. Mix thoroughly.
4. Add raisins, apple and cereal nuggets.
5. Drop by tablespoons on sprayed baking sheet. Bake about 10 minutes, or until golden brown.
6. Cool and serve. Cover and refrigerate leftovers.

Makes about 10 to 12 (3-inch) cookies.

NUTRITIONAL BREAKDOWN (Per cookie)

- Calories 56
- Protein 1g
- Carbohydrates 12g
- Fat . . . . tr
- Sodium 48mg
- Cholesterol 0mg

APPLE SORBET

2 apples, peeled, quartered
1 (20-oz.) can unsweetened crushed pineapple, drained
1/2 banana, sliced
1/2 cup low-fat yogurt
2 tablespoons low-fat buttermilk
1 teaspoon ground cinnamon
1/4 teaspoon coconut extract

METHOD

1. Combine all ingredients in a medium-size bowl.
2. Pour into an 8-inch-square pan. Cover and freeze 24 hours.
3. Remove and thaw 5 to 10 minutes. Put frozen mixture in a blender and puree until desired consistency. Serve immediately.

Makes 4 servings.

NUTRITIONAL
BREAKDOWN (Per serving)

- Calories 95
- Protein 4g
- Carbohydrates 21g
- Fat 0.5g
- Sodium 31mg
- Cholesterol 2mg

BANANA NUT POP

1/2 banana
1 tablespoon apple juice concentrate
Cereal nuggets

METHOD

1. Insert a wooden stick into cut end of banana.
2. Dip banana into apple juice concentrate and roll in cereal nuggets.
3. Place in plastic wrap and freeze until firm.
4. Thaw a few minutes before eating.

Makes 1 serving.

NUTRITIONAL
BREAKDOWN (Per pop)

- Calories 89
- Protein 1g
- Carbohydrates 22g
- Fat 0g
- Sodium 10mg
- Cholesterol 0mg

BANANA-STRAWBERRY SUNDAE

4 very ripe bananas
12 frozen strawberries
1 tablespoon no-sugar added jam or preserves
1/4 cup cereal nuggets

METHOD

1. Peel banana; wrap in waxed paper. Freeze at least 24 hours.
2. Take bananas and strawberries from freezer, break bananas in thirds and let both bananas and strawberries thaw slightly 5 to 10 minutes to slightly soften.
3. Place in a food processor fitted with the metal blade; process 5 minutes until creamy.
4. Place in sherbert glasses; top with preserves. Sprinkle with cereal nuggets.

Makes 8 servings.

NUTRITIONAL
BREAKDOWN (Per serving)

- Calories 83
- Protein 1g
- Carbohydrates 21g
- Fat . . . . tr
- Sodium 23mg
- Cholesterol 0mg

BANANA ICE CREAM

3 very ripe medium-size bananas
1/4 cup cereal nuggets
Any flavor no-sugar added preserves

METHOD

1. Peel and wrap bananas in plastic wrap or waxed paper and freeze 24 hours.
2. Take bananas from freezer, break in thirds and thaw slightly 5 to 10 minutes.
3. Place in a food processor fitted with the metal blade; process 5 minutes or until the consistency of ice cream.
4. Serve in 4 sherbert glasses with 1/4 teaspoon preserves and sprinkling of cereal nuggets on top.

Makes 4 servings.

Variations

These basic "ice cream" recipes are great for the adventurous. Try different frozen fruits (but always use some frozen banana to give it a creamy mousse-like consistency) with different extracts. For example, my family loves it when I throw in a few frozen strawberries with a drop of vanilla. Mint extract, coconut and maple extracts are wonderful, too.

NUTRITIONAL
BREAKDOWN (Per serving)

- Calories 85
- Protein 1g
- Carbohydrates 21g
- Fat . . . . tr
- Sodium 5mg
- Cholesterol 0mg

CHOCOLATE MINT BROWNIES

3 egg whites, large
1/2 cup date sugar
1/4 cup carob powder
1/2 cup cake flour, sifted
1/2 teaspoon baking powder
1/2 cup low-fat buttermilk
1 teaspoon canola oil
1 teaspoon vanilla extract
1 teaspoon peppermint flavoring
1/3 cup carob chips
1/4 cup raisins
1/4 cup dates, sliced
2 tablespoons sunflower seeds

METHOD

1. Preheat oven to 350F (175C). Spray a 9-by-5-inch non-stick loaf pan with No Stick cooking spray.
2. Whip egg whites until light. Add date sugar, carob powder, flour, baking powder, buttermilk, oil and vanilla. Mix with an electric mixer on low speed until thoroughly mixed.
3. Add peppermint flavoring, carob chips, raisins, dates and sunflower seeds. Mix by hand to combine.
4. Pour into pan. Bake 30 to 40 minutes or until knife inserted in center comes out clean.
5. Remove from pan and cut into bars or squares.

Makes 16 servings.

Variation

Substitute brown rice syrup or barley malt syrup for date sugar.

NUTRITIONAL
BREAKDOWN (Per brownie)

- Calories 104
- Protein 2g
- Carbohydrates 17g
- Fat 2g
- Sodium 42mg
- Cholesterol . . . . .tr

CHOCOLATE MOUSSE

1/2 (1/4-oz.) envelope unflavored gelatin
1/4 cup water
1/2 cup canned skim milk
1/2 cup part-skim ricotta cheese
1/4 cup unsweetened cocoa powder
1/2 cup brown rice syrup
1 teaspoon vanilla extract
1 large egg white

METHOD

1. Sprinkle gelatin over water. Set aside to soften.
2. In a food processor fitted with the metal blade, combine the milk, ricotta cheese, cocoa, brown rice syrup and vanilla. Process until combined.
3. Heat gelatin until dissolved. With motor running, add gelatin to cheese mixture.
4. Whip egg white until stiff peaks form.
5. Add chocolate mixture to the egg white and blend with a whisk until well mixed.
6. Pour into 6 dessert glasses, cover and refrigerate at least 4 hours.

Makes 6 servings.

NUTRITIONAL
BREAKDOWN (Per serving)

- Calories 117
- Protein 6g
- Carbohydrates 18g
- Fat 3g
- Sodium 58mg
- Cholesterol 7mg

CHOCOLATE ORANGE CAKE

1 cup all-purpose flour
2 teaspoons baking powder
1/4 cup unsweetened cocoa powder
1 cup brown rice syrup
1/2 cup egg substitute
1/2 teaspoon ground cinnamon
1 teaspoon vanilla extract
Grated peel of 1 orange
2 tablespoons canola oil
3/4 cup shredded zucchini
2 tablespoons no-sugar added orange marmalade

METHOD

1. Preheat oven to 350F (175C). Spray a 7-inch round cake pan with No Stick cooking spray.
2. Combine flour, baking powder and cocoa in a medium-size bowl.
3. Add brown rice syrup, egg substitute and blend well.
4. Add cinnamon, vanilla, orange peel and oil; mix well. Stir in shredded zucchini.
5. Spoon into pan and bake 30 minutes. Reduce heat to 325F (165C) and bake 30 minutes more.
6. Heat marmalade until melted. Drizzle marmalade over cake and serve.

Makes 1 (7-inch) round cake or 12 servings.

NUTRITIONAL
BREAKDOWN (Per serving)

- Calories 128
- Protein 2.5g
- Carbohydrates 24g
- Fat 2.5g
- Sodium 110mg
- Cholesterol 0mg

CREAMY ONE-MINUTE FRUIT DESSERT

1 cup blueberries
1/2 teaspoon vanilla extract
2 tablespoons apple juice concentrate
1 cup non-fat yogurt

METHOD

1. Combine blueberries, vanilla and apple juice concentrate in a blender and puree.
2. Add yogurt and blend 10 seconds or until thoroughly blended.
3. Cover and refrigerate until chilled.

Makes 2 servings.

Variation

Substitute 1 cup strawberries, 2 bananas or 2 peaches for blueberries. Substitute your favorite extract for vanilla.

NUTRITIONAL
BREAKDOWN (Per serving)

- Calories 133
- Protein 7g
- Carbohydrates 25g
- Fat . . . . tr
- Sodium 88mg
- Cholesterol 2mg

CREAMY RICE PUDDING

1/2 cup evaporated skim milk
1/2 cup water
2 tablespoons cornstarch
1/4 cup brown rice syrup
1 teaspoon vanilla extract
1-1/2 to 1-3/4 cups cooked, chilled white rice
2 tablespoons raisins (optional)
Cinnamon

METHOD

1. Cook milk, water, cornstarch and brown rice syrup in a small saucepan, stirring, until mixture thickens. Add vanilla and mix well.
2. Add rice and raisins and mix well.
3. Spoon into 4 parfait glasses and chill. Sprinkle with cinnamon before serving.

Makes 4 servings.

Variation

Warm your favorite jam or jelly, pour over pudding instead of cinnamon and chill.

NUTRITIONAL
BREAKDOWN (Per serving)

- Calories 196
- Protein 5g
- Carbohydrates 43g
- Fat . . . . tr
- Sodium 47mg
- Cholesterol 2mg

FRUIT COMPOTE

1/2 cup sliced fresh or frozen peaches
1 cup sliced fresh or frozen strawberries
1 cup fresh or frozen blueberries
1/2 teaspoon grated orange peel
1 cup orange-pineapple juice
1/4 cup sherry

METHOD

1. In large bowl, combine all ingredients.
2. Cover and refrigerate at least 1 hour before serving.

Makes 4 servings.

Variation

Add mint leaves when serving.

Drizzle 1 or 2 drops of your favorite flavoring extract on top!

NUTRITIONAL
BREAKDOWN (Per serving)

- Calories 88
- Protein 1g
- Carbohydrates 17g
- Fat . . . . tr
- Sodium 1mg
- Cholesterol 0mg

FRUIT MEDLEY GELATIN MOLD

1 (1/4-oz.) envelope unflavored gelatin
2 cups apple-cranberry juice
1/2 cup unsweetened crushed canned pineapple
1/2 cup seedless grapes, cut in half
1/2 cup unpared apples, pureed in processor

METHOD

1. Sprinkle gelatin over juice in a saucepan. Let soften. Heat gelatin until dissolved. Cool slightly.
2. Spray a 4-cup mold with No Stick cooking spray. Add fruit to gelatin mixture. Pour into mold.
3. Cover and refrigerate until firm.

Makes 8 servings.

Variation

Substitute 1/2 to 1 cup fresh cranberries (crushed in processor), and 2 to 3 tablespoons apple juice concentrate for one of the above fruits.

NUTRITIONAL
BREAKDOWN (Per serving)

- Calories 62
- Protein 1g
- Carbohydrates 15g
- Fat . . . . tr
- Sodium 4mg
- Cholesterol 0mg

GLO'S COOKIES

2 cups regular rolled oats
1 cup all-purpose flour
1/2 teaspoon baking soda
1/2 teaspoon baking powder
1 teaspoon grated nutmeg or allspice
1-1/2 teaspoons ground cinnamon
1-1/2 teaspoons vanilla extract
1 cup apple juice concentrate
1/2 cup raisins
2 egg whites
1 cup crushed pineapple, drained
1 medium-size orange, juice plus grated peel
2 tablespoons canola oil

METHOD

1. Preheat oven to 350F (175C). Mix all dry ingredients in a medium-size bowl.
2. Mix remaining ingredients in a medium-size bowl.
3. Combine all ingredients and let stand 2 or 3 minutes to absorb.
4. Spray a non-stick baking sheet with No Stick cooking spray. Drop by teaspoonfuls onto sprayed baking sheet.
5. Bake 12 to 15 minutes or until brown.

Makes about 40 cookies.

Variation

Add carob chips for youngsters.

NUTRITIONAL
BREAKDOWN (Per cookie)

- Calories 53
- Protein 1g
- Carbohydrates 11g
- Fat . . . . .tr
- Sodium 20mg
- Cholesterol 0mg

KID'S KANDY

1/4 cup peanut butter
1 tablespoon honey
2 tablespoons non-fat milk powder
Unsweetened cocoa powder

METHOD
1. Mix peanut butter and honey together in a small bowl. Stir in dry milk.
2. Form into 6 balls and roll in cocoa powder.
3. Refrigerate.

Makes 6 balls.

NUTRITIONAL
BREAKDOWN (Per serving—3 balls)
- Calories 230
- Protein 8g
- Carbohydrates 18g
- Fat 14g
- Sodium 60mg
- Cholesterol . . . . tr

LEMON MOUSSE

1 (1/4-oz.) envelope unflavored gelatin
1/3 cup fresh lemon juice, strained
1/3 cup brown rice syrup
1/4 cup egg substitute
Grated peel of 1 lemon
2 teaspoons cornstarch
1/2 cup part-skim, no-salt, ricotta cheese
2 egg whites

METHOD

1. Sprinkle gelatin over the lemon juice to soften. When soft, add the brown rice syrup, egg substitute, lemon peel and cornstarch and mix with a whisk until all lumps are dissolved.
2. Cook over very low heat until mixture thickens. Turn mixture into a food processor fitted with the metal blade and add ricotta cheese. Blend until smooth.
3. Whip egg whites until stiff peaks form. Slowly add the lemon mixture incorporating thoroughly, but lightly, with a whisk.
4. Pour into 6 parfait glasses.

Makes 6 servings.

Variation

Lemon Mousse Bars: Sprinkle cereal nuggets into an 8" x 5" loaf pan. Drizzle apple juice concentrate over the cereal nuggets. Top with mousse mixture. Spoon into pan and refrigerate at least 3 hours. Cut and serve. Makes 12 bars.

NUTRITIONAL
BREAKDOWN (Per serving)

- Calories 43
- Protein 3g
- Carbohydrates 6g
- Fat 0.8g
- Sodium 29mg
- Cholesterol 3mg

ORANGE GELATIN DELIGHT

1 (1/4-oz.) envelope unflavored gelatin
1 cup water
1/2 cup frozen orange juice concentrate
1/8 cup dry sherry

METHOD

1. Sprinkle gelatin over 1/4 cup of the water. Let stand to soften.
2. Heat until gelatin dissolves.
3. Add remaining water, orange juice concentrate and sherry.
4. Pour into 4 parfait glasses and refrigerate 3 hours before serving.

Makes 4 (1/2-cup) servings.

Variation

Add a few pieces of seedless oranges or sliced bananas.

NUTRITIONAL
BREAKDOWN (Per serving)

- Calories 30
- Protein 4g
- Carbohydrates 4g
- Fat . . . . tr
- Sodium 0mg
- Cholesterol 0mg

PEARS WITH FRUITED YOGURT SAUCE

4 pears, peeled
1 cup white wine
1 cup water
1 cup low-fat yogurt
4 tablespoons raspberry, or other fruit, no-sugar added fruit
   spread
1 teaspoon almond extract
4 mint sprigs

METHOD

1. Poach pears in white wine and water 7 minutes or until tender but firm.
2. In a small bowl, combine yogurt with 1 tablespoon raspberry fruit spread; mix well. Add 1/2 teaspoon almond extract to mixture.
3. In another bowl, combine remaining 1/2 teaspoon extract with remaining 3 tablespoons fruit spread.
4. Pour 1/4 cup yogurt mixture on each of 4 dessert plates and spread into 5-inch circles.
5. Make 2 thin circles with fruit spread 1/2-inch apart in each yogurt circle. Bring knife across yogurt and fruit spread at 1-inch intervals to make pattern.
6. Place a pear in center of each plate. Garnish with mint.

Makes 4 servings.

Variation

Substitute 2 cups apple juice for wine and water.

NUTRITIONAL
BREAKDOWN (Per serving)

- Calories 131
- Protein 3g
- Carbohydrates 30g
- Fat . . . . tr
- Sodium 45mg
- Cholesterol 1mg

PINEAPPLE CLOUD PARFAIT

1 cup low-fat yogurt
2 ripe bananas, sliced
2-1/2 tablespoons no-sugar added orange marmalade or apricot
    jam
1 cup unsweetened canned crushed pineapple
1 tablespoon apple juice concentrate

METHOD

1. Put yogurt and 1-1/2 bananas in a blender; blend just to combine, about 15 seconds. Do not liquify.
2. Pour into a medium-size bowl and add remaining ingredients.
3. Mix well and put into 4 sherbert glasses. Place in refrigerator
   8 hours or overnight.

Makes 4 servings.

Variation

Substitute other varieties of diet jams or preserves for changes
in color and taste.

Sprinkle with cereal nuggets or chopped chestnuts.

NUTRITIONAL
BREAKDOWN (Per serving)

- Calories 126
- Protein 4g
- Carbohydrates 28g
- Fat 1g
- Sodium 42mg
- Cholesterol 3.5mg

PINEAPPLE ICE CREAM

2 large bananas
1 (8-oz.) can unsweetened crushed pineapple, drained
1 tablespoon non-fat yogurt
1 teaspoon coconut extract

METHOD

1. Follow frozen banana preparation in Step 1 for Banana Ice Cream, page 342.
2. Freeze pineapple in a plastic container. Thaw banana pieces and pineapple to soften slightly.
3. Place banana pieces, pineapple, yogurt and coconut extract in a food processor fitted with the metal blade. Process until creamy.
4. Spoon into 4 dessert dishes and serve immediately.

Makes 4 servings.

NUTRITIONAL
BREAKDOWN (Per serving)

- Calories 139
- Protein 1g
- Carbohydrates 35g
- Fat . . . . tr
- Sodium 14mg
- Cholesterol . . . . tr

PINEAPPLE ORANGE PIE

Crust:
2 cups oat bran flakes, crushed to make 1 cup of crumbs
3 tablespoons orange juice concentrate
1 teaspoon no-sugar added orange marmalade

Filling:
1 (1/4-oz.) envelope plus 1 teaspoon unflavored gelatin
1/2 cup water mixed with 1/2 cup orange juice concentrate
5 ice cubes
1/2 cup unsweetened canned crushed pineapple
2 teaspoons no-sugar added marmalade
1 cup low-fat yogurt

METHOD
1. Preheat oven to 400F (205C). To make Crust, mix crumbs with orange juice concentrate and marmalade in a medium-size bowl until moistened. Spray a 7- or 8-inch glass pie plate with No Stick cooking spray.
2. Press crumbs onto pie plate firmly with back of a spoon.
3. Bake 10 minutes. Cover edges with foil to avoid overbrowning. Then reduce heat to 250F (120C) and continue baking 4 or 5 minutes. Cool.
4. Sprinkle gelatin over water and orange juice concentrate mixture in a medium-size saucepan. Heat until dissolved.
5. Add ice cubes and stir until melted. Add pineapple and marmalade. Using fork or whisk, add yogurt.
6. Pour into crust and chill until firm.

Makes 8 servings.

NUTRITIONAL
BREAKDOWN (Per serving)
- Calories 120
- Protein 4g
- Carbohydrates 25g
- Fat 0.8g
- Sodium 28mg
- Cholesterol 2mg

PINEAPPLE PUDDING

2 cups unsweetened canned crushed pineapple, drained, juice reserved
1/3 cup cornstarch
3 tablespoons pineapple juice
4 large strawberries

METHOD

1. Puree all ingredients except strawberries in a blender.
2. Pour into the top of a double boiler and cook, stirring, until mixture thickens.
3. Cool slightly and pour into 4 sherbet glasses. Refrigerate.
4. Top each with 1 strawberry and serve.

Makes 4 servings.

NUTRITIONAL
BREAKDOWN (Per serving)

- Calories 124
- Protein . . . . tr
- Carbohydrates 31g
- Fat . . . . tr
- Sodium 1mg
- Cholesterol 0mg

RICH POUND CAKE

2 cups whole-wheat pastry flour or half whole-wheat and half
   white flour
1 teaspoon baking soda
1 teaspoon baking powder
1 teaspoon ground cinnamon
1/4 teaspoon ground coriander
1/2 cup brown rice syrup
3/4 cup egg substitute or 6 egg whites
1 teaspoon almond extract
1 teaspoon butter flavor extract (optional)
1/4 to 1/2 cup non-fat buttermilk (start with 1/4 cup, if batter
   is too stiff, add extra 1/4 cup)
1 tablespoon plus 1 teaspoon canola oil
1 cup non-fat yogurt

METHOD
1. Preheat oven to 350F (175C). Spray a 9-by-5-inch loaf pan
   with No Stick cooking spray.
2. Mix dry ingredients in a small bowl.
3. Mix liquid ingredients in a large bowl.
4. Add dry ingredients to liquid ingredients a little at a time,
   beating with mixer after each addition.
5. Pour batter into sprayed pan.
6. Bake 50 to 60 minutes, until golden on top and a wooden
   pick inserted in center comes out clean.
7. Cool 15 minutes and then turn out onto a wire rack.

Makes 14 servings.

Variation
Serve strawberries, blueberries or any sliced fruit with cake.

NUTRITIONAL
BREAKDOWN (Per serving)
- Calories 99
- Protein 2g
- Carbohydrates 15g
- Fat 3g
- Sodium 135mg
- Cholesterol 1mg

RUM RAISIN ICE CREAM

1 very ripe banana
1 teaspoon low-fat yogurt
1/4 teaspoon rum extract
1 tablespoon raisins

METHOD

1. Follow frozen banana preparation in Step 1 for Banana Ice Cream, page 342. Thaw banana pieces to soften slightly.
2. Place banana pieces and remaining ingredients, except raisins, in a food processor fitted with the metal blade. Process until smooth. Stir in raisins.
3. Spoon into a dessert dish and serve immediately.

Makes 1 serving.

Variation

Recipe can be doubled or tripled to suit your needs.

NUTRITIONAL
BREAKDOWN (Per serving)

- Calories 122
- Protein 1g
- Carbohydrates 31g
- Fat . . . . tr
- Sodium 8mg
- Cholesterol . . . . tr

STRAWBERRY PIE I

Crust:
1-3/4 to 2 cups oat bran flakes
1/3 to 1/2 cup pineapple juice concentrate

Filling:
1 quart strawberries   **1/2 cup apple juice concentrate**
3/4 cup water   **2 bananas, sliced**
3 tablespoons cornstarch

METHOD

1. Preheat oven to 325F (165C). To make crust, blend oat bran flakes into fine crumbs in a blender or food processor fitted with the metal blade. Add pineapple concentrate. Place in a pie plate and pat into bottom and up side of dish. Bake 15 minutes, until browned and firm.
2. To make filling, slice enough berries to make 1 cup. Simmer sliced strawberries with water in a small saucepan 5 minutes. Combine cornstarch and apple juice concentrate. Stir into strawberry mixture; bring to a boil and cook until thick, stirring constantly.
3. Line crust with sliced bananas. Place whole strawberries on top of bananas and pour cooked strawberries on top.
4. Refrigerate 4 hours and serve.

Makes 10 servings.

Variation

Strawberry Pie II: Make crust as stated above except bake 10 minutes. Line crust with 2 sliced bananas. Place 1 quart strawberries on top of bananas. Mix 1/4 cup apple juice concentrate and 1/3 jar strawberry fruit spread. Pour over strawberries and bake at 325F (165C) 20 minutes.

NUTRITIONAL
BREAKDOWN (Per serving)

	I	II
• Calories	120	93
• Protein	2g	1g
• Carbohydrates	27g	23g
• Fat	1mg	tr
• Sodium	3mg	1mg
• Cholesterol	0mg	0mg

ORANGE FROST

1/2 cup orange juice
1/2 banana, frozen
1 tablespoon non-fat milk powder
Dash cinnamon or nutmeg
2 ice cubes

METHOD

1. Place all ingredients in a blender. Blend until creamy.
2. Serve in 2 chilled glasses.

Makes 2 servings.

Variation

Substitute apple juice and one-half frozen peeled apple for orange juice and banana.

NUTRITIONAL
BREAKDOWN (Per serving)

- Calories 68
- Protein 1g
- Carbohydrates 16g
- Fat . . . . tr
- Sodium 12mg
- Cholesterol 12mg

PIÑA COLADA

4 ice cubes
1/2 cup skim milk or 1 tablespoon non-fat milk powder plus
   1/2 cup water
1/4 teaspoon coconut extract
1/4 cup pineapple juice concentrate
1/2 very ripe banana

METHOD

1. Place all ingredients in a blender; blend 1 to 2 minutes until creamy. Pour into 2 tall chilled glasses.

Makes 2 servings.

NUTRITIONAL
BREAKDOWN (Per serving)

- Calories 76
- Protein 1g
- Carbohydrates 18g
- Fat 0mg
- Sodium 17mg
- Cholesterol . . . . tr

POPCORN SNACK

2 cups air-popped popcorn
1/2 cup oat bran flakes
1 teaspoon onion powder
1 teaspoon garlic powder
1 tablespoon grated Parmesan cheese

METHOD

1. Toss all together while popcorn is still warm.

Makes 2-1/2 cups.

NUTRITIONAL
BREAKDOWN (Per recipe)

- Calories 154
- Protein 4g
- Carbohydrates 30g
- Fat 2g
- Sodium 95mg
- Cholesterol 4mg

EVERYDAY MEASUREMENTS

1 medium-size apple	= 3/4 cup chopped
1 medium-size banana	= 1/3 cup mashed
1 medium-size lemon	= 3 tablespoons juice
1 medium-size lime	= 2 tablespoons juice
1 medium-size orange	= 1/3 cup juice or 4 teaspoons shredded orange peel
1 medium-size pear	= 1/2 cup sliced
3 cups strawberries	= 1-1/2 cups puree
6 to 8 medium-size carrots	= 2-1/2 cups diced
1 medium-size garlic clove	= 3/4 teaspoon minced
1 large bell pepper	= 1 cup diced
1 lb. onions	= 3 onions
1 medium-size onion	= 1/2 cup chopped
1 medium-size potato	= 1/2 cup mashed
1 large sweet potato	= 1-1/2 cups diced
1 medium-size zucchini	= 1 cup sliced
1 lb. large dried beans	= 2 cups uncooked or 5-1/2 cups cooked
1 lb. small dried beans	= 2-1/3 to 3 cups uncooked or 5-1/2 cups cooked
2 egg whites	= 1 whole egg
1 cup kasha	= 2-1/2 to 3 cups cooked
2 oz. spaghetti	= 1 cup cooked
1 cup uncooked rice	= 3 cups cooked
1 lb. flour	= 3-1/2 to 4 cups
1 quart milk	= 4 cups
1 to 1-1/3 cups non-fat milk powder	= 1 quart
1 tablespoon fresh herb	= 1- to 1-1/2 teaspoons dried
g	= grams
mg	= milligrams
tr	= trace

APPROVED PRODUCTS

There are thousands of products in supermarkets that claim to help benefit the public nutritionally. My staff and I spend many hours in various food stores reading labels and evaluating new products. The products are then brought back to our test kitchens to see if they meet our standards. In order to gain approval, these foods must meet the following criteria:

1. Must develop good taste when mixed with other ingredients.
2. Must be quick and easy to prepare.
3. Must be low in calories, carbohydrates, fat, sodium and cholesterol.
4. Must be as good as the company claims.

The following are some of the approved products used in our classes. Please keep in mind all products must be used with discretion.

Products that are readily available in food stores throughout the country do not show complete company address or telephone number. All other products show contact for further information.

Order of products listed does not indicate any particular preference.

BEANS

Green and Red Lentils, Split Peas	Arrowhead Mills P.O. Box 2059 Hereford, TX 79045
Gourmet Bean Soup Mix	Health House 2219 Oddie Reno, NV 89431
Raw beans in packages	All brands

BEVERAGES

Mineral water, all flavors	Artesia Waters, Inc. San Antonio, TX
Natural Mineral Water with Pure Fruit Juice	All brands
Natural Spring Water	Evian
Natural Fruit Nectar	Black River Juice Company Mississauga, Ontario L4X 2E2 Canada
Sparkling Fruit Juices, Apple Juice & Cider	Martinelli's Gold Medal P.O. Box 549 Watsonville, CA 95077
Better Than Milk (Non-Dairy Beverages)	Sovex 1-800-227-2320

BREAD

Arnold Brick Oven Light, 100% Whole Wheat	Arnold Bakery
Molenberg Whole Grain	Maier's Bread Co.
Norwegian Crispbread	Kavli
No fat, no sugar added Pita Bread	All brands

Shiloh Farms 5 Grain	Shiloh Farms
Susan's All Natural Oat Bran	Gold Mark Enterprises
	1-908-290-9060
The Natural, Bagel Dough Energy Bar	The Bagel Place, Inc.
	1-714-547-0787
Wild's Oatmeal, Sour Dough, Pumpernickel	Wild's Baking Co.
	Englewood, NJ

CANNED FISH

(See Fish, Canned)

CANNED FRUIT

(See Fruit, Canned)

CEREALS

Health Valley, cold cereals (all varieties)	Health Valley
4 Grain Cereal	Arrowhead Mills
Rice and Shine	Box 2059
	Hereford, TX 79045
Grape-Nuts	Post
Nutri-Grain Nuggets	Kellogg's
Puffed Kashi	Kashi Co.,
	P.O. Box 8557
	La Jolla, CA 92038
Cream of Wheat	Nabisco
All Puffed Wheat	All brands
All Puffed Rice Cereals	All brands
Nabisco Shredded Wheat 'N Bran	Nabisco
Wheatena	American Home Foods, Inc.
	New York, NY
Quick N' Creamy	Pacific Rice Products
	Berkeley, CA 94710
All Good Shepherd Organic Cereals	Sovex
& Wheat-Free Cereals	1-800-227-2320

CHICKEN STOCK

Campbell's Low Sodium Chicken Broth	Campbell's Soup Co.
Health Valley Chicken Broth	Health Valley
Pritikin Chicken Broth	Pritikin

COOKIES

Carissa Creme Sandwich Cookies	Carissa's Inc.
	Highland, IN 46322
	1-800-222-5886
All Health Valley Cookies	Health Valley
Snack Well's Chocolate Chip Cookies	Nabisco
Snack Well's Oatmeal Raisin	Nabisco

CRACKERS

Crispini, Sodium Free Flatbreads	Burns & Ricker
Ryvita, Toasted Sesame, Rye	Shaffer, Clark & Co.
	1-800-431-2957
Snack Well's Cheese, Cinnamon Graham & Wheat	Nabisco

DAIRY PRODUCTS

Polly-O, Lite and Free Mozzarella Cheeses	Polly-O
Polly-O, Lite and Free Ricotta Cheeses	Polly-O
Polly-O, All Natural Lite String Cheese	Polly-O
Cottage Cheese, Low Fat and Non-Fat	All brands
Yogurt, Low Fat and Non-Fat	All brands

DRESSING

Good Seasons Fat Free Dressing	Good Seasons
Salad Dazzlers	American Spoon Co.
	1-800-222-5886

All flavors Walden Farms Low Fat, Fat Free, and Low Salt	Walden Farms

EGG SUBSTITUTES

Egg Beaters	Fleischmann's
Healthy Choices	Con Agra

FILLO DOUGH

Apollo Athens Fillo Dough	Athens Food 1-800-837-5683

FISH, CANNED

Chicken of the Sea Chunk Light Tuna in Spring Water	Chicken of the Sea
Chicken of the Sea Chunk Light Tuna with Canola Oil	Chicken of the Sea
Chicken of the Sea Solid White Tuna in Spring Water	Chicken of the Sea
Chicken of the Sea Solid White Tuna with Canola Oil	Chicken of the Sea
Chicken of the Sea Pink Salmon in Spring Water	Chicken of the Sea

FLAVOR EXTRACTS

Bickford Flavors	Bickford Laboratories 1-800-283-8322

FROZEN FRUIT

(See Fruit, Frozen)	

FRUIT, CANNED

	All brands packed in own juice

FRUIT, FROZEN

Any fruit concentrate	All brands (no sugar added)
Frozen/fresh lemon juice	Minute Maid
Minute Maid 100% Lemon Juice from Concentrate	

FRUIT SPREADS

No sugar added fruit spreads (all flavors)	Clearbrook Farms 1-800-888-3276
All Fruit Spreads	Polaner
Great Valley Mills Fruit Spreads and Butters	Great Valley Mills 1-800-688-6455

HERB TEAS

	Stash Tea Co. 1-800-547-1514

MAPLE SYRUP

Cary's Sugar Free	Cary's 1-800-ADA-DISC

MUSTARDS

Dijon-style Mustard	Reine de Dijon
Green Chili & Garlic	Napa Valley Mustard Co. P.O. Box 125 Oakville, CA 94562

OILS & SPRAYS

All canola oils	All brands
All canola and olive oil sprays	All brands
Smartbeat Spread	Heart Beat Foods
Toasted Sesame Oil	Eden Foods 1-800-248-0301
Loriva, all flavored oils	Loriva Supreme Foods, Inc. (516) 231-7940

368

PANCAKE, WAFFLE MIX

Old Fashion Buttermilk Pancake Mixes	Vermont Cider Mill 1-802-483-2400
Great Valley Mills Pancake, Waffle Mix	Great Valley Mills 1-800-688-6455

PASTAS

All Homemade Organic Pastas	Eden Foods
Lupini Pasta	International Nutrition & Genetics
No Yolks Noodle Substitute	Fould's, Inc.
Pasta Mama	Pasta Mama's Inc. 1-800-456-4045

PIEROGIES

Mrs. T's Potato and Onion	Ateeco 1-800-233-3170

PICKLES

Unsalted Pickles, Relishes, etc.	B&G

POTATOES, FROZEN

Ore-Ida Lite Crinkle and Home Style Dinner Fries	Ore-Ida

RICE/GRAINS

Wild Rice	McFadden Farm Potter Valley, CA 95469
Brown and wild rice	Lundberg Farms Richvale, CA 95974
Brown and wild rice	Voyageur Box 35121 Minneapolis, MN 55435
Casbah Couscous Pilaf and Falafel Mix	Sahara
Quinoa Grain	Eden Foods
Near East Couscous	Near East
Wolff's Kasha	The Birkett Mills Penn Yan, NY

SALSAS

Chili 2000	Food 2000, Inc. 1-802-223-0774
Hot Cha Cha	Allied Old English Port Reading, NJ
Ortega Thick and Chunky Salsa	Nabisco
Smokey Chipotle, Hot Sauce	Sauces & Salsas, Ltd.

SAUCES

Shoyu-Tamari	Erewhon
Shoyu Soy Sauce and Wheat-Free Tamari Soy Sauce	San-J International 1-800-446-5500
Enrico's Salsa	Ventre Packing Co., Inc. Syracuse, NY 13204
Hot Cha Cha	Allied Old English Port Reading, NJ 07064
Enrico Homemade No Salt Sauce Spaghetti	Ventre Packing Co., Inc. 1-315-463-2384
Low Salt Shoyu Tamari	Eden Foods, Inc.
Low Sodium Tamari Lite	San-J International
Mrs. Dash Steak Sauce	Alberto-Culver, USA, Inc.

SEASONINGS/SPICES

"Instead of Salt" (all varieties)	Health Valley
Hickory-smoked yeast	Sovex
Tabasco sauce	Mc Ilhenny Co.
Brown Rice Miso	Eden Foods 1-800-248-0301

Parsley Patch (all varieties)	McCormick & Co.
All Chili and Tex-Mex Spices	Pecos Valley Spice Co. 212-628-5374
Eden Hot Pepper Sesame Oil	Eden Foods 1-800-248-0301
All Jane Butel Mexican & Chili Spices	Pecos River Spice, Inc. Sante Fe, NM
Chopped Garlic, Salt Free	Polaner
Hot Chopped Jalapeno	Polaner
Mama Dash, Papa Dash	Alberto-Culver Co.
Mama Dash Steak Sauce	Alberto-Culver Co.
Molly McButter	Alberto-Culver Co.
Butter Buds	Cumberland Packing Corp. Brooklyn, NY
Low Sodium Worcestershire Sauce	Worcestershire Co.

SNACKS

Edensoy, Non-Dairy Drink	Eden Foods 1-800-248-0301
Lundberg Sweet Brown Rice Crunchies	Lundberg Farms Richvale, CA 95974
Popcorn	Any brand to be *air popped*
Pizsoy Pizza	Tree Tavern
Smart Temptations No Oil Tortilla Chips	American Speciality Foods 1-800-621-3318
Unsalted Sour Dough Hard Pretzels Pretzel Minis, and Olde Tyme Pretzels	Snyder of Hanover 1-800-233-7125

SWEETENERS

CaraCoa Carob Powder	El Molino Mills City of Industry, CA 91746
Date Sugar	Shiloh Farms
Premier Japan Brown Rice Syrup and Barley Malt Syrup	Edward & Sons Trading Co. Union, NJ 07083
Brown Rice Syrup and Barley Malt Syrup	Eden Foods 1-800-248-0301
Brown Rice Syrup	Lundberg Farms Richvalle, CA
Apple Cider Syrup	Vermont Cider Mill 1-802-403-2400

TEAS

All Decaf Teas	All brands
Sportea	Ultimate Performance Products 1-303-322-3871

TOMATO PRODUCTS

Tomato sauce, puree, paste	All brands no-salt tomato products
Tomato and green chiles	Ro-Tel
Life All Natural Tomato Ketchup	Liberty/Ramsey Imports Carlstadt, NJ 07072
Nutra Diet No Salt Tomato Juice	S&W Fine Foods

TOMATOES, SUN DRIED

Just Tomatoes	Just Tomatoes 1-209-894-5371
Timber Crest Minced Dried Tomatoes	Timber Crest

VINEGARS

Chinese white wine rice vinegar	Any brand
Red wine vinegar without sulfites	Any brand

WINE

Ariel Dealcoholized Wines, white zinfindel, blanc, chardonnay, cabernet, sauvignon	Ariel

370

My storeroom is loaded with cookware sent to me by companies hoping I would endorse their products. Everything from enamel, porcelain, aluminum, glass, copper, non-stick, etc. They are now gathering dust on my shelves.

The final decision was the selection of Health Craft Waterless and Greaseless Stainless Steel Cookware, food processors and kitchen equipment. I use this cookware in my home as well as in the Gourmet Long Life Cooking Schools.

When you set up your new healthy kitchen and begin to prepare my healthy recipes invest in the best for your family. I use Health Craft Products and recommend them for every kitchen. Give Health Craft a call at 1-800-443-8079 and they will be more than happy to send you a brochure, or you can write to them direct at:

Health Craft
5414 Town N Country Blvd.
Tampa, FL 33615·

Index

A

Angel Cheese Cake 336
Angel Food Cake 337
Appetizers 145-156
Apple Burgers 197
Apple-Cinnamon Muffins 313
Apple Cinnamon Raisin Cookies 338
Apple Sorbet 339
Approved Products 366-370
Arthritis Interview 6-10
Artichoke Dressing, Creamy 324
Artichoke Dressing, Creamy
   Cucumber 325

B

Baked Stuffed Potatoes with Spinach 272
Baked Zucchini, Eggplant &
   Tomatoes 274
Banana Ice Cream 342
Banana Nut Pop 340
Banana-Strawberry Sundae 341
Barbecue Sauce 134
Barley Soup, Pea, Mushroom & 174
Bars, Lemon Mousse 353
Basic Nutritional Information 59-80
Basic Vinaigrette 322
Basil Green Beans, Garlic 282
Bean & Vegetable Soup, White 180
Bean Salad, Mexican 261
Bean Soup 159
Bean Soup, Mexican 171
Beans & Beef 198
Beef & Pasta 199
Beef Stock 138
Beef Stroganoff 200
Beef with Noodles, Szechuan 208
Beef, Beans & 198
Black-Eyed Peas, Natalie's Rice & 311
Bouillabaise 182
Bouillon Cubes, Frozen 142
Brazilian Holiday Chicken 214
Breaded Zucchini 281
Breads 312-320
Breakfast Muffins 314
Broccoli & Pasta 301
Broccoli Bisque 158
Broiled Flank Steak 201
Brown Rice Cheese 240
Brownies, Chocolate Mint 343
Burgers, Apple 197

C

Cabbage Soup 179
Cabbage, Sweet & Sour Red 296
Cacciatore, Chicken Wings 235
Cake, Angel Cheese 336
Cake, Angel Food 337
Cake, Chocolate Orange 345
Cake, Rich Pound 359
Cakes, Corn 315
Can Opener Chili 249
Cancer Interview 11-16
Carrot Gnocchi, Sweet Potato & 277
Carrot Salad 255
Carrot Soup, Curried 162
Carrots, Glazed 283
Casablanca Chicken 215
Casserole, Chicken Lentil 211
Casserole, Lima Bean 212
Cauliflower Soup, Italian Zucchini-167
Charts and Tables
   Avoid High-Fat Animal Protein 67
   Calcium Equivalents 77
   Choose Low-Fat Protein Sources
     Using Your Animal Protein
     Comparison Chart 66
   Compare the Percentages 63
   Fast Food is Fat Food! 70
   Fiber—Which is Best For You? 80
   Fish Containing Omega-3
     Fatty Acids 72
   Foods Low in Sodium and High in
     Potassium 75
   High Sodium Foods to Avoid 75
   Hints for a Slim Waistline and a
     Healthy Heart 79
   How to Choose Foods Low in
     Cholesterol and Saturated Fat
     64-65
   How to Figure Fat Calories in
     Food 78
   Know Your Milks! 77
   Know Your Poultry 210
   Nutrition Labels 78
   Oils and Fats 68
   Painless Ways to Reduce Fat 69
   Save Fat and Calories 71
   Sodium Levels 73
   The Gloria Rose Gourmet Long
     Life Daily Meal Plan 60
   The Sweet Facts 76

Typical American Diet Daily Meal Plan 61
What Do You Eat on a Daily Basis? 62
Where's the Sodium? 74
Cheese Cake, Angel 336
Cheese Mixture, Italian 143
Cheese, Manicotti with Vegetables & 246
Chicken Dijon 217
Chicken-Escarole Soup 160
Chicken Korma 219
Chicken L'Orange with Mushrooms 220
Chicken Lentil Casserole 211
Chicken or Turkey Curry 216
Chicken Orange Salad 256
Chicken Salad, Mushroom- 262
Chicken Salad, Pineapple 264
Chicken Stock 139
Chicken Tetrazzini 221
Chicken Wings Cacciatore 235
Children, Good Snacks for 115
Chili con Carne 202
Chili, Can Opener 249
Chili, Microwaved 204
Chili, My Favorite 206
Chinese Fish 183
Chocolate Mint Brownies 343
Chocolate Mousse 344
Chocolate Orange Cake 345
Cholesterol Interview 17-21
Chowder, Manhattan Clam 170
Cinnamon Muffins, Apple- 313
Cinnamon Raisin Cookies, Apple 338
Clam Chowder, Manhattan 170
Clear Mushroom Soup 176
Cocktail Sauce 323
Confetti Macaroni Bake 239
Cookies, Apple Cinnamon Raisin 338
Cookies, Glo's 350
Corn Cakes 315
Corn Chicken, Creamed 223
Corn Relish 257
Cottage-Cheese Spread 147
Cranberry Chicken 222
Cranberry Relish 258
Cream Cheese, "Our" 135
Creamed Corn Chicken 223
Creamy Artichoke Dressing 324
Creamy Cucumber Artichoke Dressing 325
Creamy Garlic Italian Dressing 326
Creamy One-Minute Fruit Dessert 346
Creamy Rice Pudding 347
Creamy Tofu Tomato Soup 161
Crepes 144
Crispy Chicken 224

Croutons, Garlic 270
Cucumber Artichoke Dressing, Creamy 325
Cucumber-Herb Dressing 327
Cucumbers in Herbed Yogurt 259
Curried Carrot Soup 162
Curry Dip 147
Curry, Chicken or Turkey 216
Curry, Lentil & Mushroom 250
Curry, Vegetable 278

D

Delicate Snow Pea Soup 163
Desserts & Snack 335-364
Diabetes Interview 22-28
Dilled Potato Salad 260
Dip with Toasted Pita Chips, Salmon 153
Dip, Curry 147
Dip, Hummus Party 148
Dip, Mexican 149
Dip, Onion 151
Dip, Sardine 154
Dip, Tuna 155
Dressings, Spreads & Sauces 321-335

E

Egg Drop Soup 164
Eggplant & Tomatoes, Baked Zucchini, 274
Enchiladas 156
Exercise Interview 55-57

F

Fabulous Turkey Breast 225
Fats or Oils 1
Fish Stock 140
Fish, Chinese 183
Fish, Lime-Broiled 187
Fish, Vegetable-Topped Baked 195
Flank Steak, Broiled 201
Flank Steak, Marinated 203
Flavored Oils 4
French Dressing 329
French Toast 316
"Fried" Fish Fillets 184
Frozen Bouillon Cubes 142
Fruit Compote 348
Fruit Dessert, Creamy One-Minute 346
Fruit Dressing, Orange Chiffon 333
Fruit Medley Gelatin Mold 349

G

Garbanzo Soup, Grandma's Greek 166
Garlic Basil Green Beans 282
Garlic Croutons 270
Garlic Dressing, Greek 330
Garlic Italian Dressing, Creamy 326
Gingered Orange Sauce, Poached
  Chicken in 229
Gingered Sole 185
Glazed Carrots 283
Glo's Cookies 350
Gloria's Ravioli 302
Gnocchi, Spinach 289
Gnocchi, Sweet Potato & Carrot 277
Golden Hash Brown Potatoes &
  Zucchini 284
Good Snacks for Children 115
Gourmet Quick Rice Pilaf 303
Grandma's Greek Garbanzo Soup 166
Grandma's Pasta with Kale 304
Greek Garbanzo Soup, Grandma's 166
Greek Garlic Dressing 330
Green Beans Stir-Fry 292
Green Beans, Garlic Basil 282
Green Goddess Dressing 331
Green Peas with Curried Mushrooms
  285.
Grilled Chicken Tarragon 213

H

Hawaiian Muffins 317
Heart Disease Interview 29-33
Herb Dressing, Cucumber- 327
Herbs and Spices 3
Hot & Spicy Chicken 226
Hummus Party Dip 148
Hummus Sandwich Filling 247
Hypertension Interview 34-42

I

Ice Cream, Banana 342
Ice Cream, Pineapple 356
Ice Cream, Rum Raisin 360
Italian Cheese Mixture 143
Italian Dressing, Creamy Garlic 326
Italian Zucchini-Cauliflower Soup 167

K

Kabobs, Pineapple Steak 207
Kale, Grandma's Pasta with 304
Kasha, Mexican 305
Kid's Kandy 351
King of the Sea Primavera 186

L

Lasagna Curls, Vegetable 242
Lasagna, Spinach Mushroom 244
Lemon Mousse 352
Lemon Mousse Bars 353
Lentil & Mushroom Curry 250
Lentil Casserole, Chicken 211
Lentil Soup, Luscious 169
Lentil Stew Creole 251
Lima Bean Casserole 212
Lima Bean Soup 168
Lime-Broiled Fish 187
Lime Chicken Shish Kabob 227
Lime Sauce, Scallops in 192
Luscious Lentil Soup 169

M

Macaroni Bake, Confetti 239
Macaroni Salmon Loaf 188
Manhattan Clam Chowder 170
Manicotti with Vegetables & Cheese
  246
Marinade Sauce 328
Marinara Sauce 332
Marinated Flank Steak 203
Mayonnaise, "Our" 136
Meat Entrees 196-210
Meat Surprise, Midweek 205
Meatballs, Turkey 233
Meatless Moussaka 241
Menus for Diet Plan for Overweight
  Child 117-123
Menus for Diet Plan for Pregnant
  Women 125-131
Menus for Weight Loss Diet for Men
  85-91
Menus for Weight Loss Diet for
  Women 100-106
Menus for Weight Maintenance Diet
  for Men 92-98
Menus for Weight Maintenance Diet
  for Women 107-113
Mexicali Tortillas 209
Mexican Bean Salad 261
Mexican Bean Soup 171
Mexican Dip 149
Mexican Fiesta Omelet 252
Mexican Kasha 305
Mexican Potatoes 272
Mexican-Style Scallops 189
Microwaved Brown Rice 306
Microwaved Chili 204
Midweek Meat Surprise 205
Minestrone Soup 172

Miso 2
Moussaka, Meatless 241
Mousse, Chocolate 344
Mousse, Lemon 352
Muffin Surprise Deluxe, Oat Bran 318
Muffins, Apple-Cinnamon 313
Muffins, Breakfast 314
Muffins, Hawaiian 317
Muffins, Oat Bran 319
Muffins, Piña Colada 320
Mulligatawny Soup 173
Mushroom & Barley Soup, Pea, 174
Mushroom-Chicken Salad 262
Mushroom Curry, Lentil & 250
Mushroom Lasagna, Spinach 244
Mushroom Soup, Clear 176
Mushroom Spread 150
Mushrooms in Wine 286
Mushrooms, Chicken L'Orange with 220
Mushrooms, Green Peas with Curried 285
Mushrooms, Spinach Casserole with 273
Mushrooms, Stuffed 294
My Favorite Chili 206

N

Natalie's Rice & Black-Eyed Peas 311
No Fats! No Sugars! No Salts! 1-5
Noodles, Szechuan Beef with 208
Nut Pop, Banana 340
Nutrition Interview 47-54

O

Oat Bran Muffin Surprise Deluxe 318
Oat Bran Muffins 319
Oils, Flavored 4
Omelet, Mexican Fiesta 252
Onion Dip 151
Onion Soup 165
Orange Cake, Chocolate 345
Orange Chicken 228
Orange Chiffon Fruit Dressing 333
Orange Frost 362
Orange Gelatin Delight 353
Orange Pie, Pineapple 357
Orange Salad, Chicken & 256
Orange Sauce, Poached Chicken in Gingered 229
Orange Sauce, Poached Salmon in 190
Oriental Pasta Salad 263
"Our" Cream Cheese 135
"Our" Homemade Basics 133-144
"Our" Mayonnaise 136

"Our" Sour Cream 137
Overweight Child 114

P

Pancakes, Potato 152
Parfait, Pineapple Cloud 355
Pasta Cheese Bake 245
Pasta e Fagioli 175
Pasta Salad, Oriental 263
Pasta Salad, Spring Garden 267
Pasta with Kale, Grandma's 304
Pasta, Beef & 199
Pasta, Broccoli & 301
Pasta, Rice & Grains 300-311
Pasta, Roman Style 307
Pasta, Skillet Scallops & 193
Pasta, Slim Zucchini 308
Pea, Mushroom & Barley Soup 174
Pears with Fruited Yogurt Sauce 354
Pepper, Stir-Fry Snow Peas & Red 275
Pie, Pineapple Orange 357
Pie, Strawberry I 361
Pie, Strawberry II 361
Pilaf, Gourmet Quick Rice 303
Pineapple Chicken Salad 264
Pineapple Cloud Parfait 355
Pineapple Ice Cream 356
Pineapple Orange Pie 357
Pineapple Pudding 358
Pineapple Steak Kabobs 207
Pineapple Turkey Salad 265
Piña Colada 363
Piña Colada Muffins 320
Pizza, Quick 248
Poached Chicken in Gingered Orange Sauce 229
Poached Salmon in Orange Sauce 190
Popcorn Snack 364
Potato Pancakes 152
Potato Salad, Dilled 260
Potatoes & Zucchini, Golden Hash Brown 284
Potatoes with Spinach, Baked Stuffed 272
Potatoes, Mexican 272
Potatoes, Scalloped 287
Potatoes, Stuffed Baked 293
Potatoes, Twice Baked Sweet 297
Poultry Entrees 210-237
Pound Cake, Rich 359
Pregnant Woman, The 124
Pudding, Creamy Rice 347
Pudding, Pineapple 358
Pudding, Zucchini 299

Q

Quick Pizza 248
Quickie Chicken L'Orange 232

R

Raisin Cookies, Apple Cinnamon 338
Raisin Ice Cream, Rum 360
Ravioli, Gloria's 302
Recipes 132-364
Relish, Corn 257
Relish, Cranberry 258
Rice & Black-Eyed Peas, Natalie's 311
Rice Cheese, Brown 240
Rice Pilaf, Gourmet Quick 303
Rice Pudding, Creamy 347
Rice Soup, Spanish 178
Rice, Microwaved Brown 306
Rice, Spanish 309
Rich Pound Cake 359
Rum Raisin Ice Cream 360

S

Salads 254-271
Salmon Dip with Toasted Pita Chips 153
Salmon in Orange Sauce, Poached 190
Salmon Loaf, Macaroni 188
Salmon Spread 266
Salmon Surprise 191
Salt 2
Sardine Dip 154
Sauce, Barbecue 134
Scalloped Potatoes 287
Scallops & Pasta, Skillet 193
Scallops in Lime Sauce 192
Scallops, Mexican-Style 189
Seafood Entrees 181-195
Shepherd's Pie 253
Shoyu, Tamari or 3
Skillet Scallops & Pasta 193
Slim Zucchini Pasta 308
Snow Pea Soup, Delicate 163
Snow Peas & Red Pepper, Stir-Fry 275
Sole Stuffed with Spinach 194
Sole, Gingered 185
Sorbet, Apple 339
Soufflé, Spinach 291
Soup a la Athens 177
Soups 157-181
Sour Cream, "Our" 137
Soy Sauce 3
Spaghetti Squash Primavera 288
Spanish Rice 309
Spanish Rice Soup 178

Spices, Herbs and 3
Spinach Casserole with Mushrooms 273
Spinach Gnocchi 289
Spinach Mushroom Lasagna 244
Spinach Puff 290
Spinach Salad, Tropical 270
Spinach Soufflé 291
Spinach, Baked Stuffed Potatoes with 272
Spinach, Sole Stuffed with 194
Spread, Cottage-Cheese 147
Spread, Mushroom 150
Spread, Salmon 266
Spring Garden Pasta Salad 267
Squash Primavera, Spaghetti 288
Steak Kabobs, Pineapple 207
Steak, Broiled Flank 201
Steak, Marinated Flank 203
Stir-Fry Beef 231
Stir-Fry Chicken 230
Stir-Fry Snow Peas & Red Pepper 275
Stock, Beef 138
Stock, Chicken 139
Stock, Fish 140
Stock, Vegetable 141
Strawberry Pie I 361
Strawberry Pie II 361
Strawberry Sundae, Banana 341
Stroganoff, Beef 200
Stuffed Baked Potatoes 293
Stuffed Mushrooms 294
Stuffed Shells 243
Stuffed Tomatoes 295
Substitutes 82
Sugars 1
Summer Ratatouille 276
Summer Tomato Salad 268
Sundae, Banana-Strawberry 341
Sweet & Sour Red Cabbage 296
Sweet & Sour Sauce 334
Sweet Potato & Carrot Gnocchi 277
Szechuan Beef with Noodles 208

T

Tabbouleh 310
Taco Salad, Tex-Mex 269
Tamari or Shoyu 3
Tex-Mex Taco Salad 269
Toast, French 316
Tofu Tomato Soup, Creamy 161
Tomato Salad, Summer 268
Tomato Soup, Creamy Tofu 161
Tomato Wine Sauce, Turkey
    Meatballs in 234

Tomatoes, Baked Zucchini, Eggplant & 274
Tomatoes, Stuffed 295
Tortillas, Mexicali 209
Tropical Spinach Salad 270
Tuna Dip 155
Turkey Breast, Fabulous 225
Turkey Meatballs 233
Turkey Meatballs in Tomato Wine Sauce 234
Turkey Salad, Pineapple 265
Turnovers, Vegetable 146
Twice Baked Sweet Potatoes 297

V

Vegetable Curry 278
Vegetable Lasagna Curls 242
Vegetable Mixture 279
Vegetable Paella 280
Vegetable Soup, White Bean & 180
Vegetable Stock 141
Vegetable-Topped Baked Fish 195
Vegetable Turnovers 146
Vegetables & Cheese, Manicotti with 246
Vegetables 271-299
Vegetarian Entrees 238-253
Vegetarian Stir-Fry 231

Vinaigrette, Basic 322
Vinegars 3

W

Weekender on Weekdays 237
Weekender Sandwich 236
Weight Control Interview 43-46
Weight Loss Diet & Weight Loss Maintenance Plan 81-131
Weight Loss Diet for Men 84
Weight Loss Diet for Women 99
White Bean & Vegetable Soup 180
Winter Squash Medley 298

Y

Yogurt Sauce, Pears with Fruited 354

Z

Zucchini-Cauliflower Soup, Italian 167
Zucchini Pasta, Slim 308
Zucchini Pudding 299
Zucchini, Breaded 281
Zucchini, Eggplant & Tomatoes, Baked 274
Zucchini, Golden Hash Brown Potatoes & 284

Metric Chart

Comparison to Metric Measure

When You Know	Symbol	Multiply By	To Find	Symbol
teaspoons	tsp	5.0	milliliters	ml
tablespoons	tbsp	15.0	milliliters	ml
fluid ounces	fl. oz.	30.0	milliliters	ml
cups	c	0.24	liters	l
pints	pt.	0.47	liters	l

When You Know	Symbol	Multiply By	To Find	Symbol
quarts	qt.	0.95	liters	l
ounces	oz.	28.0	grams	g
pounds	lb.	0.45	kilograms	kg
Fahrenheit	F	5/9 (after subtracting 32)	Celsius	C

Fahrenheit to Celsius

F	C
200-205	95
220-225	105
245-250	120
275	135
300-305	150
325-330	165
345-350	175
370-375	190
400-405	205
425-430	220
445-450	230
470-475	245
500	260

Liquid Measure to Milliliters

1/4 teaspoon	=	1.25 milliliters
1/2 teaspoon	=	2.5 milliliters
3/4 teaspoon	=	3.75 milliliters
1 teaspoon	=	5.0 milliliters
1-1/4 teaspoons	=	6.25 milliliters
1-1/2 teaspoons	=	7.5 milliliters
1-3/4 teaspoons	=	8.75 milliliters
2 teaspoons	=	10.0 milliliters
1 tablespoon	=	15.0 milliliters
2 tablespoons	=	30.0 milliliters

Liquid Measure to Liters

1/4 cup	=	0.06 liters
1/2 cup	=	0.12 liters
3/4 cup	=	0.18 liters
1 cup	=	0.24 liters
1-1/4 cups	=	0.3 liters
1-1/2 cups	=	0.36 liters
2 cups	=	0.48 liters
2-1/2 cups	=	0.6 liters
3 cups	=	0.72 liters
3-1/2 cups	=	0.84 liters
4 cups	=	0.96 liters
4-1/2 cups	=	1.08 liters
5 cups	=	1.2 liters
5-1/2 cups	=	1.32 liters